TRIBUTES TO TED ROGERS

"Ted Rogers was a man who lived large, who dreamt large and, to use a phrase he often used himself in praising the work of others, who 'built better than he knew.' The underdog whose achievements changed the communications landscape here in Canada but also in the United States. An inspiration. A leader."

—**Alan Horn, chairman, Rogers Communications**

"I started with Ted in 1969, and in personnel terms, there are few who lasted as long. Ted was *go, go, go,* 24 hours a day. When you worked with Ted, you really worked. When you were with Ted, you were either in the tent or out of the tent, there was no halfway. But if you got in the tent, you were right beside him. At three o'clock in the morning, if that was when he wanted to talk, that's when you had to talk. Ted has said that he was lucky, but he was more than lucky, he was persistent. It was the sheer inability of Rogers to take no for an answer. Ted just worked harder, drove harder, pushed harder than anybody else. That is a great part of his success. Other guys had a chance to buy Canadian Cablesystems, or Premier, or Maclean Hunter, or Microcell, but they called it off or said it was too hard to do or it wasn't worth the effort. But for Ted, anything that he really wanted was worth the effort."

—**Phil Lind, vice-chairman, Rogers Communications**

"There was no-one better at the art of the deal. While his approach was often audacious and unorthodox, he got deals done that other people didn't think of, or that others initially scoffed at when Ted thought of them. Ted Rogers literally worked his heart out to make up for his brilliant father's short life (he died at age 38). He more than made up for his father, and in the process became a great Canadian, a great community builder, a great businessman and a very special boss to 30,000 Canadians."

—John H. Tory, former president and CEO, Rogers Media,
former president and CEO, Rogers Cable

"Ted Rogers was the hardest-working person we ever met. He was driven, but more importantly, he was a visionary. There were many projects in which we worked together with Rogers, and some in which we competed against each other. On one project, there was a serious bet—the winner got steak for dinner, the loser got wieners and beans. We can't remember who won, but everything for Ted was about winning, and he hated wieners and beans."

—J. R. Shaw, executive chair,
Jim Shaw, CEO and vice-chair, Shaw Communications Inc.

"You could be his competitor, but you always had to respect him. There were two things about him: determination and an unbelievable capability to take risks. He's had a few strikeouts—but the home runs were many times more frequent. And if you don't have any strikeouts, you've never tried anything."

—Jean C. Monty, former chairman and CEO, BCE

"I first met Ted Rogers when he was a law student looking for an articling position. He had been so busy dealing with other matters that he was about eight months late seeking a position. I had already hired all the students we required for the year and I normally would not have interviewed him. However, I took him to lunch with my brother, Jim, and we decided to hire him because there was something unique about him that was difficult to identify at the time. A few years later he asked me if I would join the board of directors of Rogers Radio Broadcasting Limited, which owned CHFI, a small FM radio station in Toronto. Over the ensuing years, he built that little company into Canada's pre-eminent telecommunications company. Someone once described this process as 'a series of peaks and valleys.' From my perspective as a director, I think this is an accurate description, and I tried to help him where I could. However, looking back, I don't think Ted ever saw any of the peaks or valleys. For Ted, what others saw as peaks were times to formulate new visions, and valleys were either opportunities or learning experiences. Ted's whole career was built upon an uncanny instinct for what his customers would want in the future, coupled with an extraordinary ability to command the respect of those around him and to motivate them to get things done. He was a man of great vision, dedication and loyalty and was certainly one of Canada's most successful entrepreneurs. He was also a strong believer in Canada. He will be sorely missed by all who knew him."

—John A. Tory, director, The Woodbridge Company,
director, Rogers Communications

"I've always been proud to call Ted Rogers my friend. Although I live in Vancouver and Ted lived in Toronto, we saw each other regularly as directors of TD Bank, to which we both owed large sums of money. Ted was totally fearless when it came to disagreeing with the bank management. I, on the other hand, was a coward who sat quietly by, not wanting to get the bankers mad at me. I admired Ted's courage, and the more I got to know him, the more my fondness for him grew. Recently, Ted was in downtown Vancouver speaking to a business audience. He started off by saying, 'It's Jimmy's birthday today,' and he led the audience in singing 'Happy Birthday.' When he sat down, I said, 'Ted, today is not my birthday,' to which he answered, 'It doesn't matter, that was a lot of fun.' Ted was deeply devoted to his wife, Loretta, and to their four children. When Ted said goodbye to me, he would almost always say 'God bless.' Well, God blessed Ted Rogers with many good things in this life, and Ted blessed millions of people with his life, his vision, his giving and his inspiration. God bless you, Ted. And Ted, for you, the best is yet to come."

—Jim Pattison, Chairman, president and CEO, The Jim Pattison Group

"Ted Rogers and I were friends in high school, in university and in politics. I was an usher at his wedding to Loretta. To say that Ted was driven is an understatement. He gave everything he had, first to his family and then to the remarkable communications empire that bears his name. Canada has been short on genuine entrepreneurs who dare to step into the unknown. Ted was one of the truly great. When the definitive history of Canada's communications industry is written, Ted will be seen standing proudly beside his father. That is how he would have wished it."

—Henry "Hal" N. R. Jackman, former lieutenant-governor of Ontario

"Ted Rogers will be remembered in history as one of Canada's greatest entrepreneurs, no question. But to many, many of us he was much, much more, touching us at a very deep and personal level. Everyone has a Ted story or two. When I was appointed to the Rogers board, he invited my wife, Shabin, to attend as a surprise to me. It meant a lot to us as a family. Always family."

—Nadir Mohamed, president and CEO, Rogers Communications

"My father and I had the honour of knowing and working with Ted for many years, and his passing is a sad day for all of us. Ted's passion, especially for new technology, was contagious. I looked forward to his frequent visits to Philadelphia, when we would share ideas and test new technologies. He was a devoted family man as well. When he entrusted his son, Edward, to us for one of his first jobs in the cable industry, I think my father felt that was one of the highest compliments he ever could have received. Ted was a good friend and a loyal business partner, and we will miss him tremendously."

—Brian L. Roberts, chairman and CEO, Comcast,
chairman, CableLabs

"Mr. Rogers was one of Canada's greatest telecommunications entrepreneurs. His visionary business acumen was evident as early as 1960 when, as a law student in his mid-20s, he bought all the shares in Canada's only FM radio station, CHFI, when only five per cent of Toronto households had FM receivers. This prescient investment in FM radio led him to invest in cable television, wireless telecommunications, broadcasting and publishing. He touched the lives of countless Canadians outside of his business ventures through his generosity in professional sport, health care and education. He and his wife, Loretta, have made substantial contributions, including contributions to Ryerson University and Toronto-area hospitals. In 1990, Mr. Rogers was appointed to the Order of Canada, our country's highest civilian honour. We will never forget one of our greatest Canadians."

—Stephen Harper, prime minister of Canada

"He was a very energetic friend and made a really fundamental commitment to the Canadian community. He was a Conservative and I was a Liberal. But he was ready to talk and ready to listen, and we got along fine. He had all the right instincts. He was a great Canadian success story."

—John Turner, former prime minister of Canada

"Ted Rogers was a businessman for whom risk did not exist. For him, it was: 'We're charging ahead; we'll figure it out tomorrow!'

Throughout his career, he developed services his clients did not even know they needed. In that sense, he constantly surpassed himself and saw beyond the limits of technology."

—André Chagnon, founder of Vidéotron, president and CEO of the Fondation Lucie et André Chagnon

"You'd be amazed at how he was always pushing, looking for more to do. The big cable move was Maclean Hunter. I still remember how he walked over to my office at Scotiabank by himself, and he had some maps and wanted to talk about something. He lays out these maps showing where all the cable systems are, and asks, 'What do you think?' What do I think? He needs a billion plus, probably closer to two billion, all in. He says, 'Should I go for it?' I thought he should, personally, but of course, I didn't have the authority to do that. But that could never have stopped Ted, anyway. He walked out saying, 'Well okay, it's done.' The next thing I know he's off buying Maclean Hunter. I've never seen a man work harder."

—Peter Godsoe, former president, chairman and CEO, Bank of Nova Scotia, lead director of Rogers Communications

"When Ted got his first cable licence I became one of his first subscribers. I didn't know anything about cable, but the person selling for him had been my principal at Brampton Central Public School for years. So I kept reminding Ted that it was the principal who really set him on the road to success, not anything that Ted did. I was teasing, of course. He was a great Canadian, fun to be with, very enthusiastic about everything he did. I think we owe him for many advances in the field. I will go home and watch the news tonight and I will be watching it through Rogers Cable. Others will tell you about the visionary nature of the individual and how hard he works, but I hope some people will remind the world just how generous he was."

—Bill Davis, former premier of Ontario

"Today, we salute the memory of a man who was not just a leader in telecommunications, but also one of the greatest, if not the greatest, businessman Canada has ever known. Ted Rogers was never afraid to forge ahead, and he took enormous risks over the course of a career that was crowned with great success."

—Pierre-Karl Péladeau, president and CEO, Quebecor

"Ted Rogers was one of the greatest entrepreneurs and builders our country has ever seen. I admired him enormously. For us at CTVglobemedia, he was both a wonderful partner and a very tough competitor. But at all times, he was a gentleman, and his word was his bond."

—Ivan Fecan, president and CEO, CTVglobemedia, CEO, CTV

"Ted Rogers was an extraordinary businessman in every sense of the word. He never hesitated to invest up to his last hundred dollars in his projects. In the past, he even mortgaged his house to pay his employees! I remember him as a visionary and a formidable but generous businessman, one who never hesitated to get his hands dirty in every sector of his company."

—Senator Francis Fox

"Ted was kind and gracious, and totally obsessed with business. During the mid-1990s, I remember we flew out to a board meeting in Winnipeg. We ran into heavy snow, and we didn't get there until four in the morning. We were all tired, but Ted was working the entire time. The next morning he was up at 7:30 for a breakfast townhall meeting. Then we went to a board meeting, and after that he had to make a speech at the Chamber of Commerce. Everyone else was starting to fade, but Ted stood at the door and shook everybody's hand as they came in. Then he made a fabulous speech. This was in the early days of Cantel, before it became Rogers Wireless, and we were competing with Bell at the time. After his speech Ted said, 'Anyone who switches their phone to Cantel will get $100!' And he pulled out a load of cash. So what does all that speak to? That Ted was sensitive to people, totally energetic, totally competitive—and the hardest-working man I have ever met in my life."

—David R. Peterson, former premier of Ontario,
director of Rogers Communications

"I first met Ted Rogers when he was a student at the University of Toronto and chair of the Youth for Diefenbaker committee, preparing for the leadership convention in early December 1956—precisely 52 years ago this week. Ted had come down to Nova Scotia earlier and recruited me as vice-chairman (because there was no other volunteer!) and ensured he got me and all our delegates to the convention to support our hero, Diefenbaker. At that convention so long ago, I saw in Ted the qualities that would mark his brilliant life and career: he was a leader—inspirational, curious, ambitious, thoughtful, dedicated, exuberant—who was imbued with a deep love for Canada. As a builder, entrepreneur, and philanthropist, Ted exhibited those qualities throughout the decades and across the nation he loved. I will always remember Ted with genuine affection and respect because of the loyalty, kindness and friendship he showed me—and many others—throughout his life."

—Brian Mulroney, former prime minister of Canada

"Through many business dealings with Ted Rogers, I have had the great privilege of getting to know him both professionally and personally. He was tough but not confrontational, and bold and confident enough in his abilities to challenge Goliath and defeat him. Ted's business savvy has created a lot of wealth for those who believed in him, and in my opinion he is the Canadian entrepreneur extraordinaire. In his 75 years, Ted touched the lives of many people who no doubt are remembering him with great fondness. I send sincere condolences to his family and friends, who have suffered a great loss but were blessed by having this remarkable man in their lives. Canada mourns the passing of this beloved Canadian who reciprocally loved his country dearly."

—Danny Williams, premier of Newfoundland and Labrador

"A great Canadian has died. It's a loss for our country, and he should be an example for all of us . . . . He knew where wireless would be in five to ten years, but he was also a visionary because he knew his business and his industry so well. He knew the details, and that made him a visionary."

—Isabelle Marcoux, vice-chair and vice-president of corporate development, Transcontinental Inc., director of Rogers Communications

"Ted had an amazing ability to anticipate which industries would become very important in the future. He did that with cable in the early days, he did it with FM in the early days, and he certainly did it with the wireless business. He could spot industries like that, then he could get in on the ground floor and grow them. He'd loyally stick with them, and he'd finance them however he could. He used to say that he'd lever up the petty cash fund if he had to in order to do what he wanted."

—George Fierheller, former president, Premier Cablesystems, former chairman and CEO, Rogers Cantel

"I remember that Ted had just had his heart bypass surgery in 1992, and the doctors were checking on him in post-op. Ted talked them into giving him his cellphone and proceeded to call me, satisfying them that he was in full possession of his faculties and keeping his promise that he would let me know he was fine. Satisfied, the doctors left, but they forgot to take back his cell.

Ted then thought it would be a good idea to make some other calls. In between transferring the calls, I was frantically trying to get someone at the hospital to find Dr. Gosevitz, who was conferring with the surgeons. On the next call from Ted (and this was probably the seventh call) what I did hear in the background was Dr. G's voice saying 'Ted, give me that phone!'"

—Jeannie Hastie, executive assistant to Ted Rogers for 17 years

"With Ted's passing we mark the loss of a true pioneer and a giant in Canadian business. With an unyielding entrepreneurial spirit, he thrived on innovation, competition and the strength of business in Canada. We mourn the loss of a great man whose vision helped shape the Canadian communications industry."

—Darren Entwistle, president and CEO, Telus

"Ted was not just one of our neighbours, but a long-time friend. He was a Canadian business icon and leader, and his legacy will continue."

—W. Galen Weston, chairman and president, George Weston Ltd.

"Ted was generous of spirit, with a wicked sense of humour. My best memories are of the laughs we had together. He was a huge piece of my life, and I am grateful to have known him and worked with him. While we had our business differences, and often disagreed loudly, we usually got to the right place and went on to the next challenge. His death leaves a big hole."

—Colin Watson, former president and CEO, Rogers Cable, director of Rogers Communications

"Like his father, Ted was both a graduate of the University of Toronto and a great man. To mark the 100th anniversary of his father's birth, Ted decided to make a gift to his alma mater.

He made the largest personal gift in the history of the university, $25 million in support of science and technology. It was breathtakingly generous and an enormous boost to the university.

Ted made his decision quickly. He called me at 5:00 p.m.; I went to his office at 5:30 p.m.; he proposed a gift of $1 million but opened the possibility of doing more; and by the end of the hour he asked for a $25-million proposal, which he approved days later and announced two weeks after that. It was not only the university's largest personal gift, but also its fastest. All totally in character for a legendary genius and an extraordinary man."

—J. Robert S. Prichard, president emeritus, University of Toronto, president and CEO, Metrolinx

"I first met Ted in 1985, when he and Loretta donated over $2 million to help create and build a communications complex for the journalism and radio and television programs at Ryerson. At the time it was the largest donation Ryerson had ever received. [The complex] was named the Rogers Communications Centre in honour of Ted's father. Ted believed that education was most critical for building a strong, vibrant and competitive Canada. A large portion of the extraordinary donations he and Loretta made to universities was for scholarships, reflecting their deep belief that giving talented students an opportunity to excel would result in successive new generations of leaders.

Ted was a great leader who inspired us all. His imagination, innovation, risk taking, sense of urgency and above all, his passion and compassion, will live on with us."

—Brian Segal, president and CEO, Rogers Publishing

"I met Ted in 1978 and talked to him for the last time just three days before he left us. That is a long time and a lot of memories. I want to share just two. It was October 1990 and we had given Ted the budget. It was Halloween; my fax at home was spitting out one of his infamous memos, and between kids at the door, a courier arrived with yet more 'helpful' memos. The phone rang and it was that familiar voice, always with the same opening line, 'Am

I catching you at a bad time?' Without waiting for an answer he started in on all the things wrong with the budget. Just when I was about to tear the phone out of the wall, he ended by saying, 'Bill, we are really lucky you are here,' and with that he said good night. And you know the last sentence meant more than the hour of budget talk. The second memory is of visiting Ted and Loretta in Nassau with my family (Marilynne and my kids—Philip, who was 14, and Christine, who was 16) in 2004. We were a bit nervous about how this dynamic was going to work, as I was trying to sell a business (Call-Net) to Ted at the time. We knocked on the door and Ted looked at the two kids and he just lit up. They jumped in a golf cart and off they went—we could hear the laughs all the way down the road. After a little chat with me about business, Ted spent the rest of the time with our kids. He bought the company the next year, and our kids will never forget their 'afternoon with Mr. Rogers.'"

—William W. Linton, CFO, Rogers Communications

"Ted Rogers will be remembered by us all, not only as a competitor who played fairly, but more importantly as a reliable business partner and personal friend. Through his visionary leadership, he first pioneered the build-out of the Canadian cable industry and almost single-handedly positioned Rogers as a leader in the wireless and broadband age. While his place in history is secure, the future will demonstrate even more the true impact of his life's work. His business legacy will perhaps be surpassed only by his philanthropic work, which will benefit Canadians forever."

—Leonard Asper, president and CEO, Canwest Global Communications

"During my career as an investment banker, I had the chance to pitch Ted Rogers on an idea I had dreamed up. The only problem was, it would require him to part with control of an asset, which I soon learned was not what Ted was about. Bob Fung and I arranged the call, and a 30-page pitch book was sent over. We were convinced that the concept made eminent sense, and our only challenge now was to convince the two sides that it was in their interest. The idea was simple: marry up the assets of Rogers Media with those of Torstar Corp. Rogers had magazines and radio stations, Torstar had newspapers, books and weeklies, and the footprints matched up perfectly. We thought that Ted could vend his Rogers Media division into Torstar, and join the voting trust as a full-fledged member. We hadn't checked with Torstar, but in investment banking, that's a small detail to work out later. At the appointed hour, we called Ted up on his cellphone and stated our case. There was silence. Then Ted asked: 'You want me to sell?' 'No, we want you to partner,' we replied. 'One plus one equals three.' 'Sounds like you want me to sell,' was all he said. And the line went dead. Classic. The appropriate ending to a bad idea."

—**Mark McQueen, president and CEO, Wellington Financial**

"Ted was a bold patriot—a chance-taker, but a loyalist, who took seriously his obligations, his friendships and his country.

We first met in the heady aftermath of Mr. Diefenbaker's election sweep of 1958. Ted was unmistakably Toronto, not the Prairies, but there was an inherent populism to him that meshed with the sense of the future which Mr. Diefenbaker evoked. They were both evangelists, both visionaries, both nationalists in their pride and optimistic about what Canadians could do.

Then, and always, Ted was an enthusiast, excited by challenge, able to arouse others. I was a young undergraduate at the University of Alberta, and Ted visited Edmonton and recruited me on the spot to serve with him on the national executive of the Progressive Conservative Student Federation. So he introduced me to my national party, which introduced me to my country. For that, and for his consistent, contagious capacity to look forward, I am in his debt."

—**Joe Clark, former prime minister of Canada**

"What we all loved about Ted Rogers was the joy he took in upsetting the status quo to make things better (from his point of view). The funny thing was that his uncanny ability to ruffle everyone's feathers was coupled with the ability to seamlessly smooth them, and then move on to the next adventure as though nothing had happened. The childish enthusiasm he brought to the execution of each new project was accompanied by his famous relentless drive to see it through. Ted's ego didn't come first: if you stuck by your guns and debated Ted well enough, he would listen and turn in your direction if he thought you were right. Ted's courage to battle both the odds and the critics to see an idea through made Rogers Communications successful beyond even his own dreams. Once he got to one plateau, there was always another. The culmination of all these plateaus is a company that will be a Canadian icon for generations to come. Ted lived for the future, not in the past; because of that, we will be thinking and missing him for many years yet to come."

—Craig McCaw, founder of McCaw Cellular (now part of AT&T Mobility) and Clearwire Corporation

"Ted was a proud Canadian, an exceptional business leader and entrepreneur, and the fiercest of market rivals—no one better defined competition and no one won our respect more than Ted. On a personal note, having faced off against Ted since the introduction of wireless to Canada in 1985, I've lost a friend whose wisdom and constant drive for innovation was a source of both inspiration and motivation. He will be sadly missed but long remembered."

—George Cope, president and CEO of BCE

"For the last 23 years, he battled a series of cardiovascular events, many of which were life-threatening. He tackled each of his problems head on. He was never fearful. He was always brave. He always looked to the future."

—Dr. Bernie Gosevitz, long-time friend and family doctor

"I remember talking to Ted about whether or not we should buy the Blue Jays, and I actually suggested that maybe it wasn't the wisest investment we could ever make. He looked at me and said, 'Tony, you have been my trusted media advisor for 25 years, and I very much appreciate your opinion.' The next day, of course, he bought the Blue Jays."

—Tony Viner, president and CEO, Rogers Media

"In 1969 Ted Rogers needed a high antenna to service his expanding cable TV business in Ontario. He asked me if he could install the antenna on the top of the newly completed TD Tower (Toronto's highest building at the time). Rogers would pay significant money for a long-term lease, and I agreed to the proposal. After the installation was completed, I was amazed at the size of the antenna and I realized Mies van der Rohe, the architect of the TD Centre, would be very annoyed. I phoned Ted and explained Mies' philosophy of 'less is more,' and that TD would never even put a sign on top of the building. Ted immediately agreed to remove the antenna and cancel the lease. He recognized we had both made a mistake and he took quick action to correct it. Forty years later there still is no sign—and no antenna—on top of the TD Bank Tower."

—Richard M. Thomson, former chairman and CEO, TD Bank Financial Group

"[Rogers] was a man of his word. One time he called me up and said 'You know Ian, I have such faith in what you're going to do with pay television, that we've started to buy shares on the open market.' He ended up buying slightly over 20% of the company. He said 'I just want to assure you that this is in no way a hostile act, because I firmly believe in family enterprises and I respect your family. I just want you to know this is strictly an investment and in no way is this meant to be a hostile investment.' He did buy 20% of the company and I offered [Rogers Communications] a seat on the board. And then at some point during that time it was decided that this investment was not a core holding and that he was going to sell it. Just as easily as he bought it on the open market, he could have sold it on the open market, [but] he called me and said, 'I want you to know this is not a reflection of my lack of confidence in you as an operator, it's just that I've got my own issues financially and people have suggested that I sell off some non-core holdings. I don't want to upset you and I don't want to upset the marketplace by putting such a large block on the market at one time, so maybe we can work together and have an orderly sale.' The reason I tell that story is because it shows the kind of person he was, how fair-minded and compassionate he was with people, particularly family enterprises. I have often classified Ted as one of my business heroes. And because I've said that many times internally, upon his death I must have received at last 20 e-mails from employees across the country expressing condolences on my losing a very close friend. I'm truly very saddened by his loss. He had no qualms about calling me on a weekend or late at night, and it was like he was talking to me as if it was 3 o'clock in the afternoon—which I never minded. He'd be upset about something and he'd want to know if I could come see him, and the next day I was always there. If I put something on the table in response to something he had heard or that somebody in the company had told him about, he'd listen, and if he felt he was wrong and I was right, he would immediately say, 'Ian, I'm sorry, you're absolutely right, let's go forward.' He wasn't an obstinate, inflexible, stubborn person. I have only the utmost admiration for the man."

—Ian Greenberg, president and CEO, Astral Media Inc.

"Ted was not a baseball fan. But after I announced I was leaving the Sun he said to me, 'I want you to come and run my ball club.' This was over breakfast at his house. So I said, 'Ted, two things: one, I didn't know you owned a ball club, and two, I didn't know you were a sports fan.' He said, 'You're right, I'm not a sports fan and I don't own a ball club, but with your help I'd like to buy one.' Ted moved in at the right time. He knew when to do things, same with buying the SkyDome. He knew changing the name would be difficult, but calling it the Rogers Centre was a smart move. It branded his input into the community. He took a lot of things out and he wanted to put more back in."

—Paul Godfrey, CEO, National Post,
former CEO, Sun Media and the Toronto Blue Jays

RELENTLESS

TED ROGERS

RELENTLESS

THE TRUE STORY OF THE MAN BEHIND ROGERS COMMUNICATIONS

WITH ROBERT BREHL

HarperCollins*Publishers*Ltd

Relentless
Copyright © 2008 by ELM² Inc.
All rights reserved.

Published by HarperCollins Publishers Ltd.

Originally published by HarperCollins
Publishers Ltd in a hardcover edition: 2008
This trade paperback edition: 2009

No part of this book may be used or
reproduced in any manner whatsoever
without the prior written permission of
the publisher, except in the case of brief
quotations embodied in reviews.

All photographs courtesy of Ted Rogers,
unless credited otherwise.

HarperCollins books may be purchased for
educational, business, or sales promotional use
through our Special Markets Department.

HarperCollins Publishers Ltd
2 Bloor Street East, 20th Floor
Toronto, Ontario, Canada
M4W 1A8

www.harpercollins.ca

Library and Archives Canada Cataloguing in
Publication

Rogers, Edward S., 1933–2008
Relentless: The true story of the man behind
Rogers Communications
Robert Brehl. — 1st ed.

ISBN 978-1-55468-027-6

1. Rogers, Edward S., 1933–2008
2. Rogers Communications.
3. Businessmen—Canada—Biography.
4. Telecommunication—Canada—Biography.
I. Brehl, Robert
II. Title.

TK5243.R6A3 2008
384.5092
C2008-901917-2

RRD 9 8 7 6 5 4 3

Printed and bound in the United States.

Text design by Sharon Kish.

To my wife, Loretta,
and to Lisa, Edward, Melinda, Martha
and the future generations of Rogers.
We did it all for the family.

ESR

To Cobi, Aidan and Charlotte.
And to Paul and Eric; I can still hear your encouragement,
though neither of you is here to see the finished book.

RGB

CONTENTS

Prologue

THE ART OF THE DEAL

It was a sweltering hot July day in San Antonio, Texas, in 1982, when Phil Lind and I arrived. We were in town for a crucial meeting to renegotiate cable rights with Angelo Drossos, the owner of the San Antonio Spurs basketball team. As we headed downtown and drove past the Alamo, I thought about how tough this meeting would be. We were saddled with a bad deal that was sucking more than $1 million a year out of the company. Like Davy Crockett and his men at the Alamo, we just couldn't hold out much longer. We had to get this ironclad, 15-year deal changed.

Drossos held all the cards, and he knew it. Drossos was an entrepreneurial legend in San Antonio, a second-generation Greek American who started out as an Arthur Murray dance instructor and went on to make his fortune in car dealerships, restaurants and pretty much anything else he backed in and around San Antonio. He was known as one of the toughest negotiators in the Lone Star state, with a reputation for being tighter than bark on a tree when hammering out a deal.

Renegotiating this deal was essential for the long-term success of Rogers Cable in the United States. Had we failed to get a new deal, would we be put out of business? No, not likely. But with double-digit interest rates in the early 1980s and our rapid expansion forcing us to borrow more and more, we just couldn't afford to waste money. This deal might not have had a direct impact on our Canadian operations, but it might well have pushed us out of the U.S., a market we would vacate eight years later on our own accord with a $1.5 billion profit. We used that money to invest in the emerging wireless industry in Canada. In hindsight, this meeting takes on even greater meaning than I had thought at the time.

In those days, the cable TV industry in the United States was in a gold rush frenzy. It's largely forgotten now, but cable in Canada was a decade or more ahead of the U.S. in its development. Just as the demand for American programming spurred the growth of Canadian cable in the 1960s and 1970s, it was HBO and my friend Ted Turner's WTBS Super Channel and CNN that ignited U.S. cable growth during the Ronald Reagan years. Those were some of the most exhilarating years for cable, days that will never return.

For cable operators like us, there were two ways to get in the U.S. game back then: either go to various city councils around the country and apply for the cable franchise in that area; or buy up fledgling cable systems that had been awarded the franchise already. Phil Lind, who was then chairman of our U.S. operations, and his team had won scores of these franchises from local councils in cities in California, Oregon, Minnesota and elsewhere. And with Colin Watson, president of our cable operations, we were building out systems like mad across the U.S.

San Antonio was different. In this case, we had bought an existing franchise. The city was growing so fast and furious that the franchise looked like a gem, notwithstanding the lopsided and unfair contract with the Spurs basketball team. In a nutshell, the contract's terms dictated that we pay the Spurs a minimum of $1 million a year to carry their games on our cable system for 15 years. We had to pay the Spurs every year, regardless of whether we had 100 or 1 million paying customers. And the more customers we had, the more we'd have to pay. Looking back, I can see why the previous owners structured the deal this way. It was the early days of pay-per-view and there was a mentality not unlike the late '90s dot-com euphoria. The other reason they took Angelo's bait was that this deal ensured that the San Antonio council would issue them the cable franchise. As I said, Angelo was a shrewd negotiator.

Don't get me wrong, pay-per-view has been extraordinarily successful, both for cable operators and for customers who receive the programming they want when they want to watch it. But it took some time to get there, and in the meantime Rogers Cablesystems was shelling out millions of dollars to the Spurs for literally nothing in return.

In San Antonio, we had a terrific young woman named Missy Goerner working for us. She still works for us today on U.S.-related issues, such as programming rights. I had called Missy a while back and said the deal with the Spurs was too onerous, that we would have to get out of it. She gulped and told me it was all laid out in black and white. In fact, she said, our payment was overdue and we owed Angelo $1 million *right now.* Over the next few weeks, Missy gathered information on the Spurs and, in particular, on Angelo, the majority owner (he had 32 minority partners, including car dealer Red McCombs, who now owns the NFL's Minnesota Vikings). Even with all those partners, Angelo was clearly in charge, and I knew we would have to do something big to get him to renegotiate a signed deal.

Missy turned up some great information. Angelo had a gambling, carny-like personality. He is widely credited with the three-point line in basketball that has added so much excitement for fans. He once won one of his players in a tennis match with another owner, according to Missy's information. There was another legendary story about his spat with Commissioner Mike Storen of the old American Basketball Association (ABA), which later merged with the NBA. Storen made a ruling against the Spurs that Angelo thought was patently unfair. Sports sections in newspapers across Texas and around the United States reprinted the wonderful missive Angelo sent to Commissioner Storen: "F you . . . stronger message to follow." The matter went to court and Angelo won.

We had our work cut out for us. Missy set up a lunch meeting with Angelo in his office in the penthouse of one of San Antonio's tallest office towers. Because Phil and I sometimes have punctuality issues, Missy warned us numerous times in briefing notes and on calls that we must not be late because Angelo was absolutely obsessed with punctuality.

Well, we were running late. Missy was already in Angelo's office. She told me later that Angelo was very cordial to her, but firm. "He let it be known very clearly that this was going to be an unpleasant meeting and if these Canadians thought that they were gonna come in and push him around then they were in for a real shock," Missy recalled. At exactly 12 noon, the lunch was wheeled in. Then, at two minutes past noon, Angelo told Missy: "They're late. Let's start eating." He took the warming covers off not only his plate, but our plates as well. The two of them ate in silence. "It was awkward and I could see him get madder and madder by the minute," Missy said.

Finally, at 17 minutes after noon, we arrived. Angelo's face was a red inferno. He could barely shake our hands he was so mad. Angelo had a horrible temper but he was also a total gentleman in front of women. It was a good thing Missy was in the room. I apologized for being late, but it didn't seem to help. I figured I might as well cut to the chase and tell him the deal was problematic and unfair. Later, Missy told me she was beside herself at this point watching Angelo seethe. She figured I might have blown it. All Angelo said—over and over again—was, "You owe me a million dollars."

"Yes, yes," I said. "I know we're a bit late, because of the transfer of operations."

And Angelo just repeated: "You owe me a million dollars!"

"You're right, you're right," I said. "I brought it with me."

On that cue, two burly Brinks guards brought in two big trolleys filled with bags of cash, $1 million in five-, 10- and 20-dollar bills. There was money everywhere. The look on Angelo's face was priceless. In came a photographer we had hired to take pictures of Angelo and his money. He had a smile on his face as big as Texas. We laughed then shook hands. Angelo said, "You're right, Ted. The deal is unfair. Let's make it fair."

Missy has told me that the new deal saved us at least $5 million over the next eight years, at which time we sold our U.S. cable operations. Angelo was a good man who died too young, at age 68. He repeated that story so many times over the years that it was even told at his funeral in 1997. I once asked him if he'd caught flak from his minority partners for renegotiating. Angelo said he did, but that it was more important to be fair, and that there's nothing better than being partners with someone who understands the art of making a deal. That was a great compliment, and I have cherished it for many years.

Some readers may be wondering why a proud Canadian like me would begin his story in Texas. After all, I have lived my entire life in Canada. My beautiful wife, Loretta, and I have raised four terrific children in Canada, and they all proudly still live in this country with their children, the newest generation of Rogers. In Canada, I reclaimed a family communications business that was lost when my father died when I was only five years old. I like to think our products and services have enriched the lives of millions of Canadians, over my 50 years in business. At times, I have partaken in the cut and thrust of Canadian politics, especially alongside John Diefenbaker, one of the greatest and most underrated prime ministers in our history. I have had a great life in Canada. And I love this country.

So, why start in Texas? That's a fair question.

First, I have always been an outsider, whether in boarding school from ages seven to 17, or in starting businesses that much of corporate Canada routinely scoffed at first, from FM radio and cable TV to wireless phones and high-speed Internet. Even though Angelo Drossos was a like-minded entrepreneur, I was a true outsider riding into San Antonio that steamy July day. Second, I have always loved the art of the deal, the human interaction in business. There is a reason my business card reads: "Ted Rogers, Senior Salesperson." This deal was one of the finest finesse jobs of my entire business career. Angelo was a tough nut who had to be handled the right way. Clearly, I was taking a risk. He could have thought our actions to be a foolish ploy and tossed us out of his office, demanding we honour the original contract. I have long been labelled a risk taker, even a "riverboat gambler," as author Peter C. Newman once called me. But I found out as much as I could about Angelo beforehand to make sure the stunt had a better than 50–50 chance of success. Third, few Canadian companies go down to the United States and really, truly compete and win. Sure, Canadian comedians do, but few Canadian companies. There are more Dan Aykroyds, Jim Carreys, Martin Shorts, Mike Myers and John Candys than there are Research in Motions and Cirque du Soleils. But we did it. Rogers was one of the best and most innovative cable companies in the U.S. throughout the 1980s. And I am proud of that fact.

Lastly, the story is fun. I don't take myself too seriously. And I think more people in business should have fun and not take things so seriously all the time. I can just see former colleagues, and maybe even my current colleagues, chuckling at this statement coming from Ted Rogers. Yes, I admit I have driven people hard, maybe too hard at times, but I do truly believe you have to have fun in life and in business.

And I acknowledge that over the years there have been times when I have taken myself and my work a little too seriously. For this, I have been called a micromanager, or worse. But I simply love to work; and it has taken me a few years to realize that not everyone works like I do. Work and family are my life.

At publication of this book in the summer opf 2008, Rogers Communications Inc. is valued at about $25 billion on the stock market. We own the country's biggest cable TV and wireless phone companies. In media, Rogers has 52 AM and FM radio stations, five Citytv stations, OMNI multicultural television stations, the Shopping Channel (TSC), Rogers Sportsnet regional stations, and some of the nation's best-known magazines, including *Chatelaine, Maclean's, Flare, L'Actualité* and *Canadian Business*. We also own the Toronto Blue Jays baseball club and the building the team plays in, the Rogers Centre (formerly SkyDome).

I don't know quite how to put this: I have been very lucky in so many ways, but I am also pretty ordinary. I was never really good at school. I pushed my way through but I was certainly no scholar. I enjoy making speeches, but I don't use long words because I can't pronounce them properly and I don't know what they mean. I've almost gone bust a couple times and I've had episodes of poor health. So, it's pretty hard to become arrogant with these challenges. I suppose I could become arrogant now that the company's doing better, but I think that's sowing the seeds of destruction that have ruined so many other people and companies. So, I keep living in my memories and remembering all these stories over the years. Sometimes when I tell these stories people laugh and say, "My God, did that actually happen?"

I am an overachiever who comes from strong stock: grandparents and great-grandparents who were highly successful entrepreneurs and philanthropists (one co-founded the internationally acclaimed Hospital for Sick Children in Toronto). My father was nothing short of a genius whose name might well have been as well known as Edison and Marconi had he not died at an early age. My mother was an incredibly strong woman who instilled in me persistence and a great capacity to work hard. Her weakness was alcohol, but she later proved her mettle with pioneering work in Toronto for Alcoholics Anonymous.

I think I have mellowed over the last few years. I have a perspective today at age 75 that is far different from what it was when I was 25 and starting out. I have made mistakes. I have learned lessons, lots of them. I have made bets, big bets. I still make them. In fact, the greatest success of my business life came in the twenty-first century, and it involved two major deals totalling almost $3.5 billion that occurred over one week.

I am an entrepreneur. Was I born that way or did I become one? It's the old nature versus nurture argument. Who can say for sure? Would I have achieved what I have if my father had not died when I was only five years old? Would I be where I am today if not for my mother's relentless push to regain what the family lost? Who knows? But I am not unique. Many successful people, particularly entrepreneurs, lost their fathers when they were young children. The list is endless, but it includes Tim Hortons co-founder Ron Joyce; Canada's longest serving prime minister, Mackenzie King; FedEx founder Fred Smith; Kentucky Fried Chicken's Colonel Harland Sanders; many U.S. presidents from Andrew Jackson to Bill Clinton; philosophers Aristotle and Nietzsche; writers Leo Tolstoy, Robert Frost, J.R.R. Tolkien and Ralph Waldo Emerson; scientist Isaac Newton; and many, many more from all walks of life. As a youngster, you don't truly realize the impact when a parent dies young, but you do later—it defines the rest of your life.

Someone once pointed out to me a fascinating study about successful entrepreneurs, and the "seven factors" that seem to repeat over and over in their lives caught my attention. The study was conducted by sociologists Cary Cooper and Peter Hingley and the findings were published in their book *Change Makers*. These factors are negative early childhood experiences (including death of a parent and/or separation from parents); being self-sufficient loners; self-assurance, motivation and drive; a belief system that eliminates failure as a possibility; early career responsibility; charismatic leadership style; and good communications skills. As you read through these pages of my life, you may see some of these factors; perhaps you'll see some in your life, too.

I have come to the conclusion that eight things have defined my life: a mother bridging the gap between father and son; being alone at boarding school from ages seven to 17; getting the Rogers family back into communications; borrowing money to build businesses and shareholder value; having the determination to never give up and always go after the market leader, not the fourth- or fifth-place entity; marrying a wonderfully supportive wife and partner; overcoming health setbacks and never taking life for granted; and, finally, using tax deferral or tax postponement strategies to help ensure prosperity for future generations of the family.

It's been a good life, a fun life. And as I always like to say, "The best is yet to come."

Chapter 1

ROMANCE IN RADIOLAND

anadians come from many cultures and influences. This diversity is what has made this country so special, not only to us who live here but in the eyes of the world. Though this is changing, our British roots and proximity to the United States have produced an interesting hybrid that has dominated our culture over the last two centuries. I have proud roots in both countries, I might add.

I am by no means an historian, but this is what I know about our name and my ancestors. The Rogers name comes from England and dates back to 1066 and the Norman Conquest by William the Conqueror. Our branch of the family has been traced back to 1508 to a man named John Rogers the Elder, in Moulsham in the County of Essex. With the exception of two men, my ancestors in England were fairly average people, who worked hard to feed and house their families. The two exceptions were Sir Edward Rogers, who rose to be part of Queen Elizabeth I's inner circle of advisors as a member of the Privy Council, and John Rogers, who was burned at the stake for his "heretical" Protestant beliefs during the religious wars of the sixteenth century.

The first of my ancestors to cross the Atlantic to the New World was James Rogers, who boarded the galleon *Increase* from the London docks on the Thames River in April 1635 when he was only 20 years old. Less than two months later, James Rogers landed in Stafford, Connecticut. He was one of the first—but certainly not the last—great entrepreneurs in this branch of the Rogers family. A merchant trader, James Rogers was the wealthiest man in New London County, Connecticut, when he died in October 1687.

Over the next century, the Rogers in New England would prosper and grow. In March 1785, Timothy Rogers Jr., the great-, great-, great-grandson of James Rogers, moved farther inland to Shelburne, Vermont, and began farming land overlooking beautiful Lake Champlain. Timothy Rogers was a spirited and restless man, a natural leader who was persistent in achieving his goals throughout his entire life. He was a devout Quaker, a movement that began in 1660 in England as the Religious Society of Friends and evolved into a faith that shuns many of the trappings of Big Religion and concentrates on the congregation, who often meet in people's homes. Quakerism sprung to life as a reaction to the dogma of organized religions and it had its greatest growth and influence in the United States beginning in the late seventeenth century under William Penn in Pennsylvania. Then, as today, Quakers embrace many meaningful ideals, including hard work, community, family, pacifism and humanitarianism. During Timothy Rogers's time many Quakers found themselves uncomfortable as the U.S. colonies fought against England in the revolutionary war that began in 1775 and ended in 1781.

Not long after the end of this war, Timothy Rogers received a land grant for farmland on Yonge Street, north of the Town of York, later called Toronto. It was enough land for 40 farms of almost 50 hectares each. He set in motion plans to bring several families from New England to Upper Canada to start a new Quaker settlement.

Was Timothy Rogers a Loyalist of the British Crown or a pioneer who longed to make a better life for his family, open new settlements and establish new Quaker meeting houses? My guess is he was more loyal to the ideals of Quakerism than to the Crown. And he was a man who stood by his principles. Before leaving for Upper Canada, he was threatened with prosecution under the Fugitive Slave Law in the United States for harbouring two escaped slaves. With his emigration plans well under way, he could simply have skipped town. Instead, he paid $700—a huge sum of money 200 years ago—to buy the slaves and then promptly gave them their freedom.

In the winter of 1801, Timothy Rogers and his wife, Sarah, and their 15 children ages one to 24 loaded seven sleighs with their possessions and headed to Upper Canada from Vermont. Several weeks later they arrived in Newmarket and began clearing land to farm and building homes and new lives in Canada. It didn't take long for Timothy's restlessness to reappear. After establishing the Quaker settlement in Newmarket in 1801, he pushed farther east to Pickering, Ontario, in 1809 to establish a second Quaker settlement and operate a mill. Unfortunately, these were sad years. Seven of his children, including five married daughters, died during a flu epidemic in 1809–10. Sarah also perished after witnessing the deaths of so many of her children. Timothy remarried at age 57 and had four more children before his death in 1828, at age 71.

My family's direct link to Timothy Rogers comes through his daughter Mary, one of his children who died in the flu epidemic. Mary had wed a man who shared her surname, Asa Rogers, in 1799 and they had four children before Mary died in 1809 at age 27. Mary and Asa Rogers's son Elias later became the father of Samuel Rogers, who was born in 1835 and who is my great-grandfather. He was an exceptional man in many ways.

The name Samuel is an important part of our family heritage. My father was the first Edward Samuel Rogers and I am proud to be Edward Samuel Rogers Jr. In fact, as a boy I was known as Sammy, never as Ted or Edward. Today, my son is Edward Samuel Rogers III and his son is Edward Samuel Rogers IV. Tall and burly with a full beard, Samuel Rogers was a visionary entrepreneur whose Quaker roots instilled in him a sense of community and philanthropy. Samuel foresaw the importance of oil soon after it was discovered in 1858 in Petrolia, Ontario, now recognized as the cradle of the world's oil industry.

He started Samuel Rogers & Company and distributed oil in Ontario from the Petrolia area and from Pennsylvania. By the 1880s, his company held the exclusive Ontario distributorship for the products of Standard Oil Company of New York. The company grew, but competition became fierce when 16 Ontario refineries formed the Imperial Oil Company. With his sons Joseph and Albert (my grandfather) now in the business, Samuel Rogers & Company held its own and merged with Standard Oil to create Queen City Oil Company in 1898.

Behind Samuel's business acumen was a compassionate man, especially when it came to children. He was the co-founder, along with John Ross Robertson, of the world-renowned Hospital for Sick Children in Toronto. The original four-storey 320-bed facility opened on College Street in Toronto in May 1892. His philanthropy extended to education, in particular Pickering College, a private school founded in 1842 just east of Toronto. While Pickering College, which is now located in Newmarket, is no longer a denominational school and is non-sectarian in its program, it values the roots of its Quaker foundation. The Quaker precept that "the object of education is to give every opportunity for the good principle in the soul to be heard" remains central to the school's educational philosophy. When Pickering closed in 1885 following a philosophical rift among the Society of Friends, it was Samuel Rogers who came to the rescue, giving money and soliciting contributions from Quakers around the world to reopen the school in 1892.

When fire all but destroyed the school in 1905, Samuel's son Albert Stephen Rogers was chairman of the campaign to reopen the institution on the site of the original Yonge Street Quaker settlement of Timothy Rogers. The land was purchased by my grandfather and donated to the school, and the main building of

Pickering College is named Rogers House. Samuel died in 1903 at age 68, and eventually Imperial Oil took over Queen City Oil in 1912. Samuel's two sons, Joseph and Albert, were directors of Imperial Oil for the rest of their lives and, true to their Quaker traditions, they insisted that all Queen City employees be treated as though they had always worked for Imperial Oil as part of the sale agreement of Queen City Oil. My grandfather Albert Rogers married Mary Elsworth in 1897 and they had three children: Katherine Mary, Joseph Elsworth and Edward Samuel Rogers, my father, who was the youngest and born June 21, 1900.

My father was a genius and a visionary who always ran ahead of the pack. He was an inventor full of dogged determination whose business skills were also excellent, albeit overshadowed by his scientific accomplishments. (His life has been chronicled in a fine book by Ian Anthony entitled *Radio Wizard: Edward Samuel Rogers and the Revolution of Communications*.) I do not wish to go over well-trodden ground, but I must write about my father because he is such a big part of my life, even though he died 70 years ago, when he was only 38 years old.

I am not sure that *idolize* is the correct word to describe how I feel about my father—but it would be close. He and his spirit are obviously central to who I am. And over the first four decades of my life, my mother instilled in me a drive to excel and to win back the family businesses we lost after his death.

This story may shed some light as to what I mean. A few years ago, when I was 70 years old, my longtime friend John H. Tory, who held several important executive positions at Rogers before moving into politics and becoming leader of the Progressive Conservative Party in Ontario, asked me when and if I would retire. It was around the time when my school chum Hal Jackman, who built a successful financial services empire and went on to become Ontario's lieutenant-governor, decided to retire. We were having a casual conversation as we walked down the birch log steps to the dock at our cottage in Muskoka. I told John I couldn't retire because it would dishonour my father because my work was not yet finished. This answer came naturally to me, and I thought nothing of it. That's just the way it was. But it surprised John a lot. He told me later that he was taken aback and at a loss for words, a rare occurrence for my good friend. That day at Lake Rosseau, John had expected my answer to be that I couldn't because I wouldn't know what to do with myself if I wasn't working. But the answer was about my father and his—and, by extension, our—family's unfinished story.

John later went on to say how extraordinary and exemplary it was for a man who has achieved as much as I have over the years to hold his father's legacy so near and dear. John is very kind, but as I said earlier, that's just the way it is for me: I am incredibly proud of both my father and my mother. Sure, they both had their faults, like every human being, but they were exceptional people and I don't see why my feelings would change over time.

When talking about my father, I am at a disadvantage because I didn't really know him. During those first five years of my life, he worked so hard and he played so hard that I didn't see him much. But I remember this: he was a happy man. And he had friends who were happy, people like broadcast pioneer Harry Sedgwick and eclectic thinker Henry Parker, a futurist like my father who worked on the radio manufacturing side of the business. When they were together, they laughed a lot—all the time, it seemed. I have cherished that childhood memory for 70 years.

My dad loved to work, dream and have a great time. He would often work through the day and the night, maybe get a couple hours of sleep, work through the next day and then drive to New York with my mother, where they would go to the clubs and party with all sorts of friends. He was a young man in a hurry to do a lot of things. He enjoyed life. My great sadness is that I really didn't play with him much or have many pictures taken with him. I think there are only one or two pictures of the two of us together, whereas my son Edward and daughter Melinda—the only two of our offspring who have so far blessed Loretta and me with grand-children—must have 10,000 pictures of their children with them. I think that's great and maybe I should have spent more time with my kids, too. I realize that the technology of picture-taking has advanced greatly and that it is so much easier to take photos today than it was in the 1930s. Still, I wish there were more pictures of Dad and me.

My father's accomplishments were extraordinary, from a very early age up to his untimely death. Edward S. Rogers Sr. was born on the cusp of a great communications revolution. As a youngster, Dad set up a laboratory in the attic of his family home at 49 Nanton Avenue in the Rosedale neighbourhood of Toronto. By age 11, he was monitoring telegraph reports of the sinking of the *Titanic* while at the family cottage at Pointe au Baril on Georgian Bay. At age 13, he made newspaper headlines as the kid who picked up a report on his telegraph set of the shipwreck of the S.S. *Haverford,* which ran aground on rocks off of Queenstown, Ireland. The next year, on August 3, 1914, he was one of the first in Canada to hear the First World War being declared while listening to shortwave broadcasts from London at the family cottage. I understand he never lost the impish side of his nature, which may explain why later in life he was able to enjoy people from such diverse back-grounds—artists, scientists, business people. He was not the sort to be scared off by eccentrics.

My father attended Pickering College, the private boarding school endowed by his father and grandfather, and then went to the University of Toronto's School of Practical Science, where he "graduated" in 1922. I put quote marks around "graduated" because Dad left school early, without formally graduating, but he was later given his degree in recognition of his achievement as an inventor. His mind rarely wandered from radio and other electronic matters. He was so passionate about radio and communications. It's funny how genes work. My passion for the communications business is what has kept me going all these years through the many ups and downs of business and physical health.

When he was only 24, my father invented the alternating current radio tube by which people could simply plug their radios into a wall socket instead of relying on cumbersome and messy batteries. Today, when telephones are so small they fit into your pocket and are powered with tiny batteries that last days and days, it is hard to imagine just how bulky radio batteries once were and what a leap forward the batteryless radio was. Those old batteries were heavy and they would often leak fluids all over the floor. My father knew plug-in radios were the answer. But radio engineers at the time kept telling him it could not be done because using an AC current to heat the filament inside the tube would cause a near-deafening hum. He was just a kid in his early twenties and he didn't listen to them, thank goodness. On August 1, 1924, his groundbreaking work produced an innovative tube that electromagnetically and electrically shielded the input and output circuits and eliminated the hum. "Just plug in and tune in!" was an early marketing slogan for the radios.

With his father, Albert, mentoring and his older brother, Elsworth, working for him, Ted Rogers set out to manufacture radios and created the Standard Radio Manufacturing Corporation Ltd. In 1925, these new radios were selling for prices ranging from $110 to $370 apiece, or roughly the equivalent of $1,400 to $4,600 today. There is no doubt he revolutionized the radio industry: within five years almost every radio set sold was a batteryless, and prices dropped to as little as $39 for basic models by 1931. Along the way, Standard merged with Grigsby-Grunow Company of Chicago, which made Majestic Electric radios, to form Rogers-Majestic Corporation Limited in October 1928 and do battle with the giants like Westinghouse and General Electric. Rogers-Majestic was by then the single largest radio manufacturer in Canada.

My father then started radio station CFRB (Canada's First Rogers Batteryless), which went on the air in February 1927. It was yet another brilliant stroke, because he could use the radio station's programming to increase the demand for radio sets. CFRB and Rogers-Majestic started cross-promotion advertisements in Toronto newspapers and employed other advanced marketing tactics for the times, like driving a truck around town with loudspeakers tuned to CFRB and carrying New York programming through a deal with William S. Paley, president of Columbia Broadcasting System (CBS), a contemporary and friend of my father.

CFRB quickly grew to be the biggest and most powerful radio station in the country and Rogers-Majestic had trouble filling all the orders, even when they were pumping out more than 500 radio sets a day at the Toronto manufacturing plants. Even the Great Depression couldn't slow things down: Rogers-Majestic was selling more than $500,000 worth of radios each month and employing more than 600 people. When jobs were scarce and bread lines long, my father provided many jobs to help many families. At the time, he received offers to move much of the radio manufacturing to the United States. There were lucrative incentives in each offer, but he refused even though part of the company was now owned by Americans. He was a proud and loyal Canadian.

During the same decade, my father was also experimenting with a new medium called television. In August 1933, he had radio personalities Foster Hewitt and Gordon Sinclair take part in a closed-circuit TV experiment in the Eaton's College Street store. Their images and voices were transmitted via wires to rudimentary television sets in the store that turned the heads of fascinated shoppers.

Dad began experimenting with radar concepts in 1936 in the basement radio laboratory of his home. This new technology would help the Allies win the Battle of Britain only four years later in 1940. Admittedly, it is unlikely that his work with radar ultimately helped Sir Robert Watson-Watt perfect the technology, but it illustrates how my father was always looking ahead and trying new things, especially when it came to radio waves. His mind was always racing and his genius was framed by tenacity. He worked long hours, often through the night, testing a theory, discarding it, and testing another theory. Legendary broadcaster and newsman Gordon Sinclair, a CFRB mainstay for many years, once said this about my father: "Genius has often been described as an infinite capacity for taking pains. And that describes Ted Rogers."

My father was also a good listener. He would listen to people's ideas and build upon them. For example, in April 1924 he travelled to Pittsburgh on a research trip to meet legendary inventor Frederick S. McCullough, who was experimenting with alternating-current tubes. The two worked together and my father bought the Canadian rights to the experimental tube and returned to Toronto to perfect it and develop it into a workable device. This ability to listen and connect the dots may be the greatest gift my father gave me. Over the years he would visit different laboratories and factories, take the best idea from each one, add his own versions and ideas and bring it all together. I've tried to do the same in my business life. People say to me, "How could you possibly come up with all this?" I tell them that I listen, I write a lot of notes and I ask someone to write background papers for me. Then I ask another person to write a background paper on something that is relevant or related but not the same. And then I sort of put it all together. That's what my dad did, as well.

During those heady days of radio, it is a wonder my father had any time to meet my mother, let alone court and eventually marry. But he met Velma Melissa Taylor in the late 1920s at a University of Toronto social function; he was immediately smitten by the statuesque, strikingly beautiful auburn-haired debutante daughter of William and Minnie Taylor of Woodstock, Ontario. My mother was born June 19, 1906, and was almost exactly six years his junior. She graduated with a bachelor of arts degree from University

College in 1925, a rare occurrence for women in those days, especially for someone still a teenager. In January 1930 my mother accepted my father's proposal and they were married days later, on February 1. The timing was typical for a man who moved quickly and whose business motto was "It can be done." The local newspapers dubbed theirs "The Romance of Radioland." The wedding took place at St. Paul's Anglican Church on Bloor Street East in Toronto, a block from our Rogers Communications headquarters today, with another ceremony at the Quaker Meeting House in Newmarket. They honeymooned in Florida, Jamaica and Cuba.

I was born on May 27, 1933. I was not the healthiest child. There have been reports written over the years that I was so sickly at birth that the doctors told my parents I might not make it through the night. I don't know if that is true and I cannot recall my mother ever telling me that. Over the years, there have been similarly incorrect prognoses about my business ventures, too, so I wouldn't be surprised if it had happened. I can tell you that as a child I was painfully thin due to an infant celiac condition that disrupted my digestive system and metabolism and even caused the loss of most of my sight in my right eye during my first year. (Later in life, I would also battle glaucoma, but thankfully I have not gone blind.) As a youngster I was fed sugar pills, which I detested, until age six as a way to strengthen me and to add weight. I was a skinny little fellow, but I was a fighter.

I remember my mother telling me when I was a boy that "God, in his wisdom, didn't give you a body for football and such, but he did give you something to balance that, a good brain—but you are the one who has to use it." Mother was a good woman with good judgment. Like everyone, she was only human, but she was at the core a wonderful person. For example, during the Depression she pawned many of her personal possessions to help provide crucial financing for the family businesses which, in turn, helped Dad keep hundreds and hundreds of jobs in Canada helping Canadian families.

Within a year of my birth, we moved into a bigger, more comfortable home on Glenayr Road in the Forest Hill neighbourhood of Toronto. Though immersed in business and all the paper-shuffling and decision making, my dad was still hands-on when it came to experimenting with various electronic technologies of the day. He set up his laboratory in the basement of the new house and he would head down there most every night. Toward the end of the decade, the grind of the Depression was beginning to ease and my father's commercial interests were all hitting their full stride. He and his businesses were on the cusp of creating ever more great things, including a lasting legacy. But after the events of May 4, 1939, my life would never be the same.

Chapter 2

THREE OF THE BEST

In the spring of 1939, the clouds of war were gathering over Europe. Seemingly distant from those threats, life in Canada was peaceful, but certainly not easy after a decade of Depression hardship. On Wednesday May 3, 1939, Toronto was drenched by an afternoon thunderstorm. The streets were still slick in the early evening as my father drove his white Packard automobile up Spadina Road to our home at 405 Glenayr Road. It had been an exceedingly busy and long work day for my dad at the radio manufacturing plant, but this was not unusual.

That evening, as was so often the case, he and mother entertained several dinner guests. They both enjoyed the company of their many friends. I was sent off to bed and could hear laughter and talking as I drifted off to sleep. It is odd how memories are imprinted on us: I can remember little else first-hand about my father other than his laughter. At the time, I was five years old and still an only child. I was excited about my sixth birthday approaching.

After the dinner party that night, my mother went to bed and my father headed to his workshop in the basement. It was quite normal for him to unwind in the evening by heading downstairs to his laboratory to try out one theory or another. After a couple of hours, he retired to bed. My mother told me years later what happened next. She steadfastly refused to tell me these details until I was an adult.

She was awakened in the middle of the night on May 4 by sputtering coughs and moans coming from the bathroom. She called out to Dad but he didn't reply. She jumped out of bed and ran to the bathroom. The door was slightly ajar. She grabbed the handle and burst into the room to find a scene that would haunt her for years. Dad was hunched over the sink, seemingly unconscious. There was blood everywhere: in the sink, all over the floor, splattered across the wallpaper. An aneurysm had ruptured and my father was dying.

An ambulance arrived and he was rushed downtown to Toronto General Hospital, about 10 minutes away. At the hospital the doctors discovered that an ulcer, caused by the extreme stress of overwork, had burst and hemorrhaged at the same time as the aneurysm ruptured. A weaker man would have died instantly. Surgeons worked on him and blood transfusions were pumped into him. Remember, this was 1939, even before the Second World War had started. Medical technology was not what it is today. Still, Dad battled and it looked as if his condition was improving. But the hospital was running out of blood. His radio station, CFRB, which was only on-air dawn to dusk in those days, came back on the air Thursday night, urging people to donate blood to save my father. As the dinner hour approached on Friday, he appeared to rally. But it was not to be. A second attack occurred that night and he passed away early Saturday morning on May 6, 1939, at the age of 38.

During those tumultuous 72 hours from the late-night attack to his death, I was sent to stay with a distant cousin named Wendy Rogers and her father on Roxborough Avenue, unaware that I would never see my father again or hear his jovial laugh. His death was a shock to so many people, not only to his family but to the Toronto business community and to his many admirers in the radio industry around the world. The news of his passing was widely reported, wherever radio waves could carry it. To me, perhaps the most telling and poignant report ran in the *Globe and Mail:*

Edward Samuel Rogers gave the world his electric radio receiver before he had reached his middle twenties. He was a young man who declined to let obstacles stand in the way of success. His invention conferred great blessings on mankind. Like the inventor of the telephone and electric light, Ted Rogers often "burned the midnight oil" before he worked out the problem which had baffled older heads. He spent long hours in laboratories and worked his tiny transmitter at night, sending signals across the seas. Young folks and old were thrilled by his success. It provides a lesson for other young men inclined to the defeatist attitude.

That says it all. He was a man filled with perseverance. His motto was "It can be done." And he got things done. I am proud to have inherited a measure of the tenacity and perseverance that were so much of his makeup. Without my mother's relentless drive to make sure these qualities came to the fore in me, would this perseverance and determination of Dad's be so much of who am I, too? Probably not as strongly, but I am sure they are in my DNA. Nothing in business drives me crazier than people coming to me with a list of why things can't be done, especially highly paid executives who are richly rewarded to tell me how things *can* be done.

Dad's funeral was held on May 8, 1939. CFRB president Harry Sedgwick, a wonderful man and a loyal friend to Dad and later to me, read a special tribute over the air:

Canadians may well be proud that the first all-electric radio in the world was made by Ted Rogers here in Toronto. Since that time, he made many outstanding contributions to the science of radio communication; and broadcasting, as we know it today, is heavily indebted to him. He guided the destinies of CFRB from the outset, and Mr. Rogers was more than an executive head of this station. From his earliest years the miracle of wireless communication was his governing obsession. He was, however, to all, high and low, kindly, generous and considerate.

Just before 3 p.m. CFRB played Handel's poignant and haunting *Largo* and then the station fell silent for two hours as a mark of respect during the funeral. With friends, dignitaries, colleagues, and business associates, including U.S. radio executives, in attendance, Ted Rogers Sr. was laid to rest in Mount Pleasant Cemetery in Toronto on that drizzly, dark day.

Later that month, close to my birthday, Dad's will was probated and the estate was valued at $384,243, a significant amount of money that was left to mother and me. But it could have been a lot more, especially when one considers the success of the radio manufacturing business and CFRB, the country's largest radio station. Rogers-owned enterprises employed close to 1,000 people at the time. I am not crying poor, mind you, but I feel the need to point out that, at the time of his death, there was a perfect storm that prevented the Rogers family from retaining control of what my father had built.

First, by sheer coincidence, the new Canadian "death tax" came into law in 1939 just weeks before Dad's passing. I cannot recall exactly how much the estate paid to Ottawa, but it was significant. The death tax would remain on the books until 1972, when the capital gains tax replaced it. Second, Dad died without life insurance. This was a much different era from today and it was not unique for men with young families to be without life insurance. And third, there was a family feud between mother and Dad's older brother, Elsworth.

I can only guess that there were many reasons for the feud, from Uncle Elsworth's feelings of inadequacy because he had worked only for his father (my grandfather Albert) or for his younger brother (my dad) all his life to a simple personality conflict. Mother was naturally protective of her husband, and she always felt Uncle

Elsworth would put down his little brother at any opportunity, despite my dad's indisputable successes. Elsworth could be a real bugger, a real bastard. For years I would send him a Christmas card and write at the bottom: "Love to see you," but he never replied. Grudges often fester and grow within families. Regardless of the reasons, this feud hindered any chances for the Rogers family to retain control, and it may have led to Elsworth's giving mother poor advice in February 1941, when she relinquished power over the companies Dad had built.

The bottom line: all of my father's businesses were sold or shuttered. I have always believed that my father's estate got screwed. Some may say this is sour grapes, but I believe otherwise. Regardless, what transpired nurtured a drive to fight and get back what was lost, and to do my utmost to ensure that the Rogers family does not lose control after *my* death. It is one reason why I have thought about death throughout all stages of my life and why I set up my first estate trust in 1968 when I was only 35 years old .

After my father's death, Rogers-Majestic Ltd., also known as the Canadian Radio Corporation, was taken over by British Rediffusion Inc., a communications company headquartered in London, England. W.C. Thornton Cran, an officious man who managed British Rediffusion, came in to the company's offices and took down all reminders and pictures of my father. It was as if he wanted to erase all of my dad's accomplishments. For years to come he would be a thorn in my side. He even kicked me off the CFRB property and banished me from the station my father founded. I would exact a measure of revenge against "Winks" in 1960, but more on that later.

CFRB, where Uncle Elsworth remained a vice-president after his brother's death, was separated from the manufacturing company, and eventually sold to the conglomerate Argus Corporation. Dad had given Harry Sedgwick a lifetime contract and Argus honoured that contract, in no small part because they recognized the talent in the man. Sedgwick was a radio pioneer and staunch defender of private broadcasting in Canada. He held the distinction of serving a remarkable 14 consecutive years as president and then chairman of the Canadian Association of Broadcasters, from 1935 to 1948. Like my father and my mother, Sedgwick was posthumously inducted into the Canadian Broadcast Hall of Fame. (I have also been so honoured, which means all the more, being next to my father, my mother and Harry Sedgwick.)

Philips Electronics Ltd. soon acquired British Rediffusion and continued to manufacture Rogers-Majestic radios. (As a youngster in the 1940s, I remember seeing the latest models on display at the Canadian National Exhibition, where, coincidentally, Dad had introduced his first batteryless radio to the world in 1924.) Philips discontinued the Rogers brand name altogether in 1964.

The months after Dad died were sad times, indeed. I was too young to appreciate what it all meant, losing both my father and the family businesses, but more personal challenges lay around the corner. My mother started to drink heavily after Dad died, very heavily. And when I was seven years old, mother received advice that would have a great impact upon me. Mom was connected to the medical community through her brother, Dr. Allen Taylor of Windsor, Ontario, and some doctors were urging her to send me away to boarding school "because I needed male influence in my life." Dr. Alan Brown, a pediatrician, convinced mother that it would be best to send me away. Now, I can't blame mother, really. It would have been difficult to argue against a man like Dr. Brown, who was physician-in-chief at the Hospital for Sick Children and one of the co-inventors in 1930 of Pablum. He was also strong, aggressive and domineering and he never doubted that he was right. Dr. Brown's advice to my mother might have been appropriate for a 12- or 13-year-old boy, but I was only seven.

Nonetheless, in September 1940, as the Battle of Britain raged overseas, I faced my own personal blitz when I was shipped off to Montebello, Quebec, to a boarding school called Sedbergh, 500 kilometres from home. I went from living at home with a nanny who helped me with everything to getting bullied if I didn't do something right or sometimes simply because I was small and skinny. I just *hated* it. I wanted my mother, not boarding school. I am sure it was and is a fine school, but I should never have been sent there at that very young age.

Immediately, I knew I couldn't stay in the place. I ran away a couple of times but that didn't work. So I hatched a plan to get home. As with any challenge in life, you have to be determined to find a solution. After three weeks, I wrote to my grandmother, Mary Ella Rogers, and persuaded her to intervene. She went to my mother and said, "Velma, I'm a very old lady and Sammy is so far away at Sedbergh. I never see him and I'm going to die one of these days, and I'm asking you to bring him back and put him in a school in Toronto, where I can see him."

It worked. Mother put me in Upper Canada College, where I boarded even though it was only blocks from our house. My family could visit me and I went home three weekends per term. (Grandma lived another five years, until May 1946, so I got to see her a lot more than I would have if she had not appealed to my mother.)

In June of 1941 I got a second father when my mother married a remarkable man named John Webb Graham, a lawyer six years her junior. John served overseas as a major in the Royal Canadian Armoured Corps during the war, and later became general counsel with the Imperial Life Assurance Company. He truly was my second father and a steadying hand for years in both my business and personal development. John and I had an instant bond because he had been only 14 when his father passed away.

The wedding took place at the Church of the Messiah on Avenue Road, and was followed by a reception at the top of the Park Plaza Hotel in a restaurant with an outdoor patio, where guests could look out over the entire downtown Toronto area. Boy, the city looked great from up there that day. Some military people attended the reception, including a general covered with ribbons and medals. I went up to him and asked, "Are you more important than my new daddy?" He looked at me and said, "Not today, son, not today."

When the reception was over, I followed my mother and John downstairs. And as they got into the car that was the first step to leaving on their honeymoon, I jumped in too. Somebody pulled me out and I was very confused. I said, "Don't children always go on the honeymoon with their parents?" All the adults laughed.

While they were away, Grandma came and lived with me. I remember thinking it might be the end of my boarding school days because now I had a dad and the male influence in my life that Dr. Brown told my mom I needed. But it was not to be. John was shipped off to Europe to fight the war and I was sent back to Upper Canada College. All told, I was a boarder from ages seven to 17, when I went to the University of Toronto and finally returned to live full-time at 405 Glenayr Road. Those 10 years shaped me a great deal. When other young boys were being sent to their cozy beds with a glass of milk and a hug from their mothers or nannies, we were being marched off, sometimes after a caning for misbehaviour, to our cots in a lights-out dormitory.

I was nicknamed "Bones" and was teased a lot. Even with one bad eye, I decided to get into boxing at school. My advantage was that I had greater reach than kids in my weight class. My disadvantage was that I didn't pack much firepower in my punch because I was so scrawny. When I started boxing, I got knocked out a lot, but I was determined. By fifth year, I actually won my weight class. It just goes to show that you can achieve anything if you are persistent enough.

I remember many a night falling asleep not counting sheep, but wondering how I was going to get control of CFRB back into the hands of the Rogers family again. Often I would worry that

Uncle Elsworth's son Stephen would beat me to the punch. These are pretty deep bedtime thoughts for a boy of that age, but that's just the way it was.

Upper Canada College had a definite caste system when it came to the boarders and the day students. Day students often looked down their noses at boarders and didn't associate with us simply because we were boarders. People often think I come from Toronto's establishment but I really didn't get to know many of the kids from that echelon at UCC because they were all day students. Some day students, like Bill Boultbee, of whom you'll hear more later, befriended me. My best friend, Toby Hull, was also a day student. And what a friendship! Toby has been there for me through thick and thin and he has served graciously and ably on the board of Rogers Communications for more than 40 years, through the many peaks and valleys.

Boarding at UCC affected me in many ways, and it is difficult to know exactly the full toll. For example, when my mother became pregnant, she and John told me the great news in the school's parking lot. They couldn't take me home or to a restaurant because it was not one of the three weekends in the term when I was allowed out. When my wonderful little sister, Ann, was born on September 25, 1943, I saw little of her for the first seven years of her life. I love her dearly and I think we missed an opportunity to bond even more during those early years.

Then there was the time, at age 12, when I experienced real emotional hurt, genuine pain, for the first time in my life. I am talking about something much deeper than being teased or bullied. When the war ended in 1945 and their dads came home, a lot of the boys who were boarding left the school. When John came home, I thought my time in boarding school was finally up. I was wrong. John probably thought that, because he was only my second father, my mother should have the final say. My mother wasn't well; she was drinking heavily and it wasn't a happy situation at home, so she opted to leave me at UCC. I remained in boarding for five more years, until 1950, which is about the time she turned the corner and beat her addiction and became a stalwart member of Alcoholics Anonymous.

It wasn't all bad at boarding school. I don't want to create the impression that it was a prison. It wasn't. We had a lot of fun at different times, especially during my teenage years. I was mischievous and I got into a lot of trouble.

When I was about 15, my friend Harry Wasylyk and I were the bookies of Upper Canada College. We had discovered that the racetrack makes money by taking money out of the betting pool and then dividing the remaining money up among the winning ticket holders. We figured we'd take bets and do the same thing. It was a mathematical game, not really gambling on our part. Or, so we thought. When players won, we paid them the amount reported in the newspaper, which was after the racetrack took its cut. We even listened to race results on CHUM radio, and if a guy bet after the race had been run and he happened to have the winner, then we'd just say that we were sorry, the race has been run and we can't take the bet. But if he wanted to bet and he didn't pick the winner, then we might just accept his bet and let him see the results in the next day's newspaper.

We took bets for a term or two until several people started winning all of their bets. We couldn't figure out how they were doing it. At first, we thought they must be pretty lucky. Then we found out that a Hamilton radio station called CHML ran the results a few minutes before CHUM did. These wise guys outsmarted us by listening to the earlier CHML broadcast and then running down and placing bets with one of us. We had done okay booking bets until this came along, but we figured we better close our horserace operation before any teachers found out.

At school, I loved debating, and I still do. Participating in school debates is such wonderful training for business. It sharpens the mind and teaches you to focus on what you say. In my final year at Upper Canada in 1950, I won the Wallace Rankin Nesbitt Cup for extemporaneous speaking when I put forth the benefits of universal medicare.

Lorne "Butch" McKenzie was the principal of Upper Canada for most of the time I was enrolled there. Debates were important to him; he really liked to win. Butch was missing a finger and he was a very tough guy; I found him very intimidating. One day he passed me in the hall and said he was looking forward to the big debate coming up the next Saturday against another private school. "Rogers," he said, "Good luck. Do your best, do what it takes."

"Okay," I said. "Yes, sir."

That Saturday, the opposition proved to be a much more mature debating team than we were, and we started to lose badly. All I could think of was what Butch had said to me about doing whatever it took, and an idea came to me. I stood up when it was my turn.

"Mister Chairman, we've listened here with awe and are impressed by the information that's being provided by the other side with all sorts of statistics that they've given us, which is also very impressive. But you know, fortunately this debate is taking place in a library. Now a library is the place for the truth and the facts. They can't be changed or embroidered and so in the book that's on the shelf up there, if you turn to page 167 and I quote . . ." I then pretended to quote from some book, utterly destroying the other side's case. It was absolute nonsense, pure fiction. But no one called my bluff, no one picked up the book that I referred to and checked what I said. We won the debate. Afterwards, someone finally opened up the book to page 167, and of course it said something altogether different. But by that time we had won and were out celebrating. But Butch McKenzie found out.

After the Monday morning announcements over the intercom, Butch came on: "Will Ted Rogers come to my office immediately."

When I arrived there, he said, "You've disgraced us. It's an outrage, it was a lie. There was no book. The head of the losing school has phoned and he's complaining. What do you have to say?" Steam was coming out of his ears while he waved that hand with the missing finger.

"Sir," I said, "you remember we met each other passing in the hall, right?"

"Yes, I do," he snapped.

"You said to me, do what it takes, do what it takes. I did what it took and we won."

"Get out of my office. Get out," he said.

I had him and he knew it. He liked me but he didn't like being had. Luckily, that time I escaped without getting caned. I wasn't as fortunate other times. For instance, we had a housemaster named Jim Biggar who would march us all off to the Anglican church each Sunday so we could pray and put our nickel in the collection plate. One Sunday I decided I would go instead to a Quaker church, or meeting place. Up until my dad's generation, my family had been devout Quakers, but I had never been to a Quaker church. Being a young rebellious teenager, I thought I'd like to go and see what the service was like.

Biggar realized that I was not at the Anglican church with the rest of the kids and later brought me into his office and told me I would be getting "three of the best" for skipping church. Just as I was about to lean over to get whacked, I asked him if I could get "six of the best" because I might go back to the Quaker church next Sunday. After I had taken a few, he realized that he was caning me for going to the church of my choice, so he stopped.

Biggar was also, without his knowledge, part of my very first communications network, in 1949 and 1950. Television was new and I wanted to pick up signals across Lake Ontario from Buffalo. I secretly rigged a four-metre antenna on the roof of Seaton House, our dormitory building at Upper Canada College. It was hidden and you could not see it from street level. I installed pulleys so that I could even lower it out of sight during the day. From the antenna I ran a cable down into my room, where it was hooked up to a TV set. Viewers were invited to gather around, for a small fee, to watch the marvel of television. I loved playing around with electronics, as my father had, but I also liked to watch the faces of my customers and knew I was delivering to them a compelling, innovative service worth every penny of their admission fee. Everything worked well until one stormy night when the antenna blew over, toppling off the roof and crashing through Biggar's window below. And so ended my first communications network, and I endured one of the severest canings of my childhood.

I may not have been able to sit down for a few days, but I certainly knew I was onto something. Just as my father had found 25 years earlier that people would pay for crystal-clear reception from a radio plugged into an electrical outlet, I found people would pay to see crystal-clear TV programming. It also dawned on me that I shared my father's two great gifts, his passion for electronics and business acumen, but that my entrepreneurial side outweighed my interest in engineering wizardry. I would always enjoy the technical aspect, but I now knew unequivocally that at my core I was an entrepreneur.

Chapter 3

THE CHIEF AND ME

I have always been a list maker. Writing lists and notes to myself has helped me plan and establish priorities. People who know me well know about the Daytimer I keep in my pocket in which I jot down ideas or even little details of my daily life. I have been writing little notes to myself for as long as I can remember. It is a constructive use of my time.

Time is one commodity I think about a lot: first, because my father was denied half the normal lifespan when he died at such a young age and, second, because I have had many health challenges over the years, including heart failure. Today, the average lifespan for a man in Canada is 78 years, a little more than 28,000 days. So far I have been granted about 27,000 days. Making lists help me make the most out of each moment.

At the beginning of the 1950s, I made a list of things I wanted to accomplish in life. At the top of that list was getting the Rogers family back in control of CFRB, the country's biggest radio station, which my father put on the air in 1927. I also wanted to finish university and get a law degree because mother kept telling me I had to have something to fall back on if I went bust with all the entrepreneurial ideas buzzing around in my head. I wanted to marry and have a family. I wanted to be a successful entrepreneur, probably in broadcasting but I wasn't about to limit myself, either. I also wanted to have some sort of impact in politics, another of my passions.

Even though I was turning just 17 years old in 1950, I knew the decade was going to be an important one as I moved into adulthood. It was table-setting time for me. I would meet so many people in the 1950s who would help shape who I was to become in both my business and personal lives. These new people would include John Diefenbaker, John A. Tory, Peter Appleyard, Joel Aldred, John Bassett and John Roland (Jack) Robinson. And, of course, Jack Robinson's daughter (and my future wife), Loretta Anne Robinson.

In the early 1950s one could see, feel and almost taste the economic prosperity, not just in Toronto but across Canada and beyond. After the Depression and the Second World War, this was a new and different world. It was exciting. Everything seemed to be expanding and growing with opportunities everywhere. And I was busting to get out and find my way.

First there was school. As I have said, I wasn't much of a student. If I am remembered at all at Upper Canada College, it would be for my hijinks and tinkering with my radio and TV equipment, not for my schoolwork. I was more apt to be phoning stockbrokers during recess or running over to CFRB to watch live radio programming than cracking a book or turning out for college battalion marching drills.

One year my mother and my second father, John Graham, really leaned on me to work harder on my lessons. For a term I applied myself and rocketed up to the top of the class standings, but what a dreadful time it was. No fun at all. When the marks came out, I said to John and mother: "There, I've shown you I can do it, and now I'll go back to believing that if you get 50 percent you'll get ahead just as fast as the person who gets 90 percent." That wasn't the brightest thing I ever said or did. My grades slipped so badly afterwards that I had to redo several courses to bring my marks up so that Trinity College at the University of Toronto would let me attend.

With my time at UCC over, I was back living at 405 Glenayr Road with my family. It was good to be home, to have my own bedroom, to see my mother, my second father and my little sister every day. I remember I used to have my friends over all the time. We used to call my house Club 405 because the address was 405 Glenayr.

Attending university was important to me. For one, it provided an opportunity to join the Sigma Chi fraternity, which has stood me well my entire life. (You never say, "I *was* Sigma Chi"; instead you say, "I *am* Sigma Chi.") Being Sigma Chi opened a lot of doors for me. For example, in the 1980s when Rogers Cable was operating in the United States, I needed to meet with Tom Frost who ran the Frost Bank in San Antonio. It turned out he was Sigma Chi too. We had a great first meeting at dinner, not just as guys looking to borrow and lend money, but also as Sigma Chi brethren.

One of the other things about the fraternity I have always enjoyed is that Sigma Chi was founded on the principle that true fellowship prospers only when people of *unlike* minds, talents and personalities come together. In other words, Sigma Chi is very inclusive, not snobby like some fraternities, and its members really widen their circle of the type of people they get to know.

I don't like snobbery and never have. We all put our pants on one leg at a time. Anyone can suffer misfortune, get sick or lose their job after a company goes bankrupt. So many things can happen in life. I don't know how anybody can be snobbish. For example, why do some overeducated people think they are better than others? Just because they know bigger words they think they're more intelligent or more worthy than the rest of us. Some people who have been handed a lot of money and have never worked a hard day in their lives are snobs. They dress better because they spend more time worrying about such matters. And they believe themselves to be real "ladies and gentlemen," with no idea what those words really mean. John Graham, for one, was a gentleman, a real gentleman. He had class without having to show off. But some people put on airs and have to flaunt what they have.

John Graham was unique. He took credit for nothing, but did so much, especially for me. John helped me get into every school I ever intended. My marks were never any good. And whether it was Upper Canada College or Trinity College or Osgoode Hall Law School, he always was the one who got me in. He would say, "It's up to you to get out, but I'll get you in if I can."

I remember talking to him one time about a large portrait of my father that hung on the second floor of our home on Glenayr. (I still proudly display it in my home.) I said to him, "Look, I think we should probably take that down and I'll put it in my room or somewhere else because you're married now to my mother." And he said, "No, no, no. It is right to leave the picture up."

John Graham really was a dad to me. He taught me many things, including the value of keeping meticulous financial records, which I have from the time I was 13 years old. I kept a ledger of what I earned and what I spent, from $14 shoes bought at Eaton's to subscriptions to financial newspapers. I still have those old-fashioned green ledgers somewhere around the house. This training from a young age has been very important, not just in business but in every aspect of my life. You have to have an accounting of how you're doing to be able to make clear decisions on where you want to go.

John Graham took me to my first political meeting in 1949, a Progressive Conservative nomination meeting, which ignited a lifelong passion for politics. A fellow Sigma Chi, Larry Skey, was a candidate, and George Drew, the leader of the federal Progressive Conservative Party at the time and a former Ontario premier, was speaking at the event. I loved the atmosphere, the excitement in the air. I got the political bug that night.

Drew was a decent man who had been a good premier. After the war, he brought planeloads of people from Europe to Ontario to build new lives. But Drew later ruled the federal Progressive

Party with rigid control, much like Paul Martin did years later with the Liberal Party. Drew and his cronies did not like John Diefenbaker for exactly the reasons I was drawn to him: Dief was a populist who represented the voice of rebellion in the party. The people of privilege, those who backed Drew, wanted Diefenbaker stopped. But he couldn't be stopped. People loved Dief, who had lost his first wife to cancer, because he was like them: a small-town guy who wanted everyone to get a fair shake, not just the privileged. People could identify with him, understand him. He was like them. He was ordinary, but also extraordinary.

In the early 1950s, I was elected president of the Toronto Young Conservatives and chairman of the National Progressive Conservative Student Federation. It was only a matter of time before I would butt heads with the party establishment because I envisioned a party of inclusion, which Diefenbaker personified.

One day I came up with this idea to invite Dief to speak at a luncheon at the Albany Club on King Street East in Toronto, a tony Tory hangout. The Young Conservatives had a little bit of money left in the treasury, and I used it to subsidize the price of tickets for the younger people and to pay for a photographer. I knew Dief would draw several standing ovations, but just to be safe I also planted friends who would get to their feet at key moments. I told the photographer not to take pictures of Diefenbaker or the people cheering him on. Instead, I said, take pictures of the people who are sitting glumly on their asses. He looked puzzled, but I explained that we wanted to have a record of these folks as Dief's popularity in the party grew.

The party establishment was none too pleased, especially Alexander David (A.D.) McKenzie, the Toronto lawyer who was at the controls of the George Drew machine in Ottawa and Ontario premier Leslie Frost's team at Queen's Park. In the parlance of politics, he was the party boss. I was summoned to McKenzie's office on Bay Street, a street where many of the establishment still hangs out. McKenzie was a brilliant lawyer with a cunning mind, cold blue eyes and a strong jaw. In 1917 he had been gold medallist at Osgoode Hall Law School. Some, like lawyer Eddie Goodman, have described A.D. McKenzie as "the greatest backroom politician that ever existed." I respected him a lot, but I was too young and naïve to fear him.

As I sat in a big leather chair in his office, he did not attempt to hide his anger. He told me it was inappropriate even to invite Diefenbaker to speak at the lunch when Drew was still the leader. Then he tore a strip off me for taking pictures of people who sat on their hands during the standing ovations for Diefenbaker. Right then and there, he told me that I was no longer president of the Toronto Young Conservatives. I impishly informed him that I had been elected and that he couldn't fire me. He just said, "We'll see" and told me to be at a meeting the following night.

The room was filled with Tories from the Toronto Establishment, but I brought along some friends, too. It was a spirited meeting. The debate about my fate as president of the Tory youth group went back and forth until one in the morning, and the final tally was 17 to 15 against me. Clearly, the Drew camp was getting nervous; the vote to oust an outspoken supporter of the renegade Diefenbaker was closer than McKenzie had anticipated. Still, it was a setback for me personally. But as with any setback I've had in life, it forced me to sit down, make a list and come up with a plan. I was still chairman of the student federation, and I would use that perch to help Dief become the next leader of the Progressive Conservative Party of Canada.

It was now 1956 and a convention was approaching in December. Under party bylaws, each university that had a Progressive Conservative Club would be awarded two votes at the convention. In those days, there were about 1,000 delegates at conventions, so if I could collect two votes from 25 universities or more, it would be a real coup for the Diefenbaker camp. I travelled the country, either forming clubs or talking to existing clubs to convince them to back Dief. I first met Joe Clark at one of these clubs in a church basement in Alberta.

The Maritimes were a gold mine because there are so many wonderful universities there. At St. Francis Xavier in Nova Scotia I met a young man named Brian Mulroney, who would be a hard-working gofer for us at the convention and a lifelong friend. There was no club at the University of New Brunswick, and I didn't know any Conservatives there, so I phoned a Sigma Chi brother named Barry Ritcey and asked him to round up 20 people for the first Conservative Club meeting the next night. "But Ted," he said, "I'm a Liberal." We laughed, but he still got 20 guys out and I got two more votes for Dief at the convention.

By the time the convention rolled around on December 14, 1956, Dief had overwhelming support from the student federation, but he was far from winning, or so it seemed. After all, Dief had come up short in both the 1942 and 1948 leadership conventions so we were taking nothing for granted. Davie Fulton and Donald Fleming were both tough candidates, too. Fulton was from the West, a smart guy and a strong Catholic. Fleming was the Toronto candidate and very powerful in the party. Undoubtedly he was the favoured choice of the Establishment.

On the convention floor we were losing the "sign war." On camera, it looked as if Fulton and Fleming had more than enough supporters and we didn't have enough. I don't relish admitting this, but I came up with an idea to win the sign war. One thing politics had already taught me was that to be successful, you've got to make decisions fast. That lesson has carried over into my entire business life. You can't run a company by committee. I am not always right, but I do know that dithering is always the death knell of success.

At the convention, I said to some of our bigger, hulkier guys, "Look, here's what I want you to do. We want to pick off the Fleming people first. So, go inside and get next to someone carrying a Fleming sign. Wait for our signal and then kick the sonofabitch right in the shins as hard as you can. He will drop the sign, grab his shin, and hobble off the floor." It worked beautifully. With Fleming out of the way we then went after Fulton's people, who were tougher to beat because they kicked back.

The rest is history. Diefenbaker carried the convention and was a first-ballot winner with 774 votes out of 1,284 cast. His victory drove the party establishment a little batty, I think. Diefenbaker wanted to turn the Conservative Party into a party of the people, not the party for the privileged. It's easy to say that, but you have to show it. Working-class districts in Manitoba still vote Tory because of him. He was a sole-practitioner lawyer, not a big-firm guy, and he took on cases often without getting paid if the person didn't have the money. He was the hero of so many people, and still is.

It was quite something for me to see this change up close. I was young, rebellious and a big activist. If I had been brought up differently, if I hadn't been sent to boarding school and had instead hung out with the Establishment kids as a day student at Upper Canada College, I probably wouldn't have become such a rebel.

Dief was a great prime minister. He made some mistakes, but he did many, many great things. For one, he was so proud of Canada and Canadians. He did not believe in hyphenated Canadians the way the Liberals did. He believed everyone was Canadian first and foremost. He helped people from different backgrounds to get ahead in politics. For example, he was the first prime minister to have a Ukrainian Canadian in the cabinet. Now there's a paradox—he was against calling someone a Ukrainian Canadian but boasted that he was the first guy to put a Ukrainian Canadian into a cabinet position.

Over his six years as prime minister, Dief did so many good things but he had never run anything but a law office with one secretary so some of it was really quite beyond him. He didn't have the management skills or flexibility that a prime minister requires.

The Conservative Party had not been in power since 1935 so Dief didn't have much bench strength, either. He did have some really fine people, such as Alvin Hamilton, a man who was decades ahead of his time in recognizing many new directions, from the value of fresh water to opening up the vast Chinese market to Canadian products. Dief had Donald Fleming as finance minister and Davie Fulton as justice minister, but he needed more experienced and visionary people in his government. David J. Walker, a terrific man whom I campaigned for several times in the Toronto riding of Rosedale, was another Diefenbaker supporter. My guess is that lacking full and total support from the party establishment didn't help Dief, either.

We had so much fun working on Walker's campaigns. During the 1957 campaign a fellow named Frank Nutbean borrowed his dad's truck so we could go around and pull up Liberal lawn signs at night. The problem was that Nutbean didn't tell his dad he was borrowing the truck so his father called the cops and reported it stolen. The police saw the truck parked as we were rounding up lawn signs and arrested everyone except me. I was so skinny back then that I managed to hide behind a tree. I ran home to tell John Graham what had happened and he went down to the station, smooth-talked the police, and got my co-conspirators out before the story made the newspapers and hurt Walker's chances.

The general election was held on June 10. That morning David Walker met with his campaign workers and started divvying up areas where we'd all go out and try to get as many Conservative voters to the polls as possible, a common practice called "getting out the vote." The plan was to phone residents to see whether they needed a ride to the poll and to hand out pamphlets near the polls, trying to persuade the undecided voter to go Conservative.

"Where are the Liberals strongest?" I asked at the morning meeting. On the map of the riding, Walker pointed to a polling station beside a Catholic senior citizens' home. Historically, Liberals have done well capturing Catholic votes. "I'll take that one," I said. I pulled together a few friends and we lined up just outside the polling station. As the seniors came out of their building next door and headed toward the polling station, we started chanting: "Vote Walker! Vote Liberal! Vote Walker! Vote Liberal!" Some of these seniors must have voted for Walker thinking he was a Liberal because there were more Tory votes from that polling station than in any of the previous elections. It was all fun and games. We didn't use any tactics the Liberals haven't done to the Conservatives in spades over the years.

Diefenbaker has gone down in history for his role in cancelling production of the Avro Arrow fighter jet. In the long run, this decision was not totally wrong but it was handled so badly, and it showed his lack of management skills. Dief should have said he supported Canada's development of fighter planes, but that we wouldn't be able to sustain the program over the long term on our own. He should have led the charge to partner with the Americans. It's like in business: if you come to the conclusion your company can no longer survive, you must shut down, sell or merge. Had we merged with the Americans we might have been able to keep some of the jobs and the advanced research and development work here in Canada.

I didn't see much of Dief while he was prime minister, between 1957 and 1963. But I do remember visiting him in his office on Parliament Hill once. Before the meeting, I was told I would have 10 minutes with the prime minister, no more, no less. I started calculating in my head: one minute to greet him and ask how things are going, another minute to sit down and get comfortable, and another minute or two because he loved to tell stories and he surely would lay one on me. I was nervous that there wouldn't be any time for me to get my pitch in.

When I was escorted into his office, Dief threw me a curve ball: he said he had to use the washroom. I panicked, thinking that I would run out of time with the prime minister. As he headed to the water closet in the next room, I didn't know what to do. Next thing I knew, I was following him into the bathroom and giving him my pitch. He always teased me afterwards that I was the only person with the gumption to go into the prime minister's washroom while he was using it!

In the end, the party establishment took out Dief. But this was a wonderful time of my life, being part of the growing populist Diefenbaker movement in the mid- to late 1950s. The Diefenbaker people were almost a fraternity. We were all abused. We were all outsiders bucking the Establishment, beaten up all the time. In the end, we lost the fight to Dalton Camp and the rest, but the Diefenbaker years were a great time in my life.

Chapter 4

LOVELY LORETTA

few days after Christmas in 1957, I met the most important
person in my life, Loretta Anne Robinson.

A new Sigma Chi member by the name of Ian Henderson
invited me down to his parents' place in Lyford Cay, Nassau,
Bahamas, for New Year's. Ian, who was studying at the University
of Toronto, was the son of the Bahamian chief justice. Their home
was two doors down from the Robinsons, who were British. Jack
Robinson was a long-serving Tory member of Parliament who
knew everyone in Britain, from Winston Churchill on down. At
their winter getaway in Nassau, they didn't host many parties, let
alone parties for their son, Richard, and their daughter, Loretta. But
this was just such a party. It was special and they had invited Ian. In
Lyford Cay when you're invited out, it is customary to ask whether
you can bring a houseguest, if you have one. So when Ian said he
had a houseguest, the Robinsons told him to bring me along.

When we got to party, Ian went in and I chatted with the
father on the doorstep. We were talking politics, of course, and
I was telling him all about John Diefenbaker and my role in the
Youth for Diefenbaker organization, and he was telling me all
sorts of things about England and its politics. We talked for about
25 minutes, between his greeting guests, and I was enthralled.

Suddenly I saw this beautiful blonde girl walk past. Jack
Robinson introduced me to his daughter, Loretta. After introduc-

tions, we danced, and danced again. Before I knew it, pretty much everybody had left the party, including Ian. Jack Robinson called out: "Would one drunk take the other drunk home!"

I was intoxicated, but not with alcohol. It had been a fairytale evening. That may sound corny, but that's how it felt. Loretta teases me to this day that I spent most of the evening talking to her father, not her, but that's not how I remember it. Anyway, after her father barked out that command to get out, I looked around the room and there was nobody else there except Loretta and me dancing and a guy named Johnny Wanklyn, on the couch. If he wasn't passed out he was sure showing signs of fading fast.

Johnny was staying in a house down the street, so I had to haul him out. But beforehand I asked Loretta if she would have dinner with me the next evening. I was 24 and she was 18. Being British, the Robinsons thought my invitation a tad forward and held a family conference where it was decided I could come over to their house for dinner and that her brother Richard would escort us out to a club afterwards.

Loretta and I talked a lot that night. She told me she was born in London on April 13, 1939, only three weeks before my father died. I told her that my dad had died when I was five and that I never really knew him. The same thing almost happened to Loretta: both her parents came close to dying when she was a baby.

On June 8, 1939, when Loretta was less than two months old, Jack and Maysie Robinson planned to fly back to London from their vacation spot in the south of France for a day or so to look after some business affairs. (Jack held the distinction of never being defeated in an election over his 33-year career in the British House of Commons. Maysie was the daughter of Clarence Warren Gasque, an American businessman who ran the Woolworths department store chain in England and owned a big part of the company.) They left Loretta and her older brother, Richard, with the nanny in a rented château while they flew home.

The regular pilot was sick and a substitute was sent from London, a man who came highly recommended, as he had often flown members of the royal family. He flew to France to pick up Loretta's parents, who were the only passengers; after refuelling he failed to do the proper checks before the return flight. They took off and got up a few hundred metres, then went into a tail-spin and crashed at the airport. The Robinsons and the pilot were pulled from the wreckage just before the plane exploded in flames. Maysie Robinson was sent to a French hospital and couldn't walk for two years after the accident. Jack Robinson was in the hospital for several weeks with compound leg fractures and other injuries. The pilot survived but lost his licence.

After the war started, Maysie was told she had to leave the French hospital because all available beds would be needed. Jack put his family on a ship for America, where they lived with various relatives in New York, Maine and Florida for the next six years.

Jack Robinson served in the Royal Air Force during the Second World War, then he returned full-time to the House of Commons and was chairman of the Conservative Commonwealth Affairs Committee from 1954 to 1964. He was knighted in 1954, and was raised to the peerage in 1964 as Baron Martonmere and appointed governor of Bermuda, where he served until 1972. Like my hero John Diefenbaker, my future father-in-law was a populist. Before the war, he was one of the leaders of the movement for paid holidays for workers. As governor of Bermuda, he was often quick to deplore government policies that harmed poorer people. He served as governor longer than anyone since the eighteenth century, which underscored his popularity on the island.

In November 1945, Loretta, Richard and Maysie returned to England to reunite with Jack Robinson after the war. In the early 1950s, when Loretta was in grade eight, she was sent to a boarding school in Palm Beach, Florida, until grade 12. Unlike me, she wanted to go to boarding school. After boarding school, she attended Wellesley College, an Ivy League liberal arts school for women near Boston. She did not enjoy the experience, as she found the staff and faculty to be heavy-handed and negative. She left after two years. From 1959 to 1961 she studied art, a lifelong passion, at the University of Miami and was incredibly happy there. During the years she was in college we maintained a long-distance relationship. It often wasn't easy but we did have fun visiting each other in Canada, the United States, Bahamas and England.

One time, she came up to Lake Rosseau in Muskoka, where I was building a cottage right next to my mother's cottage on Tobin Island. I was 25 by now and in law school, and I was running a music business on the side. I had made some money on the stock market with Rothmans shares and I was using the $30,000 in proceeds to build this getaway. Loretta, then 19 years old, teased me for meddling too much with the construction workers when I said I didn't want them to use this particular type of board here or that type of material there. Imagine the nerve of this young lady accusing me of micromanaging a project! Of course, this behaviour really only endeared her more to me. We still have the cottage and later we purchased mother's cottage, too.

It has been more than 50 years since I first met Loretta, yet I find it hard to believe that it has been that long. We've had a great life together. Sure, like any marriage, there have been ups and downs along the way, but we've been through it all together. In September 2008, we celebrated our forty-fifth wedding anniversary and I simply can't imagine what my life would have been like without her.

Chapter 5

COMRADE TED

In the spring of 1957, I was inside Massey Hall in Toronto listening to John Diefenbaker kick off his first election campaign as the leader of the Progressive Conservative Party. The hall was jammed and there was electricity in the air.

After a rousing speech by the Chief, I made my way to the stage to say a few words to him and get my picture taken with him. On my way up, I shook hands and exchanged pleasantries with the evening's master of ceremonies, Joel Aldred. It was the first time Joel and I met. Lo and behold, within a couple years John Graham would bring us together again, and Joel would be an important early partner of mine in the radio and television world.

It is safe to say that in 1957 Joel Aldred was the best-known Canadian in show business. He was the announcer on popular TV programs starring Dinah Shore, Bob Hope and Perry Como. He hosted an acclaimed drama called *Studio 57*. He was under contract to pitch products for General Motors, Rothmans and Procter & Gamble. He was effortless in his delivery, a real professional who may well have been seen on more television shows by more people in North America than anyone else at the time.

Unlike Joel Aldred, I was not famous in 1957. I knew a lot of politicians, but outside Trinity College, some Tory youth groups and my Forest Hill neighbourhood, if people heard the name Ted Rogers they thought of my father, not me. But I was beginning to make waves, or at least ripples. As chairman of the broadcasting committee of the national Progressive Conservative Students Federation, I had testified at the Royal Commission on Broadcasting (Fowler Commission) in the summer of 1956. I had made two major recommendations: the installation of an independent regulator, because the CBC had been both a broadcaster and regulator of its competitors since 1936, and the licensing of private television stations in regions capable of supporting them.

I was proud of my presentation because I passionately believed competition would stimulate content development and greater choice for consumers. But as far as exposure and name recognition by the public go, my statements were mere fish wrap by the next day.

Indeed, the most press I had received to that point came about when U.S. immigration officials thought I was a Communist. In January 1954, I flew home from Nassau. In those days, you had to fly through Miami; you couldn't get a direct flight to Nassau, or at least I couldn't. I was travelling with a friend named William C. Boultbee. This was the McCarthy era, when Americans saw Communists under every rock and compiled lists and black books filled with the names of suspected pinkos. As we were going through customs, the officers saw a "William Boultbee" on their list. They pulled Bill aside and asked me if I was travelling with him. I said I was.

"What do you do?" they asked.

"I'm a student and go to university."

"No, no," they said. "Do you work? Have you had a job?"

"Well, I worked on the Progressive Conservative election campaign last summer." As soon as I said the word *progressive* they looked at me funny and pointed: "Over there with your friend Boultbee." We were being held under the provisions of the infamous McCarran Act, which barred people suspected of having Communist affiliations from entering the United States.

They put us under house arrest at a hotel. We were there for three days. The *Toronto Star*, which has always been great at beating the anti-American drum, had a reporter write up some stories about these poor young Canadian kids being held south of the border. One of my Sigma Chi brothers at the University of Toronto named Gary Cooper wanted to help me out, so he sent me a telegram wishing me a happy new year—in Russian!

Back in Toronto some of our university chums carried signs that said "Save Rogers" and "Release Bugs Boultbee" and marched outside the U.S. consulate. The Liberals were in power in Ottawa and John Graham called some friends who got in touch with Lester Pearson, the minister for external affairs, who then called the Americans to have us released.

It was all quite funny. In one picture in the *Star*, I was on the phone with my history book open, pretending to be studying. My poor scholastic abilities were well known. When I got home, my history professor immediately said to me, "Rogers, I bet that was the only time you had that book open the entire time you were away."

"I won't lie," I told him. "It's true. But I had it taken just to please you, to make it look like I was hard at my studies."

He shook his head ruefully and said, "Well, Rogers, as usual with you, I'm not pleased."

It's not that I loathed school work. I just never really took to the discipline of formal schooling. I even flunked a year on my way to a law degree. I was attracted to so many other things in the 1950s, like politics, having fun and concocting money-making schemes to earn a few bucks.

A couple of summers I went down to Windsor, Ontario, to work at radio station CKLW, which my father's company had owned for a spell in the 1930s. The money wasn't good, but I got to see up close how the radio business worked, through jobs in the music library, newsroom and control room. I also kept myself busy showing dogs. I loved sheepdogs, and so did my mother and my sister, Ann. I had a trainer who would get the dogs ready and then I would take them to shows in places outside Toronto, like Guelph. We'd often win Best of Breed because there were rarely any other sheepdogs in the shows. Another summer I sold encyclopedias door-to-door. I was hardly a walking endorsement for higher learning, but the experience helped me hone my cold-call skills.

To be honest, during this period of my life my main business venture involved music. I love music and always have. In 1950, I launched a company called Music Services with a partner named Richard Hoyt Dameron, an old boyhood chum. We would book and supply orchestras for dances at public and private secondary schools, university fraternities and sororities, and other clubs and associations around Toronto. By 1952, I wanted to expand and get better acts and offer service in Muskoka during the prime summer months. Richard and I decided to part ways and I went out on my own. I was 19 when I launched Rogers Music Services.

By about 1955, I was getting set to enter law school but I was also enjoying the music business. I needed office space so I rented an apartment with Toby Hull at 25 Lascelles Boulevard, not far from "Club Glenayr," my mother's house, where I still lived. The building sat on property once owned by my great-grandfather's company, just west of Yonge Street near Mount Pleasant Cemetery, and was one of the few high-rise apartments in Toronto in those days. We had suite 1603. Toby, who was in the insurance business, used the bedroom as his office and I used the living room. It was naturally quite cluttered. The landlord was a man named Reuben Dennis. I liked him, but he was tough. On the second day of the month, he would invariably phone if we were late with the rent. He would say, "Ted, there seems to be a misunderstanding here."

"Yes, Mr. Dennis. What seems to be the problem?"

"You and a few others seem to think I'm in the banking business. Ted, I am not in the banking business. I'm in the apartment business. I'm not here to loan people money. You're supposed to pay your rent on time."

This happened again and again. He wouldn't put up with our hijinks. I wasn't dodging my rent payments on purpose, it's just that I occasionally had a cash flow problem. Collecting money for Rogers Music Services, paying the orchestra and then having enough money to pay our rent was challenging.

I could see real opportunity in the music business at the time. There was a growing talent pool that was being stifled by the American Federation of Musicians, the musicians' union that also represented Canadian talent. The union had a rule that immigrants to Canada couldn't join until at least one year after their arrival. After a year of digging ditches, or doing other things to pay their bills, these musicians' fingers became raw and damaged and they couldn't play their instruments. This was a real cute con game to keep talented immigrant musicians out of the business for as long as possible, sometimes for good. I thought it unfair and I could see an opportunity to hire good musicians without having to pay the high union rates. The plan worked and we had a booming business for a while.

One of the first musicians I recruited was Peter Appleyard, who years later would become the world's premier vibraphonist and who has performed with the likes of Ella Fitzgerald and Henry Mancini. He had come to Canada around Christmas 1951 from Lincolnshire, England. The union had told him to come back in a year for his card, so he was forced to take jobs as an elevator operator, a night clerk at the King Edward Hotel and a salesman at Simpsons department store. Those are all honourable jobs, but Peter wasn't using his talents to the fullest and he was frustrated. I called him up and booked him for Saturday and Sunday nights in Baysville, a tiny village in Muskoka. We found many talents like

Peter who were just itching to play and earn some money doing what they loved to do.

Of course, the union did not like me providing opportunities to these new Canadians. Typically, these thugs used threats and intimidation to get me to stop. One night at the Palace Pier on the Lakeshore in Toronto I was greeted in the parking lot by a few union guys. The boss called me over and told me that he knew what I was doing, he knew about my dad and CFRB and he knew about my ambitions in the radio industry. Bear in mind, at the time this union carried a lot of clout. The government required radio stations to play specific amounts of live music, so radio stations needed musicians and the union controlled the musicians.

The man told me I had better stop what I was doing because if I ever owned a radio station he'd make sure I didn't get any musicians if I kept this up. Some of his buddies started to push and shove me, and they busted up a couple of instruments to drive home the point. In the end we compromised: All the musicians performing for Rogers Music Services were allowed to join the union immediately without any repercussions and I would pay union rates.

There was one other story from this period that I am proud to recount. Pickering College, a private school built on the Timothy Rogers homestead land in Newmarket, which my grandfather Albert helped rebuild after a fire, hired our 10-piece orchestra. It was winter and it snowed heavily that night. The dance was to commence at 8 p.m. and only six musicians had arrived at that point. They started playing and a few more musicians arrived over the next couple of hours. But for most of the show the band featured mostly six out of its 10 members.

Someone at the school came up to me and said, "Look, we shouldn't have to pay the full amount because not all the musicians showed up, but we'll give you a proportional amount."

"No, no," I said, "our guarantee is 100 percent satisfaction or no charge."

We went back and forth a couple of times, and they finally accepted that I would not take their money if they were not 100 percent satisfied. The principal later addressed the school assembly and cited this as an example of how the students should operate when they went out into the real world, whatever profession they chose. I was tickled by this praise, but I would have preferred that they were 100 percent satisfied so I could have collected the money!

While working at Rogers Music Services I learned an important lesson in life: the people who have the worst debts or default on their debts are often the richest people, not the poorest. This says something and it has stuck with me. I am proud that no one in my lifetime has ever lost one cent in receivables or interest on a Rogers account.

At the end of the 1950s, the federal government announced it would license the first private television station in Toronto. (The CBC had had a TV station in Toronto since 1952.) I just knew I wanted to be part of this new venture. But it would be one of the most competitive licensing processes in Canadian broadcast history with powerhouses like CFRB, the *Toronto Star* and others vying for the prize.

At this point, I still had not bought my first radio station and I was articling at the prestigious Torys law firm after almost flunking out of Osgoode Hall Law School. Here I would find a lifelong friend in John A. Tory, whose father and the founder of the firm, J.S.D. Tory, thought little of my future in the legal profession. I was 25 years old and I had a beautiful girlfriend who was in school in Miami. I had a new business partner in Joel Aldred, who was 12 years older and far more famous. I had worked my tail off for a great man who was now the prime minister of Canada, with the largest majority in history.

Of all the opportunities before me in the 1950s, this new television station was the biggest, the best. It was at the top of my list. One day in 1959, I was at a law office waiting for Aldred to show for a meeting when an idea came to me. I scurried off to the nearest private spot, the law office's library, to make a phone call. Standing between several shelves of books, I made what would turn out to be one of the most important cold calls of my life. I've always believed in cold calls because if you don't ask, you don't get. And I desperately needed to meet this man.

"Who the hell are you?" barked the booming voice on the other end of the line. "I don't know you."

I sweet-talked. I told him I was Joel Aldred's business partner. I danced around. I talked up our common interests in Conservative politics. I dropped the names of politicians I knew in Ottawa. I damn near begged. After a few minutes, John Bassett agreed to meet me in his office the next morning at 9:30 sharp. "Don't be late," he said and hung up the phone.

Chapter 6

ON THE AIR

I would be hard pressed to pick just one period of my business life that I loved most. There have been so many wonderful adventures along the way. Certainly, the period when I was in my late twenties would be at or near the top. This may surprise some people because this was before there was Rogers Cable and long before Rogers wireless phones; it was the era of black and white television and bunny ears. We weren't even dreaming about video on phones or high-speed downloads or personal video recorders.

AM radio ruled the airwaves and the industry scoffed at an innovation called Frequency Modulation (FM). Though it was a new technology and nobody had the equipment to receive FM signals, I just *knew* FM was better and would win out in the long term. In our advertisements we would call it "Filet Mignon" radio because it was so superior to AM.

Over and over we proved it could be done when almost everybody else told us it was impossible. Naysayers had told my father he could not develop a radio that plugged into the electrical outlet because the hum would drown out reception, and, like my father before me, I revel in proving the herd wrong. In fact, I never want to run with the herd. Just because something is done one way doesn't mean it can't be improved upon or done a different way. I have always believed that.

While I was juggling one business deal after another in the early 1960s, I was also articling at the Torys law firm where John A. and his twin brother, James M. (Jim), worked for their father, John S. D. Tory. I was supposed to be at the law office full-time, but I was hardly ever there. Jim balked at signing the certificate stating that I had articled for him because I wasn't around enough. In the end, Jim would sign the papers only if I vowed *never* to practise law. I was so grateful I offered to shine his shoes whenever he wanted, which I have done over the years, a couple times at black-tie events in front of a crowd.

I may not have been studying law as much as I should, but I felt as if I was moving at warp speed in other areas. Although I was immersed in business, I was still learning the fundamentals of law, which have never left me and which have been an enormous benefit over the years. Laws change, some come and go, but the fundamentals don't. For example, in any deal I try to keep things as simple as possible and not argue over minutiae. I hold out for what is really important and ignore the rest. The other guy may win nine points in negotiations and I may win one, but if it's the one key item I need, then that's fine by me. A good negotiator is not bent on wringing the last nickel out of every deal. Being prepared, trying to be the most prepared person in the room—this is what studying law taught me.

There is a misconception that my quest to re-establish the Rogers name in broadcasting began in radio with my purchase of CHFI-FM in 1960. The truth is my initial foray into Canadian broadcasting actually began in television as part of the winning bid to bring Toronto its first privately owned station, CFTO-TV.

The radio and TV events occurred within months of each other and, over the years, I have been unintentionally guilty of perpetuating the myth that I got my start in radio. I really don't know why, but at most public appearances I just seem to talk more about the early days of CHFI than the origins of CFTO. And that spills over into media reports, because most articles about my early days tend to focus on CHFI more than on CFTO. In some ways, the CFTO story is more important to me and my long-term business than even CHFI, which Rogers Communications Inc. still owns and which is Canada's most profitable radio station. That may sound odd, but CFTO introduced me to powerful people like the Bassetts and Eatons.

In 1958, the Diefenbaker government overhauled the Canadian broadcasting system by creating the Board of Broadcast Governors (BBG) to regulate radio and television, a function that had been the domain of the CBC for more than 20 years. Until the BBG, the CBC was the judge and jury of Canadian broadcasting, both operating its own network and regulating its competitors. It was a ridiculous situation that many, including myself, argued against at the Fowler Commission hearings in 1956 and 1957. The BBG was the forerunner of today's CRTC (Canadian Radio-television and Telecommunications Commission).

Early in its mandate, the BBG decided it would open up the Canadian television market and license privately owned TV stations in major markets to compete with the CBC in Vancouver, Toronto, Winnipeg and Montreal. The hearing for the Toronto licence was scheduled for early in 1960. Around this time, Joel Aldred and I formed a broadcasting company called Aldred Rogers Ltd. John Graham set us up because his law partner Stan Biggs was Joel's lawyer and John thought we were a natural fit because Joel and I were both interested in applying for the private TV station licence for Toronto. Problem was that Joel thought I had money and I thought he had money. Neither of us had any real capital, although Joel had a lot more than I did at the time. It didn't take us long to figure out we didn't have a prayer of landing this TV licence on our own.

To get into the TV business, Joel and I first tried to buy the CFRB radio station with borrowed money and use its resources to apply for the TV licence. I was still obsessed with getting the

Rogers family back into CFRB, and this seemed like the perfect opportunity to kill two birds with one stone. Our $1 million offer was rejected.

Still, the offer to buy CFRB was typical of the bold moves we would make during this truly exciting five-year period from 1959 to 1964. We were always trying to do the impossible. We changed the Toronto radio market, where only about 5 percent of homes had FM receivers, into one where two-thirds had an FM radio. We were the first to bring high-fidelity FM stereo to Canadian listeners. Together with terrific partners, we fought for the first private TV licence for Toronto against several powerhouses, including the gentlemen at CFRB who stripped the Rogers family from broadcasting after my father's untimely death. We also established an AM radio station in Toronto's overcrowded frequency spectrum and kept re-engineering the signal until it was as powerful as the competition.

Sure, the company was tiny. I remember that when I convinced John A. Tory to join our board around this time he went home and told his wife, Liz, who replied, "Why would you want to sit on the board of that crappy little company?" John has never left our board, and he and Liz have been great friends of mine for 45 years, but the fact is that Liz was right back then: we *were* a little company. But without the seeds planted during this period, we never would have been able to harvest the multi-billion-dollar deals that would come later.

One such important seed was my cold call to John Bassett as part of our bid to get into the TV business. Bassett was heading up a bid for the TV licence in Toronto with the Eaton family and Roy Thomson, who was also an acquaintance of Joel's (Aldred knew everybody) and owner of TV stations in Scotland. Luckily for us, Thomson had decided to pull out of the bid and concentrate his business interests in Britain. After reading this in the newspaper, I made the cold call to Bassett from the law office library and managed to talk him into a meeting.

John White Hughes Bassett was born in Ottawa and educated at private schools in Quebec where his father, an Irish immigrant, rose to be president of the Montreal *Gazette* and later the owner of the *Sherbrooke Record*. He was almost 18 years older than I and about the same height, at six-foot-four-inches. His voice roared like thunder and he often pounded his fists to drive home a point.

Big John, as he was affectionately known, was a newspaperman, working as a reporter at the Toronto *Globe and Mail* in the 1930s before becoming a war hero as a major in the Seaforth Highlanders in campaigns in Italy and northwestern Europe. A Tory like me, he ran for Parliament in Sherbrooke in the 1945 federal election and lost. He ran again in 1962 in Toronto and again lost. I loved teasing him that he should keep moving west and run next time in Manitoba for the Conservatives. In 1952, he persuaded the owner of the T. Eaton Company department store chain, John David Eaton (grandson of company founder Timothy Eaton), to help him buy the failing Toronto *Telegram* newspaper. Ownership of the *Telly* was then vested in a trust for the benefit of Eaton's four sons (John Craig, Fredrik, Thor and George) and Bassett's three sons (John F., Doug and David). Thus was born the incredibly successful Bassett-Eaton partnership. The Eaton money and Big John's business acumen added up to a powerful force.

At my first appointment with Big John in 1959, I asked for 50 percent of the CFTO bid to go to Aldred Rogers and 50 percent to Baton Broadcasting Ltd. (the incorporated company name was a contraction of Bassett and Eaton). Put yourself in Bassett's shoes: here's this 26-year-old nobody trying to replace media tycoon Roy Thomson on his ticket and he's got the gumption to demand half! But that's one of the reasons I loved Bassett. He was an entrepreneur, and entrepreneurs can take an instant dislike or an instant liking to a person, because they make decisions quickly. Thankfully, he took a liking to me or I would have been out on the street.

Years later, Bassett would call me a "practical dreamer who

dreams his dreams and goes out and makes them work." That was a great compliment from a man of his stature; he truly was a hero to me. But I honestly believe you have to act on your dreams. What good is it to dream and then simply sit back and contemplate? It's no good at all.

At that initial meeting, Big John told me to come back in a few days after he had thought things through. At our next meeting, Joel Aldred came along and we managed to get 37 percent, even though we didn't deserve even 7 percent. Maybe I am exaggerating. But we were pleased to get as much as we did. (Our ownership diluted to 34 percent by the time of the licence hearing.)

On October 22, 1959, we signed a simple two-page agreement and formed a company called Baton-Aldred-Rogers Broadcasting (BARB) Limited with the intention of winning Toronto's first private television station, CFTO.

Bassett wasn't our only partner. Paul Nathanson, a Liberal in this otherwise Tory Blue syndicate and founder of the Odeon theatre chain, was a minority partner, as was Foster Hewitt, the voice of *Hockey Night in Canada*. The *Telegram*'s lawyers, Eddie Goodman and Charles Dubin (who went on to head the famous inquiry into the use of drugs in sports and later became Ontario's chief justice), took their fees in stock and were also partners.

On December 10, BARB made the formal application. I knew two things. First, we were in tough competition with 10 other applicants for the licence, including CFRB and the *Toronto Star*. Second, Big John Bassett was the boss of this venture. Though our BARB ownership agreement allowed for flexibility, it could and would lead to conflict, too. And Bassett held the hammer at all times, especially since Baton appointed four of the eight directors, and Bassett, as chairman, could break any deadlock. Regardless, this was a good deal for Aldred Rogers Ltd. For the next three months we prepared for the BBG hearing, set for March 1960 in the Oak Room at Toronto's Union Station.

The BBG was holding similar hearings in Vancouver and Winnipeg, so I went to Winnipeg in January 1960 and watched the proceedings closely, making lots of notes. I came up with a list of recommendations for our best strategy. In a nutshell, we had to rehearse and have our answers down pat during the question-and-answer portion of the hearing. We also needed to be humble at all times and never appear arrogant in front of the board. I witnessed first-hand the looks on the governors' faces when some stuffed shirt appeared before them in Winnipeg. In my strategy letter to Bassett and Aldred at the end of January, I wrote: "We must be humble—sincere, industrious, imbued with the challenge, confident that we can do the job—but always humble."

This advice to two such gregarious personalities as Big John and Joel (in whom humility was not an innate virtue) was essential. In fact, I believed it to be our ace in the hole because I knew Winks Cran at CFRB and my friends at the *Toronto Star* could easily wade into pools of pomposity.

We were to appear on March 14. A few days before, Toby Hull rented a suite across the street at the Royal York Hotel where we could rehearse. Toby's insurance business was taking off at this point and he hoped to land CFTO's insurance account, should we win. The suite, and all the booze, turned out to be a darn good investment by Toby.

During those days in the suite we worked hard, but had a great time and a lot of laughs, too. Tough, rigorous rehearsal of our presentation was really John Graham's idea. He told me to keep a close eye in Winnipeg on those who did not properly prepare. John's advice has become his legacy at Rogers: we always practise and prepare before every hearing. Despite our preparation for the BBG meeting, something happened that we could never have anticipated, and that probably won us the licence in the end.

At the hearing our competitors were saying how many hours of programs they'd produce, how much news, how many sports hours and so on and so forth. There was so much hot air from CFRB and others that you'd think television was nothing more than pictures for radio or reading from a newspaper to entertain viewers. In contrast, Bassett and Aldred cooked up the brilliant idea of actually producing some programs and showing them to the governors. If we lost, the cost of these programs would be written off. But we also knew the programs might actually impress the BBG. I can't recall what the specific programs were, but Joel hired people he knew to produce some news and children's programs.

We had the nearby Meridian Studio lined up where we'd roll tape and then bring the shows into the meeting room via cables hooked up to TV monitors. We rehearsed and rehearsed. Everything went well. Our pitch was that other people promised TV programming, but we actually produced it. When Bassett made that statement that was my cue to press the button and get the shows up on the TV monitors. Every rehearsal went off like a charm. Unfortunately, the night before we were to appear, the city got whacked by a heavy snowstorm. We were first up at the hearing. Bassett made his pitch to the governors and I got my cue and hit the button. As I did, I heard a crackle and then all the lights went out. We were in complete darkness: turmoil took over the room, with the audience talking and moving about.

We didn't know this at the time, but the electric ice melters outside under the sidewalk at Union Station had turned on automatically to melt the snow, and they were draining all the electricity. So when we turned on our equipment, it blew the circuits and knocked out the power. CFRB, the *Star* and our other competitors really enjoyed our problem. And the governors were bewildered.

I kept pressing the button, and Bassett kept talking, saying things like, "You know, Mr. Chairman, you see this is a test of business and entertainment. Of course there are going to be power outages and problems as we go forward, no doubt about it. But you have to choose someone who will be able to overcome these challenges."

He was just stalling for time and praying we could overcome this glitch. The transcribers kept yelling: "Stop talking! We can't write it down!" But Bassett kept talking. The amplifier wasn't working, but he didn't need it with that loud, booming voice of his. Sure enough, he kept talking long enough that the power returned and I got the programs up on the TV monitors. And the room erupted in applause. On March 24, the BBG awarded us the licence. We were to go on air on January 1, 1961—in only eight months.

Those were hectic times. Joel Aldred was named president. Now, Aldred was an outstanding guy; tall, good-looking and with a booming voice like Big John. He definitely understood television, but he was a unique chief executive. It was only a matter of time before he would clash with Bassett and the Eatons. I was named vice-president, but my being only 27 meant that I got saddled with all the menial tasks.

Aldred had the vision to design the studios for colour TV, years before colour became standard. He had the CFTO building in Agincourt built in the shape of a horseshoe so that studios could easily share resources, with the control booths in the middle encircled by studios and sets. This design lent itself perfectly to taping money-making automobile commercials, because the vehicles could drive right up onto the set. He even built huge turntables for the cars so they could spin around during the shooting.

Aldred was brilliant, with a very creative mind, but he didn't have the financial discipline to control costs. He would say, "We have to have this, no matter how much it costs." The cost overruns were getting out of control, with the studios' price tag at $4.5 million. He also didn't show up for meetings, which really drove Bassett crazy. I could see a clash—or maybe "crash" would be a better description—

coming. And you just knew Big John Bassett would be walking away from it, not Joel.

Regardless, we were all working frantically toward our on-air goal of January 1, 1961. Bassett thought I was wet behind the ears and handed me junior jobs, but I took it upon myself to find more important things to do. For instance, the Toronto *Telegram*, owned by the Eatons and Bassetts, was printing a series of articles updating the public on CFTO developments as we headed towards launch day. The *Telly* planned a special section entirely about CFTO for sometime around Christmas. I took it upon myself to go down to the *Telly*'s composing room and read the galleys of these pages before they were printed, just to make sure there were no errors.

The launch of CFTO went off without any extraordinary snafus. J. Keiller MacKay, Ontario's lieutenant-governor, cut the ribbon with Bassett and we hit the air at 9:45 p.m. with an 18-hour charity telethon. We toasted the success of the launch that night with champagne. But reality set in pretty quickly, with lower than expected ratings and higher than budgeted costs.

Both John Graham and I warned Joel about looming trouble. In March 1961, just two months after the launch, I went up to the CFTO studios with John to tell Joel that the train was running off the rails. Joel worked the strangest hours; the meeting was at 2:30 in the morning. I was not yet married with children, so I had the flexibility to meet with Joel at crazy times like that, and John was always accommodating, especially in times of crisis. Joel listened to what John and I told him but didn't really hear what we were saying. He told us that he knew television and that Bassett didn't.

Talk was cheap but operating losses spoke louder. In only the first five months of CFTO, from January to May 1961, the operating loss totalled $762,949 (or $5.5 million in today's dollars). Bassett was a man of action: in March, 58 employees were let go; in April, Aldred returned from a holiday to find Big John occupying his office, although Joel was still president. Joel was none too pleased but he knew Big John held the cards. In May, in another cost-cutting measure, my salary of $10,000 a year was cut to $1,000, while Foster Hewitt, another vice-president, saw his salary cut in half to $5,000.

The reason for the difference in pay cuts was that Big John saw me as being too loyal to Joel and was sending me a warning. Foster, on the other hand, was always obsequious to Bassett and this was his reward. Bassett used to play games with Foster, too, and this was another way he kept Foster off balance, almost giving him a false sense of security when it came to his relationship with Big John. Another time, I convinced Bassett to allow my radio antenna be placed on the 270-metre CFTO tower, which he knew would drive Foster crazy because he had a radio station, too, and would be jealous of the antenna's positioning. What did Big John do when the discussion about approval for my antenna came to CFTO's board of directors? He made Foster bring the motion to a vote and watched him seethe as it was approved.

As we headed into summer, both Joel and I knew the status quo at CFTO was not an option. We offered to sell half our interest in BARB for $500,000, to be released from the company's debt obligations, and for Joel to be paid his annual salary of $50,000 as severance for a year. Bassett turned us down, instead offering to sell us control of BARB if we could find a new partner. That signalled to us that the end of this partnership was in sight.

In August, John Graham and I were summoned to Bassett's house late one night. Some of the Eaton boys were there, along with a cadre of lawyers. Joel and I, and Bassett, had all been talking to potential partners, especially to NBC and ABC in the United States.

In the end, Baton decided they would not sell. Bassett told us that Joel was out and that I could stay on in a lesser capacity. He was not open to negotiation. He asked us to go upstairs and phone Joel with the news. John Graham reached Joel, who was quite drunk, in Montreal. John told him what had happened, and Joel replied, "Tell Bassett to go screw himself."

When we came back downstairs Bassett asked, "Did you reach him? What was his response?" Ever the diplomat, John responded, "Joel said he appreciated being informed of your views and to tell you that he will think over your proposal and give it due consideration." Bassett exploded and unleashed a flurry of four-letter bombs. He told us we had until three o'clock the next afternoon to accept his terms.

Over the next few days and weeks, the negotiations went back and forth, and ultimately Joel left. But he made a $250,000 profit on his investment. I was stripped of my vice-president title but retained 10 percent of CFTO and remained on the board, and CHFI's radio antenna stayed atop the CFTO tower, which was critical for me and my fledgling radio company.

Shortly thereafter, Joel and I parted ways as he concentrated on producing television programming and I got deeper and deeper into radio. My business relationship with John Bassett strengthened, though the road was often bumpy.

Chapter 7

PIONEERING FM RADIO

While the drama played out at CFTO, my radio interests continued to bubble. In 1960, FM radio technology produced a richer, clearer sound, far superior to AM radio. Some likened it to what colour TV looked like compared with black and white. I prefer the comparison of today's GSM digital wireless phones to the old static of analogue cellular technology.

FM was simply a better mousetrap when Aldred Rogers Ltd. paid an entrepreneur named Ed Piggott $85,000 for CHFI-FM on September 30, 1960. (Joel Aldred would leave the partnership within a year to pursue TV programming endeavours, and CHFI would be the kernel that would grow into today's Rogers Broadcasting, with its 52 radio stations and various television properties.)

Eighty-five thousand dollars may not sound like a lot of money, but this was a nascent industry where only 5 or 10 percent of radio listeners in CHFI's listening area even had an FM radio. No one really knew how many FM receivers were out there because market research was embryonic. But AM radio was definitely the undisputed king of the castle in those days. And CHFI was also the only stand-alone FM radio station in Canada, perhaps in North America. By stand-alone, I mean it did not have a big AM station subsidizing costs and providing programming to the fledgling FM outlet. To make matters worse, FM was developing much more quickly in the United States, and American stations along the border were quickly grabbing up FM slots and competing for many of the same listeners in southern Ontario as CHFI.

In one important way, this grab for spectrum by the Americans was a blessing in disguise. The broadcast regulators, in particular Board of Broadcast Governors chairman Andrew Stewart, had the vision and desire to create a vibrant FM industry in Canada. Several BBG decisions at this crucial period were beneficial for FM pioneers like us at CHFI. Still, CHFI faced formidable challenges and no one knew this better than Ed Piggott, who had started the station in 1957 with an investment of $65,000. Indeed, he once told the BBG that many people in the radio industry referred to CHFI as "Piggott's Folly."

Piggott was an entrepreneur through and through who started out supplying and servicing washroom fixtures in gas stations owned by Imperial Oil Ltd., where my grandfather Albert sat on the board of directors. (Life's little connections and coincidences can be funny at times.) By the 1950s, Piggott owned a company that sold coin-operated public toilets, and he rented TV and radio sets to hospitals. He also sold recording and broadcast equipment. He was a good salesman, but he was not a broadcaster.

The radio station faced internal challenges. Much of the broadcasting equipment used at CHFI was junk and had to be thrown out. The studios were located at 13 Adelaide Street East, at Yonge Street, in a cramped and drafty old three-storey building. On the ground floor were a convenience store and a greasy spoon. Visitors to CHFI entered between the two establishments by climbing a steep staircase amidst a decor of linoleum and fake wood veneer. My office was on the third floor, although it was called the fourth floor because it was a few steps above the third floor, but not a full storey higher. (The 1999 movie *Being John Malkovich* gives a sense of what it was like.)

In addition to the interesting smells (some at CHFI would refer to them as "pungent") emanating from the restaurant, there were cockroaches. In fact, our first chief financial officer, a less than adventurous man named John Grinksy, quit the company abruptly, claiming he couldn't tolerate going to the washroom and having cockroaches climb up his pant legs while he was on the toilet.

Despite all this, I just knew the future was FM, with its high-fidelity sound capabilities. Radio was changing dramatically. Families no longer sat around the living room after dinner listening to radio; they sat around watching TV shows like *Front Page Challenge, Ozzie and Harriet, Ed Sullivan* and *Leave It to Beaver.* Radio was becoming more personal, almost a one-on-one medium. It was experiencing a resurgence as people started listening in their cars as they commuted to and from work, or having it on in the background in their homes. CHFI's early-evening program *Candlelight and Wine* was the type of radio that fit perfectly in this new age.

Along with John Graham, Joel Aldred, CHFI's general manager Don Wright and others, we came up with a plan: first, we'd offer quality programming of great music and trustworthy news with minimal commercial interruptions. Second, we'd increase CHFI's potential audience by putting the transmitter atop CFTO's 270-metre tower out in the then-farmland area of Agincourt where the signal would be unencumbered by urban buildings and other obstacles.

Third, we had to get more FM receivers in the hands of consumers, which we did by striking a deal with Westinghouse Canada Ltd. to manufacture sets that retailed for $39.99, the lowest price for an FM receiver on the market. The custom-designed, twin-speaker table-top radios became mini-billboards for the radio station, with gold letters on the front promoting "CHFI-FM 98.1—Canada's First Station for Fine Music." By the end of 1962, two-thirds of Toronto-area homes had at least one FM radio receiver, up from 5 to 10 percent only two year earlier.

Lastly, to paraphrase the English poet John Donne, no FM radio station is an island. We urgently needed an AM counterpart to promote and introduce listeners to the benefits of FM. We embarked on one of the toughest fights of our life: finding available spectrum and squeezing a new AM radio station onto the dial already crowded with both Toronto and Buffalo stations.

The easiest parts of the plan were ensuring that we aired quality programming and moving the transmitter to the CFTO tower. (This was long before the CN Tower was constructed. Our previous transmitter was located a mere 23 storeys high, on a nearby rooftop.) I convinced John Bassett of the benefits of moving our signal to the TV tower and proposed that this could lead to an even greater sharing of services and personnel by CFTO and CHFI. Foster Hewitt didn't like the idea, but Bassett saw the potential to further control costs. Once the transmitter was atop the tower we increased power to 210,000 watts and expanded CHFI's coverage area to reach a potential audience of 3 million people, from Trenton in the east, Georgian Bay in the north, Woodstock in the west and deep into New York State to the south.

Next, it was important that more FM receivers made it onto the market. In addition to our deal with Westinghouse, we had to create demand through advertising and promotion. In April 1961 we announced a whopping $100,000 advertising campaign. The CHFI name was on billboards, subway signs and point-of-sale materials given to customers at all radio stores in the city. We bought space in newspapers and magazines. One advertisement asked: "Filet Mignon . . . or hash?" with hash, of course, being AM radio.

In that first year, from October 1960 to September 1961, I was in a daze. The work was paying off; people were beginning to notice CHFI. The U.S. trade magazine *FM* wrote, "Joel Aldred and E.S. (Ted) Rogers, neither of whom was formerly associated with FM, have taken to FM like ducks to water. Their aspirations are high: they want to put FM on the map, and put their station on the map. And they are operating on the old bank-spun philosophy that you have to spend money to make it."

By September 1961, CHFI was gaining listeners but losing money, about $200,000 in the first year. It was at this point that Joel and I parted ways. He was interested in TV, not radio. I was now the sole owner of this stand-alone, money-losing FM radio station. CFRB had already tried to crush CHFI by asking the BBG to allow them to start up separate FM programming so they could compete directly with us. Until 1961, CFRB had been simply rebroadcasting its AM programming on FM, which did not take full advantage of the superior high-fidelity sound of FM.

Late in 1960, only weeks after we bought CHFI, the BBG threw us a lifeline when it delayed CFRB's FM plans for a few months. Winks Cran proved to be his own worst enemy when his arrogance came through at the hearing. Winks was asked whether there would be enough advertising dollars in the market for CFRB to launch separate FM programming and compete head-on with CHFI. He responded by saying it didn't concern him what impact his FM plans would have on CHFI or any other FM upstart. Wrong answer.

At the time, there were only two FM stations in Toronto, CHFI and CFRB-FM (later CKFM). The BBG was looking ahead; it wanted more FM radio stations in Canada to prevent the Americans from dominating the FM dial. The governors viewed Winks's response as short-sighted and not in the public interest. Canadian FM radio needed to be nurtured at this precarious time.

But we knew that the BBG could not hold CFRB back forever and that Winks might smarten up, too. At a second hearing in the spring of 1961, Winks did wise up and CFRB said all the right things by promising to help grow the FM industry in Canada. On June 1, 1961, CFRB-FM, with all the might and resources of the colossus AM radio station behind it, became a direct competitor to CHFI.

It was now crystal clear: CHFI could not survive for long without a sister AM station. But we could not afford to buy one.

We needed to find a slot on the crowded AM dial and launch a new AM radio station in Toronto. Everyone said it was impossible. But nothing is impossible. In this case we had two brilliant engineers, Don Williamson and Ron Turnpenny, on our side and we proved the impossible could be done, again and again.

The monetary stakes for this AM venture were a trifle compared with other gambles to come. All in, it cost about $1 million. But it was a five-year battle to secure an AM frequency, one of the three toughest fights of my business life. Without victory, the Rogers name in Canadian communications could have been extinguished forever.

Chapter 8

FREQUENCY FIGHT

Aldred Rogers Ltd., later Rogers Broadcasting, was committed to blazing new trails in FM radio. After the initial investment and operating losses, we had spent $300,000 in the first year. When CFRB decided to go head to head in FM, we knew our only chance was to start a station in the more lucrative AM market and split resources and subsidize FM losses until the superior technology took hold.

There was no room on the AM dial for a 24-hour, full-power radio station, so we applied for a dawn-to-dusk licence at 1540 on the dial. It was a tough fight, especially after CFRB and its confrères raised silly objections, but we won the licence for the frequency in 1962 and went on air in August.

Within months, we knew the dawn-to-dusk solution wouldn't work in the long run. During the shorter winter days we simply couldn't get on air early enough in the morning and had to shut down during the lucrative afternoon drive home.

For technical and regulatory reasons we simply couldn't broadcast at night on 1540. AM radio signals travel much further at night and the 1540 frequency was a "protected" nighttime frequency under international rules so we could use it only during the daytime. We simply *had* to find another frequency. My chief engineer, Ron Turnpenny, and I hired a bright young engineering consultant named Bill Wright to find another spot on the dial with the fewest obstacles to overcome. After much study, Wright recommended 680.

There was a station called CHLO in St. Thomas, Ontario, about 200 kilometres to the southwest, already at 680, and WRVM, another 680 station southeast, in Rochester, New York. After drawing up complicated engineering schematics and grids, we came to the conclusion that if we set up our AM transmitters south and west of Toronto we could beam our signal to our target audience without interfering with the other markets. Or so we thought.

But these were drawings, and we were working in the real world. As hard as we tried to engineer a solution, we couldn't keep from interfering with CHLO. We had to come up with a backup plan. We offered to pay CHLO to move its signal to 1410 on the dial; everybody would be happy, at a cost to us of between $150,000 and $175,000. But it was risky: even if we paid for the move, we didn't yet have the 680 frequency licence for Toronto. The regulator could still award it to someone else.

Given our pioneering work in FM and radio experience in general, it was worth the gamble. Meanwhile, I spent $477,500 for 43 hectares of farmland in Mississauga, just west of Toronto, to put our transmitters on, even before we had the licence. It was a lot of money, but I had to take the opportunity to buy the land when it arose. (Over the years, this land near Hurontario Street and Burnhamthorpe Road in the heart of what would become Mississauga has greatly appreciated in value. At first, we used the rising value to secure more business loans. Later, under the leadership of Rob Cook, who handled the company}s real estate, we developed much of it and sold it to builders for new homes.)

We didn't anticipate the depths to which Winks Cran and CFRB would stoop. They objected to the BBG that we were "trafficking" in frequencies and acting contrary to the public good. The media had a heyday, with all the newspapers reporting Wink's accusations as if they were true, not the load of crap that they were and part of a shameless smear campaign by the station that was founded by my father. I was livid.

But when we appeared before the broadcaster governors, the sage John Graham meticulously cut down Winks's outrageous remarks with a thoughtful, penetrating and factual argument. In essence, John argued, it was indeed in the public interest to maximize spectrum in respective markets. And, John pointed out, it was only fair that the station in smaller St. Thomas incur no expense for moving down the dial to maximize the 680 frequency throughout Southern Ontario. Lesson learned: John Graham would not allow CFRB to distract us.

(In another cheap shot around the same time, the parent company of CFRB sued us for trademark infringement when we changed the name of our company to Rogers Broadcasting Limited in 1962. Even though CFRB's parent was called Standard Radio Limited, it had retained the name Rogers Radio Broadcasting Company Limited from when my father owned the company. Again, John Graham won the day by arguing that Rogers was my legal name and that I had a basic right to own and operate a company under the family name.)

Eventually we got the 680 licence, but because of the reach of Rochester's WRVM, also at 680 on the dial, we couldn't broadcast at full power during the day unless that station moved to another frequency. The owner of WRVM was a Detroit businessman named Milton Maltz, who would later go on to found both the Rock and Roll Hall of Fame and Museum in Cleveland and the International Spy Museum in Washington, D.C. I called Maltz, but he wouldn't entertain the idea of moving the station and he eventually stopped taking my calls.

A broadcast convention was coming up in Washington, and I found out from his assistant which flight Maltz would be on. He had a stopover in Cleveland, so I headed down there and booked a ticket on Maltz's flight to Washington. I asked the attendant if

I could sit beside "my pal" Milton and she said that the seat was available. If you don't ask, you don't get, as I have learned time and time again.

When I boarded the plane and sat down beside Maltz, he went berserk, saying: "You're hounding me, Rogers. You're hounding me. I can't go anywhere without you calling and now you sit down beside me on an airplane." At this point, he took off his shoe and pounded it on the armrest of his seat, like Nikita Khrushchev at the United Nations.

Before we landed in Washington, I had won him over. He said my persistence was driving him crazy and he would move the Rochester station on the dial if I paid for the switch and bought him the land he would need for new transmitters. I gladly did so.

This early battle taught me some great lessons in business, or reinforced some I had already learned:

Chart a course and act decisively and quickly.

Be flexible and always have backup plans for when things go against you (as they surely will at times).

Respect risk, but never fear calculated gambles or using leverage to attain objectives.

Never underestimate your opponents or let their dirty tricks distract you.

Tenacity and perseverance are the way to success.

Now that Rogers Communications is so big, with 29,000 employees, more than \$11 billion in annual revenues and a stock market valuation of \$25 billion or so, it is easy to forget the significant events of the early years and the important people like John Graham, Ron Turnpenny and Bill Wright who helped so much. But I don't forget. There would be lots of struggles ahead for both the AM and FM stations before they each grew into profitable pieces of the larger company, but none tougher than simply creating the AM frequency so that CHFI would not remain an FM orphan.

Chapter 9

THE NEXT GENERATION

Let me step back a couple years to catch up on some personal matters that were occurring around the same time as important business deals. On all fronts, my life was barrelling ahead. I was wrapping up articling at the Torys law firm. Things were so hectic that I could not get to law classes, so I would send my assistant to take notes for me in preparation for the arduous final series of law exams. She took meticulous notes filled with details, which helped immensely, and somehow I managed to pass and was called to the bar in 1962. I was finally a lawyer, fulfilling a promise to my mother, but my career sights were not set on the legal profession. I was not yet 30 years old.

Around this time, I was jolted twice by shocking news. The first was that my mother had cancer. She was my rock, and this diagnosis hit me hard. She had won the battle of the bottle a decade earlier, and now she embarked on another life-and-death struggle that lasted throughout the 1960s until the early 1970s.

The second jolt changed my life. In March 1963, the Robinsons were invited to New York for some gala and they invited me to join them. The four of us sat talking in their hotel suite: Loretta, her mother and father and me. Jack Robinson turned to me and said, "Son, you and Loretta have been seeing each a long time now. What are your intentions?" I gulped. Like any young man with a good thing going, I was in no great hurry to get married and be tied down. I felt a little like a prisoner in the dock with the judge peering down, demanding an explanation, and with the judge's wife and daughter as the jury. He was so forthright and a little intimidating, to say the least.

I immediately told him how much I loved Loretta. But I tried to explain that though we'd been dating since 1958, we didn't really see a lot of each other because it was a long-distance romance, with her studying in Florida or visiting them in Nassau or London. Then I mentioned that my radio station was on tenterhooks, and that I had to work so hard that it wouldn't be fair to Loretta.

My excuses didn't wash. Loretta's dad saw right through me. He told me that several young men were interested in his daughter and he wasn't keen on her forsaking these opportunities while she waited for me to make a commitment. Later on I would find out that there was a guy in England exactly one day younger than I was who had talked to Jack about Loretta's hand in marriage. Loretta likes to tease me that that chap was my twin and, like me, he even developed heart troubles later in life.

In that New York hotel suite, I knew I was cornered. But before I could say anything, the phone rang. It was the proverbial stay of execution from the governor, but in this case, Prime Minister John Diefenbaker was on the line. His office had tracked me down. Diefenbaker was asking me to run for office in the next federal election, which was only weeks away. I told him I would think about it and call him back. Talk about timing! With Jack Robinson's love of politics, the conversation immediately shifted and would not return to the topic of marriage for the rest of my visit.

As a long-time member of Parliament in Britain, Jack urged me to enter politics, but others didn't. Jack said it was quite a compliment that the prime minister would call personally to invite me to run. In the end—and with added counsel over the telephone from my mother and John Graham—I declined to run in the election because I had too much work to do in my quest to return the Rogers family to prominence in communications.

Even though Jack Robinson didn't bring up the subject of marriage again, I knew the jig was up. When I returned home to Toronto, I headed to Birks jewellers on Bloor Street and shopped for a diamond ring. I hardly had two nickels to rub together, but I talked to Bart Ellis, the boss at Birks, and he agreed to sell me a ring on credit. I picked one out that was just shy of three carats and asked if I could pay for half with free radio commercial time. In the media business, we call this type of bartering "contra." As an advertiser on CHFI, he agreed to the swap. Loretta still wears that credit-and-contra diamond ring today, more than 40 years later, and has never even had it reset. Of course, it is fully paid for now.

In April, a month after that New York hotel episode, I was visiting the Robinsons in Nassau for Easter holidays. On April 10, I took Loretta to dinner at a restaurant called Martinique on Paradise Island. Back in those days, Paradise Island really was an island; you had to take a boat to get there. Today, it is a casino and golf resort for high rollers and is connected to Nassau by a bridge. I was very nervous all through dinner with that ring in my pocket. I must have checked my pocket a hundred times to make sure it hadn't fallen out. Finally, after the bill came, I suggested we go outside for a walk. We came to a bench near the end of a stone path. She sat down and I got down on one knee and proposed.

To my great joy, she accepted and we spent some time talking and kissing. Before we knew it, it was 11 o'clock. When we walked back, all the guests from the restaurant had gone and we had missed the last guest boat back to Nassau. We then had to wait and ride back with the restaurant staff after they had finished cleaning up. We got home and Loretta's father was still up, reading a book. He was delighted by the news, as was her mother. The next day we called my mother and John Graham, and they came down the following day to celebrate and to plan the wedding. During these celebrations and toasts, Jack Robinson said to me, "What's Loretta's is Loretta's, and what's yours is negotiable." He loved to tease me.

The four parents discussed—negotiated, really—dates for the wedding. Loretta and I sat and watched in amazement until it was decided that September 25, 1963, would be the wedding day and that the ceremony would take place in London at St. Margaret's Church, Westminster, on the grounds of Westminster Abbey. St. Margaret's is the parish church of the House of Commons, and Jack was still the Member of Parliament for Blackpool South.

As the wedding approached, I was up to my eyeballs in work. CFTO was still losing money, CHFI's popularity was growing as we pushed out those Westinghouse FM receivers for $39.99, and I was before the Board of Broadcast Governors more times than I cared to remember, fighting for an AM radio licence.

I worked during the entire Atlantic crossing aboard the *Queen Elizabeth* that would take me to London for the wedding. The new Liberal government in Ottawa had thrown a monkey wrench into our plans to secure an AM licence and that meant yet another hearing before the BBG, so it was back to the drawing board before ultimate victory on the AM frequency battle could be claimed. As I sailed across the ocean, I had to prepare a strategy and supporting documents for the new hearing. Even though the nuptials were only days away, I instinctively took action and mapped out a plan. John Graham was invaluable, supplying me with material to review and build on and cabling updates and more work to the Savoy Hotel, where Loretta and I were going to be staying.

September 24, 1963, the day before the wedding, was a typical rainy, cold and foggy day in London. The streetlights were on all day. But Loretta's mother told her not to worry: "It's always nice on the day of a Robinson family wedding." And she was right. September 25 was altogether different: sunny and warm, London at its best.

Toby Hull and his first wife, Peggy, stood up for us as best man and matron of honour. The bridesmaids were my sister Ann Graham, Patricia Robinson de Mara (Richard's wife), Sally Clive, Audrey Moore and Anne Turner. The ushers were Hal Jackman, John Craig Eaton, Richard Robinson (Loretta}s late brother), Lionel Coleman and Gary Cooper (a friend now deceased, but not the movie star). There were 400 guests, very few from my side. As I said, Jack Robinson knew everyone. As a long-time chairman of the Commonwealth Parliamentary Association, he had travelled the world and the Robinsons were equally welcome in political and society circles.

Our wedding was a high-society event and the pictures were later published in the *Tatler* magazine. The reception was held in the back garden of Loretta's parents' London home. The garden courtyard was shared with a couple other homeowners who gave their permission to set up marquees. It was so nice to have the reception outside instead of having it at a hotel. We have continued this alfresco tradition at two of our daughter's weddings.

Our honeymoon was a trip to Kenya. I even got British Overseas Airways (now simply British Airways) to throw in two first-class seats in exchange for free radio commercials, again proving how contra can come in handy. We arrived shortly after the Mau Mau revolt that led to Kenya's independence in December 1963, but we were never in any danger and the trip was wonderful, until it was cut short by half. After nine days we left so that I could be back in time for the BBG radio hearing regarding the AM licence. At the time, I promised Loretta I would make it up to her with a second honeymoon, and I did three years later when I took her to the South Pacific.

After the honeymoon, we lived in an apartment in Toronto. When my in-laws came to visit a short time later, they looked around the apartment and told us we had to buy a house. I turned to Loretta's parents and said, "I can hardly afford to pay for a light bulb. I can't afford a house." Jack and Maysie then told us we could buy a house with money from a trust held in Loretta's name. But there was one condition, Jack said: "Ted, promise never to put a mortgage on the house to finance your businesses." We did end up putting two or three mortgages on the house at different times to meet payroll during the ensuing lean years. I think Jack knew but he never asked—and I didn't volunteer the information, either.

So, off we went house shopping. All four of us squeezed into the car of our real estate agent, Mary Gordon. We were driving down Dunvegan Road in Forest Hill, passing Frybrook Road, not far from my mother's home, when Mary stopped the car in front of a house. Mel Simpson, the owner, was standing outside. Mary had sold him the house only a year earlier.

"Hey, Mel!" she yelled. "Do you want to sell your house today?"

He laughed. "No, we love it."

Later that night Mel called Mary Gordon and said he'd changed his mind. They had a 325-hectare farm north of the city that his wife and four kids loved and spent every weekend at. His wife didn't like the Frybrook house as much as he did, so he said he would like to sell it after all. We agreed on a price of $168,000, and it was ours. It was another instance of the same lesson: If you don't ask, you don't get.

Of course, there could easily have been another lesson: Be careful what you wish for. I had never been in such a big house before. It felt so much above my station and I worried about whether we could afford it. I didn't have any real money at the time and we furnished it slowly. At first, we could furnish only two rooms, the bedroom and the library. I didn't need any extra motivation to succeed in business, but now I had it. Gradually, over the years, we've really fixed the house up and expanded it, including buying the property next door and adding a tennis court and an indoor swimming pool. (When we knocked the house down next door to build the tennis court, I told John A. Tory that Loretta had taken up tennis, to which he quipped: "I'm glad she didn't take up golf!") Frybrook has been a tremendous home for us for more than four decades.

The next project was to fill the house with more than just furniture. But the children didn't arrive as anticipated. So I did what I always do in private life and business: I mapped out a campaign on how to beat our fertility problem. I researched and found there were doctors trying different procedures and techniques to help couples like us have children. I went to many places in Canada and the United States and tried different procedures. Nothing seemed to work. Then I heard about a doctor in Detroit who was making great strides in this area. I am no doctor, and there were all sorts of complicated reasons why Loretta wasn't getting pregnant, but nevertheless I just *knew* this Detroit doctor had the answer. I went down to Detroit and did all the necessary tests and procedures.

I was at the cottage on Tobin Island when the letter containing the test results arrived, along with some work material. I was going through my papers and I immediately spotted the letter from the Detroit doctor's office. I felt a rush and became very nervous and excited at the same time. There were guests at the cottage so I went into the woods to be alone. I sat on an old tree stump and tore open the letter. My hands were trembling. I started reading the letter and tears came to my eyes. Medical technology had failed us. We weren't going to be able to have our own biological children.

After I regained my composure, I went back to the cottage and told Loretta. She was so wonderful; right then and there we decided to adopt a child, a decision that would lead to great joy.

A few months later, we were told by the adoption agency that they had a baby girl for us, born on October 9, 1967. Just hearing that news was wonderful, but it was eclipsed by the first moment we laid eyes on her. My eyes welled up with happy tears as soon as I saw her. She was so beautiful. In those days, prospective parents were required to visit the baby and then go away without the child to reflect and make sure they were making the right decision. Even

My father, Edward Samuel Rogers, working in his home laboratory. My dad loved to work and was always dreaming up new ideas, whether at home or at his offices at CFRB or in radio manufacturing plants.

When he was only 24 years old, my father created the world's first alternating-current radio tube, which allowed listeners to simply plug their radios into electrical outlets. Until then, radios ran on expensive, cumbersome batteries that often leaked corrosive fluids.

Dad and me sitting on the steps in front of our home at 405 Glenayr Road in Toronto's Forest Hill neighbourhood. This is one of only two or three pictures I have ever seen of us together.

Me with my mother, shortly after I was born, on May 27, 1933. I was sickly at birth and in the first year suffered through an infant celiac condition that caused me to lose most of the sight in my right eye.

As a toddler I suffered digestive problems and so was fed sugar pills (which I detested) until age six to help me gain weight and strength.

Me with my mother at the old Woodbine racetrack (later renamed Greenwood) on Lakeshore Boulevard in Toronto in the 1940s. This early exposure to the world of betting may have helped me when I later "booked" bets for classmates at Upper Canada College.

Me with my second father, John Webb Graham, who married my mother in 1941, two years after my dad died. We are standing in the same spot on Glenayr Road as my father and I were sitting in when we were pictured in the earlier photograph.

That's me (centre) at a Sigma Chi fraternity hoedown party in Toronto
in the early 1950s. Sigma Chi has been important to me all my life,
especially in business. The connections I made helped open many doors.

At the Sigma Chi 1957 convention, held in Toronto. My sister, Ann
Graham, is on the far right beside John Graham; I am standing
between my date and my mother. This was the first time the
fraternity's annual convention was held outside the United States.

John Graham (centre), engineer Ron Turnpenny and me holding one of the FM radios we had built and then sold at bargain basement prices to get them into the marketplace. When we bought the station in 1960 for $85,000, only 5 percent of Toronto-area homes and cars had FM receivers.

Soon-to-be prime minister John Diefenbaker (left) at a Progressive Conservative Student Federation rally in 1956. (I was chairman.) To my left is Pierre Panneton, who headed our Diefenbaker youth movement in Quebec. I loved the cut and thrust of politics at this time of my life.

CFTO, Toronto's first privately owned television station, went on the air January 1, 1961. This newspaper advertisement shows the four partners in the operation: (from top to bottom) Big John Bassett, Joel W. Aldred, me and Foster Hewitt, who was the voice of Hockey Night in Canada for 40 years.

My wife, Loretta, and me on the steps of St. Margaret's Church, the parish church of the British House of Commons in London, at our wedding on September 25, 1963. We were married in England because Loretta's father was still a sitting member of Parliament at the time. In the background between Loretta and me is Peggy Hull, our maid of honour, and behind her is Richard Robinson, Loretta's only sibling, who died of cancer at a young age.

Loretta's parents, Jack and Maysie Robinson, on our wedding day. Jack was the Conservative member of Parliament for Blackpool South and held the distinction of never being defeated in an election during his 33 years in politics. Maysie was the daughter of Clarence Warren Gasque, an American businessman who ran the Woolworths department store chain in Britain and owned a large part of the company.

With my mother a few years before her death in November 1971. Mother battled throat cancer courageously for a decade. She was my bridge to my father's dreams and the person who instilled in me the tenacity to never give up, even when things looked grim.

Loretta and me heading out on our honeymoon and our life together. On our wedding day, the London rain and fog lifted and it was sunny and warm, so we saw the great city at its best. The reception was held in the back garden of Loretta's parents' home.

Loretta and me standing exactly on the equator during our honeymoon in Kenya. We had to cut our honeymoon short after nine days. I was a well-known Progressive Conservative, and the new Liberal government that had defeated John Diefenbaker overturned a radio licence decision on the AM frequency of 680 in Toronto and ordered the Board of Broadcast Governors to go over the file again, forcing me to return home to Ottawa.

before seeing this baby girl, we were sure, but those were the rules. We touched her in her bassinette and left with great reluctance.

On the second visit, one of the women from the adoption agency held the baby while Loretta was allowed to gently pat her, then she slowly transferred the baby to Loretta's arms. While chatting I found out that the woman from the adoption agency was the wife of a man named Larry Fox, a nice guy in charge of the unit at Bell Canada that I was involved with in a conflict over stringing cable for our company. I liked Larry and I never fought with him personally, but of all the people in Toronto here was Larry's wife handing over our long-awaited child.

Eventually, the adoption agency awarded us the baby girl, whom we named Lisa Anne, and we took her home. I had a photographer waiting at the front door. We took Lisa inside the house and I remember her lying on a couch and then lifting her head and looking me straight in the eye. It was a joyous moment.

We told Lisa very early on that she was adopted and she has never had a problem with that. She knows she is as loved and every bit as much a part of the family as anyone else. She has tracked down her birth parents, who were two young college kids at the time, but she is a Rogers first and foremost.

Not long after Lisa arrived, I heard about the research work of Dr. C. Alvin Paulsen in Seattle. I went to see him in 1968 at the military hospital where he practised. At one point, I was lying on a gurney in a hallway along with several other men. One asked, "When are you shipping over?"

"Sorry?" I said.

"When are you going to Vietnam?"

"Oh, I am Canadian. I am not going over there."

That seemed to end the discussion and for the next hour or two I lay there thinking: I wonder why God planted me north of the border and not south? Why are all these guys going over there to fight, and perhaps die, and I am not?

I returned home not knowing whether Dr. Paulsen's procedure had worked or not. I had been disappointed before, so we put in for another adoption. Within days, Loretta was pregnant. Dr. Paulsen, whose work has garnered international acclaim, is a hero to me, and no doubt to many other fathers.

Our son, Edward Samuel Rogers III, was born June 22, 1969, followed by Melinda Mary on January 27, 1971, and Martha Loretta on April 6, 1972. All of these births were special. We even made "home movies" by recording Loretta and Edward from the hospital room on a private channel of our community cable channel. When Martha was born we did a tribute show called *Hello Loretta;* the three youngsters were in the studio with me and their mother was on the telephone from her hospital room with the new baby.

Loretta and I have also been blessed with, as of 2008, four wonderful grandchildren. Edward and Suzanne's three children are Chloe Alexandra Velma Rogers, Edward Samuel Rogers IV and Jack Robinson Miklos Rogers. Melinda and Eric's son is named Zachary Joseph Hixon.

Generally, I don't live with regrets, in business or family matters. You have to go forward, and not dwell on things in the past. But I will say, when it comes to raising the children, I would do two things differently, if given the chance.

First, I would figure out a way to spend more time with them when they are very young. I tell new fathers this all the time. I am a product of a different time when fathers generally worked long hours and didn't spend much time with the children. I was the type of dad who loved getting on the ground and rolling around with the kids when I was with them, but I wish I had been around more. When the kids were young, in the 1970s and early 1980s, I was facing some of the most challenging times for the business. But, looking back, that's not good enough: I should have carved out more time for them.

Second, if I could do it over again, I would have nannies to assist, but not nannies in charge. I deferred to our nannies a little too much. A parent shouldn't do that. We had many fine nannies, but the fact is that parents, not employed caregivers, should always be in charge.

I am proud of all my children. They have grown into adulthood to become good people. As the company became more and more successful, I often feared our wealth would have a negative impact on them. I wanted my children to work hard, no matter what they did, and to make positive contributions to the community and the lives of loved ones.

Edward and Melinda work at Rogers Communications; Edward in charge of cable and Melinda heading up strategy and development. Lisa now lives in Victoria, British Columbia, and is an accomplished triathlete with entrepreneurial businesses unrelated to communications. Martha has obtained her degree in homeopathic medicine and lives in Toronto and dotes on me, perhaps too much.

It is my fervent wish that our children—and hopefully our grandchildren and future generations—continue the legacy and keep the Rogers name at the forefront of communications in Canada. After my father's death, we lost it for a while; but we have it back now and I have worked extraordinarily hard to ensure that it stays there long after I am gone.

Chapter 10

BACK FROM THE BRINK

On Monday, March 20, 1967, I found myself walking around Toronto neighbourhoods asking people about their TV reception. Was it clear at all times? Was it better at certain times of the day? Were there "ghosts" on the screen or double images? Did they have a colour TV?

This was my market research before launching into my next great business endeavour. I had heard and read about this new technology called cable television and I had always believed people would pay for more TV content with crystal-clear TV reception. I had proved this almost 20 years earlier when I pulled in Buffalo TV signals with an off-air antenna on the roof of my dormitory at Upper Canada College. But a cable TV business, that was something altogether different—and altogether riskier. In fact, most people thought it a crazy idea back in 1967.

Trolling the streets of Toronto and asking strangers questions about their TV reception sounds a bit crazy, but I was looking for the best places to launch my cable TV business. I wasn't about to start where viewers were receiving decent signals from their bunny ears or rooftop antennas. I wanted to find areas where the over-the-air reception was poor. With debt growing in my radio business, I couldn't afford to start this cable venture in the wrong location.

Canada was in the midst of its centennial year; 1967 was one big party. If you are old enough to remember, you know what I mean.

There was so much excitement across the entire country; a festive air swept from coast to coast all year long, especially in Montreal with Expo '67. It was as if we all knew the historic significance in real time: Canada was growing up and really stretching its wings, starting so many new things, and rebuilding—not just retooling—the nation.

The birth and development of cable television aligned perfectly with Canada's vigorous renewal: cable would offer viewers more programming at a higher quality than a rooftop antenna; it would strengthen the broadcasting system so Canadian stories could be told amidst the onslaught of signals from the United States; its innovative technology would bring future services we take for granted today such as pay-per-view and specialty channels. In short, cable would play its part in stitching together the fabric of Canada just as the steel ribbons of the transcontinental railroad had done a century before.

I walked many miles over a few days that spring, and I spoke to hundreds of people. Whenever I saw a TV repair shop, I would pop in and ask the owner about his customers' reception. TV reception in those days was affected by the new skyscrapers rising in the city, or by dips in the city's topography. Even the weather could affect the picture on your television. (Satellite TV companies still have that problem today, but that's another story.) Right from the start, I knew cable TV would be a winner. But in my wildest dreams, I never envisioned that the cable industry would one day churn out billions of dollars a year in revenues.

I knew at the time that the naysayers who mocked cable as frivolous and unnecessary were wrong. A common cry from the wet blankets was, Why would anyone pay to receive television when you could pick it up free with an antenna? I do admit, that question did cross my mind, too, if only briefly. The answer was threefold: choice of programming, colour television, and clearer reception.

These answers would haunt the likes of Bell Canada and other phone companies for years to come. Perhaps no other company in the world was better positioned to seize the cable opportunity than Bell. It already had connections, both hard wires and marketing links, to millions of customers. Its territory was in the heart of central Canada, the cradle of the world's cable industry because of the population's insatiable appetite for picture-perfect U.S. programming. Instead, Bell took a pass on cable TV. Bell executives were the barons of the country, the goliaths of finance. Even with its government-sanctioned telephone monopoly and guaranteed rate of return (Ottawa would raise Bell's rates whenever the company's expenses rose for whatever reason, including mismanagement), Bell decided to string cable along its poles to customers' homes and lease the wires to cable operators rather than providing cable TV service itself.

Thankfully for cable operators like me, Bell, in its wisdom, chose to invest its money in pipelines, real estate and everything else except cable. Over the years, Bell has written off $20 billion to $30 billion through diversification, according to various analysts' estimates. Its affiliated phone company monopoly in western Canada and the Maritimes also took a pass on cable. History would be much different had Bell jumped into cable instead of mocking it.

My interest in cable television started long before I started knocking on doors that March. Unlike my father, I was no inventor, though I have always had a passion for the engineering side, which drew me to cable. I liked to tinker with gadgets. Because of my limited engineering abilities, I would simply hire cable TV engineering experts like Frank Verkaik, just as I did in radio with tremendous engineers like Ron Turnpenny and Don Williamson. The pioneering aspect of cable TV also appealed to me, as it did with FM radio. And I also wanted to foster Canadian programming.

Cable TV began rudimentarily in the 1950s as a community

television service. In other words, in communities where TV reception was poor or non-existent, pioneers such as Ed Jarmain in London and Syd Welsh in Vancouver would build a big antenna, grab over-the-air signals, string wires out to a few homes and share the strong signal from the tower. In the early days, it tended to be a rural phenomenon because TV signals in big urban centres like Toronto were pretty strong. Vancouver was an exception because of the mountains.

In his book *Kings of Convergence,* Gordon Pitts tells a wonderful story about Jarmain visiting Pottsville, Pennsylvania, in the early 1950s, where he met a TV salesman named Marty Malarkey. After the Second World War, Malarkey was selling a lot of television sets, but he had a problem: his customers kept returning the sets because the reception was so poor in the mountain-ringed town of Pottsville. Malarkey built a receiving tower on one of the mountains and strung some wires around his customers' homes and hooked them up—the birth of cable. Marty Malarkey went on to start numerous cable systems and co-founded the National Cable Television Association in the United States. I was honoured in 2002 when I joined Malarkey as an inductee into the Cable Hall of Fame in Denver, Colorado, the first Canadian to be inducted.

Back in the early 1950s, Jarmain looked at Malarkey's books and decided that this was the business for him. He returned home to launch cable television in London in 1952 by wiring up 15 homes and offering U.S. programming even before Canadian channels were available.

Though I was not one of the early pioneers in cable as I was in FM radio, I was most certainly not coming to the party late. In fact, of Canada's three big cities—Montreal, Toronto and Vancouver—Metropolitan Toronto with a population approaching 2 million was the least cabled in 1967 because of the wide selection of over-the-air channels. There were three U.S. channels coming across Lake Ontario from Buffalo, as well as the CBC's flagship CBLT and

CFTO (of which I still owned 10 percent). Many homes in Toronto could pick up other signals from nearby cities like Hamilton, Barrie, Peterborough and even Rochester, New York. Some Torontonians could receive six or more channels over the air.

In February 1967 I made up my mind that cable was where I wanted to go. Loretta and I were on our second honeymoon, a six-week trip in the South Pacific. We were having a fabulous time Down Under seeing new things and exploring. Loretta is an avid swimmer and snorkeller and there may be nowhere better for that sport than the South Pacific.

In Australia, I met with media tycoon Rupert Murdoch. This was long before he made it really big internationally, but he was already big in Australia and it was nice of him to give me a couple hours to talk about business and where broadcasting was heading. I have met him several times since and I will always remember how gracious he was to a young guy from Canada just starting out.

During this trip we went to Fiji and it was there that I cracked open a little book all about cable television and how it was the future for delivering programming. I can't even recall the title, but it really opened my eyes. When Loretta and I returned home, I got serious about cable. I just couldn't shake it. It seemed as if wherever I turned I was pointed toward cable. I would be in a store, for instance, and I would notice the racks and racks of magazines: news, fashion, sports, food, lifestyle, cars, and various hobbies. Just about everything was available and targeted in these specialty magazines. That got me thinking that cable could offer so much more programming than the standard over-the-air networks. Then I would look at all those jungles of rooftop antennas across the city and I would think that cable would eliminate those eyesores.

The timing was perfect. Colour television was newly licensed in Canada and began transmission on January 1, 1967. This was important for cable because the "ghosts" created by antennas on black and white TV were bearable to some people, but Technicolor ghosts were beyond annoying. The ghosts on colour TV sets made them almost impossible to watch.

When a Toronto cable operator called Metro Cable, which was owned by the American Famous Players movie chain, refused to carry CHFI radio on its cable to people's homes, but carried my arch-competitor CFRB's FM station, CKFM, I decided it was time to make my move. I said to John Graham, "That's it. We'll just start our own cable company." On March 19, 1967, Rogers Cable TV Limited. was formed.

Back in those days it was simple to obtain a cable TV licence for a particular territory. Anybody could go to the federal department of transport and buy a licence for $25. The real cost came in getting access to homes. The de facto regulator was Bell Canada (or the other local phone companies across the country). The local phone company strung cable along its poles and up to homes, which wasn't cheap, and I was already up to my ears in debt. Bell demanded a $200,000 deposit upfront for each territory on a first-come, first-served basis.

Loretta, who was by now a full-fledged business partner, lent me $225,000 from her family trust, and on May 3 we paid Bell the first $200,000 down payment for 600,000 metres of cable to be installed. We were now in the queue and only weeks away from Bell workers laying our cable.

There were already a few licensed cabled areas in Toronto, including my own neighbourhood of Forest Hill. I walked the streets and decided on the Borough of East York, an area in the east end of Metro Toronto, but close to downtown.

A seemingly insignificant and serendipitous event occurred that led to my getting the money I needed to build the cable company: Channel 3 in Barrie, about 100 kilometres north of Toronto, announced it was planning to move its transmitter south, closer to Toronto, which would mean that some homes would soon have problems with interference in picking up the popular Buffalo

channels 2 and 4 on the dial. If homes in Toronto developed picture interference problems, they would be more apt to buy cable
TV services, thus increasing the value of the business. Smart people,
like Big John Bassett, were quick to realize this.

Even though Barrie's Channel 3 ultimately wasn't allowed to
move the transmitter, Bassett suddenly saw value in my operation.
First, he called in his lawyers and told them he had to find a way to
get this cable thing from me and into Baton Broadcasting, where I
was still on the board of directors and a minority owner. It would be
too harsh to say he wanted to steal my fledgling cable company, but
he sure wanted to get his hands on it any way he could. His lawyer,
Eddie Goodman, told Bassett that the Baton partnership agreement
stipulated that none of the owners could own or operate a television
business to compete with CFTO within 112 kilometres (70 miles) of
the CFTO tower. With this news, Bassett then called and told me
he wanted me to hand over at no cost these cable television licences
to Baton, as per the agreement. I told him to go fly a kite.

The next thing I knew, Bassett called a board meeting. Bassett
always did things with flair. In the boardroom at the old *Telegram*
building, which is now the home of Canada's national newspaper,
The Globe and Mail, all of the Bassett and Eaton directors sat down
on one side of the table and the rest of us from the Rogers board
sat on the other.

"Ted," Bassett started off, "I've always loved you like a son."

Richard Stanbury, a wonderful man who became a Liberal
senator in 1968, was sitting next to me. He whispered, "Yeah, loves
you like a sonofabitch," loudly enough to cause a ripple. Bassett
then tabled a dreadful offer for me to turn my cable company over
to Baton at a ridiculously low price.

I stood up and said to Bassett that I also felt that I had a special relationship with him. In situations like this, there is a certain
amount of showmanship, but I was truly sincere. I told Bassett that

he was like a third father to me, after my real father and my second father, John Graham. I meant it.

I then told him I would enjoy working with him, but these cable licences were valuable and I was not about to give them away. I also pointed out that many people in the industry believed that cable was different from broadcast television and that the 70-mile rule did not legally apply. "You can sue us," I said. "But that offer of yours just might as well be put in the garbage."

He looked at me with those stern eyes while I continued: "If we're sitting here as two allies and fellow shareholders and lifelong Conservatives, I have a different proposal. We should merge."

I offered him half the cable company if Baton put in two-thirds of the money. I would run it, but he had the option to install his own choice as chief financial officer if he was worried I would spend too much.

"Done," he said, pounding the table. Just like that.

This deal was a blessing—but it also disguised a vulnerability that would eventually push me to the brink of utter destruction, the closest I would ever come to losing everything.

The first two years of our partnership were unbelievably successful and the newly incorporated Rogers Cable TV Limited was growing beyond all expectations. We started in August 1967 with a $6 million loan from a consortium of three banks, CIBC, Bank of Montreal and Scotiabank. Baton was on the hook for $4 million and I was in for $2 million.

Also part of the agreement was that Baton would have final say on any large expenditures or acquisitions. Unwittingly, I once broke that part of the agreement. When I realized I spent too much money without Baton's pre-approval, I went to Bassett and told him what I had done. "Don't worry, Ted," he said. "These things can happen. Keep up the good work." We couldn't fill orders fast enough. Every day we were laying an average of 35 kilometres of cable in East York and signing up customers by the dozens even before the service was available.

I had bought a small cable company in the Toronto satellite town of Brampton, northwest of the city, called Bramalea Telecable Ltd., in July 1967. It cost $17,000 (which I paid for from my personal bank account) and I assumed the company's $65,700 of debt. Though Bramalea had only 300 subscribers, it was the heart and soul of Rogers Cable, which offered eight crystal-clear channels and whose slogan was "Your Eye on Entertainment."

Radio was still very much on my mind as we expanded out of Toronto and bought two AM stations, CHIQ in Hamilton, which we rebranded CHAM, and CHYR in Leamington. However, cable (and later, its creditors) consumed so much of my time and energy that I soon handed over the day-to-day radio chores to Keith Dancy, a tremendous radio man whom I got to know when he bid against me for CHIQ.

Over the next year, we built and bought cable at the same time; picking up Essex Cable TV Ltd. in Windsor and Coaxial Colourview Ltd. in Toronto. Barry Ross, who owned Coaxial, stayed on and became general manager of Rogers Cable and did a superb job. I also acquired Department of Transport licences in then-rural areas just outside Metropolitan Toronto, because I knew the suburbs would one day spill over the city's boundaries into places like Markham, Vaughan, Port Credit and Streetsville. We now had licences for all these places and were ready when the housing boom was sure to come.

We also had come across a significant piece of good luck, finding a new banking partner committed to the cable TV industry, the Toronto-Dominion Bank. Richard (Dick) Thomson, a distinguished and brilliant man, was then chief general manager of the bank. He would go on to be president and then chairman and also serve as chief executive officer for an astounding 20 years, from 1977 to 1997. With him on the cable file was Robert (Robin) Korthals, a bright young star who had come to the bank from brokerage house Nesbitt Thomson. I would soon find out that Robin had experience stringing together structured financings for small cable television partnerships in the U.S. and he was convinced cable was the future of television.

I had a chance meeting with Dick Thomson in 1968 on our dock at Tobin Island. Dick, whom I had not yet met to this point, also had a cottage on the lake and on this weekend John A. Tory and his wife, Liz, were visiting Dick and his family. They went for a boat ride and, apparently, John suggested they pop by and see me and Loretta.

John told me later that he knew Dick and Robin were becoming interested in the cable business, so maybe it wasn't such a chance meeting. We had a great chat, and then Dick asked if I would be interested in working with TD Bank. It was difficult for me to hide my delight, but I tried not to look overly eager. Remember, this was only a year after we had started Rogers Cable and I knew I would need to borrow lots of money to build such a capital-—intensive business. To meet and get to know a man like Dick at this point was fortuitous to say the least. Dick then set up a meeting with Robin a few days later.

Robin arranged for an initial loan of $3 million from TD and it was the beginning of a great business relationship, as well as some wonderful friendships. It was literally a loan on good faith because I had so little collateral to offer. At one point, I mentioned the cottage to Robin and he said, "No, keep the cottage out of this."

TD became a significant lender to the cable industry. In the late 1960s both banking law and the corporate finance market in general changed significantly in Canada. TD took a visionary approach when it came to cable and others didn't.

Jean de Grandpré, head of Bell Canada and the man who would go on to form the holding company BCE Inc., told Dick that he and Robin were crazy to back cable so heavily. De Grandpré felt that people wouldn't pay for TV when they could get it for free. At the time, he was on the board of TD. I am fortunate Dick ignored the advice. Both Dick Thomson and Robin Korthals liked the fact that cable was an industry with monthly recurring revenue from subscribers, which could then be used to finance the huge amounts of capital required.

These two men were visionaries. Other banks generally stayed away from cable in the early days (or offered onerous conditions on their loans) because the way the business operated meant that there was little collateral. (Remember, we had to rent the right to hang our cables from the telephone companies' poles.) Both Dick and Robin saw the potential: that it could be done, that viewers would want more and different programming that went far beyond what the homogenized major networks were able to offer, and that they would be willing to pay for it.

Driven by Dick and Robin, the TD Bank would make a lot of money by becoming one of the top three North American banks for both the cable and cellular phone industries. But the financial picture wasn't always rosy. They lost on some loans, but never on a loan to Rogers. The most Rogers Communications has ever owed the TD Bank was $1 billion in the late 1980s, which was all paid back. In fact, once the bulk of it was paid, I was named to TD's board of directors, where I served from 1989 until the mandatory retirement age of 70 in 2003. On my fiftieth birthday, Dick and Robin gave me a $50 billion line of credit as a joke gift. I proudly hang the "certificate" in my office to this day.

In the late 1960s, we were increasing our customer base tenfold every five or six months. We had started from nothing, so gains like that were possible for several years. In November 1967 we negotiated a deal to put our "head-end," or master antenna to pick up over-the-air signals, on top of the brand new Toronto-Dominion Centre in downtown Toronto. This 20-metre-tall antenna on the roof of the 56-storey skyscraper was the highest receiver in Toronto at the time and it delivered the best picture quality.

We would eventually move it after Dick Thomson looked up one day and saw that the receiver was much bigger than he had expected. He did not think the head-end could actually be seen from the ground, but it could. Dick called me and said he knew we had a firm contract but explained that the famed architect Ludwig Mies van der Rohe, who had designed the building, was a minimalist who wouldn't even let the TD Bank hang commercial signs on the building. I agreed to move it to another skyscraper and eventually technology changed so that we would no longer need head-ends high atop buildings. With satellites, head-ends would move to ground level and we would use dishes to pick up the signals from the satellites before putting them out on the cable network.

On June 29, 1968, Toronto Mayor Bill Dennison and East York Mayor True Davidson simultaneously pushed the button to activate the Rogers cable system inside Toronto and our first customers inside the city were served. By October 1968 we had outgrown our office space and had to move our cable offices out of CHFI and next door to 25 Adelaide Street East. By February 1969 we were the fourth-largest cable company in Metropolitan Toronto with 5,812 customers. (The two biggest were controlled by American companies, Metro Cable by Famous Players Theaters and York Cablevision by CBS).

We were holding our own. Going from zero to 6,000 paying customers in eight months was a tremendous achievement. We were hardly big yet, but our trajectory was going in the right direction.

That's when the trouble began. Maybe I was too busy building the company. Maybe I got cocky during the good times. (This was a lesson I gradually learned, and today I am always ringing the alarm bells when the sun is shining because one day it will be raining.) Maybe I took my eye off the ball because I was a new father and Loretta was also now pregnant with our son, Edward. But I just didn't sense the danger until it was too late.

Around the spring of 1969, Liberal propagandists like the *Toronto Star* and others started to moan about the Bassetts and Eatons owning too many media properties in Toronto with the *Telegram* newspaper, CFTO-TV and Rogers Cable. The agitation was public and more than likely in the corridors of government, too, with lobbyists whispering in the ears of Liberal politicians. In addition to bemoaning the Eatons and Bassetts, they tossed other minority owners of CFTO into the fray, like Foster Hewitt and his radio station (CKFH-AM) and me with my radio stations and cable company. Our radio division was $2.5 million in debt and cable was already $8.5 million in debt when the Liberal government of Pierre Trudeau set up a commission headed by Liberal Senator Keith Davey to examine the concentration of media ownership.

Rogers Cable's licences were up for renewal by the new regulator, the CRTC. On July 10, 1969, just days before the first moon landing, the trajectory of our company changed completely when the CRTC ruled it would renew Rogers Cable's licences only if Baton sold its stake and got out of the cable TV business. This was devastating, perhaps the darkest day of my business life. It could very well have meant the utter destruction of my company. All my dreams of restoring the Rogers family to the heights my father had achieved in communications before his early death were being shot to pieces.

I called John Bassett to tell him the bad news, and he was magnanimous, saying he would help me find another partner, possibly even the *Toronto Star* or the *Globe and Mail*. It was too early; I was not yet desperate enough to go that route. Instead, I thanked Big John and told him Loretta and I would like to find a way to buy the 50 percent of Rogers Cable owned by the Eatons and Bassetts. I had no idea where I was going to get the money or why Bassett even agreed, but he gave me some time to raise the funds. The first thing I did was to sell back my share of CFTO, which worked out to about $1.5 million. But we still needed $450,000 to pay off the Eatons and Bassetts and more than $1 million to keep the cable company afloat. Somehow I would find a way. In 1970, six months after the CRTC decision, Bassett gave me my first "three-month deadline" to come up with the cash. That deadline would come and go and he extended it by another three months. This happened over and over throughout 1970 and into 1971.

These were lean years indeed. Loretta and I put a triple mortgage on our house, even though I had promised her father I would never do that. The people who offer third mortgages are not the nicest folks in the world. They made Loretta and me feel five inches tall when they walked around the house inspecting our things. Loretta, Toby Hull and my sister, Ann Graham, all put personal assets on the line so I could borrow money here and there. I even grabbed $20,000 from a trust we had set up for Lisa after she arrived in 1967.

I was flabbergasted when CHFI's station manager Vaughn Bjerre volunteered to put a $40,000 mortgage on his home and program director Gerry Bascombe and sales manager Harry McIntyre offered a few thousand dollars each to help us get through the crisis. It was heartwarming that these people had so much faith in me and the company.

It was around this time that one of Ann's friends from school, Phil Lind, joined Rogers, in October 1969. He must have wondered more than once what he had gotten himself into. It turned out our ancestors had done business together in the nineteenth century, so maybe there was some sort of historical bond between us. Phil started in programming at the cable company and he is today vice-chairman of Rogers Communications Inc. We know each other so well that our business relationship has been compared to that of an old married couple. Maybe so, but I can tell you it was no honeymoon during his first few years because the company was constantly teetering on bankruptcy.

We didn't have sufficient cash to pay all the suppliers during much of this period. After meeting payroll, I would put all the bills in a hat and keep drawing invoices until our chief financial officer Pel Bell-Smith shouted: "That's enough. No more money." Can you believe that some creditors didn't appreciate such innovation? They would shout at me over the telephone. I often got a headache and asked them to stop yelling. With anger in their voices, they'd ask me what I would do if they kept yelling. "Very simple," I'd say. "I won't put your bill in the hat next week!" Nobody sued—they all got paid, with interest. As I have already said, no one in my lifetime has ever lost one cent in receivables or interest on a Rogers' account.

By the summer of 1970, it was an open secret that I was in trouble and the company was on the brink. A gossip column in the *Globe and Mail* read: "Rumor: Ted Rogers, the ambitious and high-flying owner of CHFI and Rogers Cable TV Ltd., has run out of money. Explanation: the CRTC has ordered John Bassett and John David Eaton to get out of radio and cable. So there goes Rogers' bankroll. He admits that 'over the next year it will be difficult to finance growth' even though his radio stations and his cable company are profitable." At this point, I was the riverboat gambler that Peter C. Newman had called me. I was in the water and hanging on to the side of the boat, hoping for landfall.

Then the worst news of all finally came from John Bassett: he would offer no more extensions. He explained that they were taking Baton Broadcasting public in the fall of 1971 and selling the *Telegram* newspaper. (With no success in finding a buyer, they instead simply shut it down after selling the *Telly*'s subscription list to the *Star.*) He said they needed out of Rogers Cable TV (read: pay up, Ted) in order to go public with Baton. The final deadline was set for July 15, 1971.

I looked everywhere to raise money, from the Bay Street financial community to private equity or public shares, but with no luck. The banks wouldn't give me anymore, even the TD Bank, despite the fact we were nearing 50,000 cable subscribers. At a conservative value of $200 per subscriber (today cable subs are valued in the $4,000 range), the company was worth $10 million, or $1.5 million more than what was owed to the banks. Still, I could not raise money, probably because guarantors Eaton and Bassett were vacating.

I needed a minimum of $1 million, but really I needed more. I was so desperate that I went to a bunch of companies and offered half of Rogers Cable for that $1 million with the stipulation I would continue to run it, just as I had done with the Eatons and Bassetts. I asked real estate companies, a pension fund, the Odeon theatre chain and media companies like the *Montreal Star.* Everyone turned me away. Selkirk Communications Ltd. offered more money but it wanted to run the company. I wasn't prepared to let it do that.

I even approached the *Toronto Star,* which shows how desperate I was. The *Star* was one of the great enemies of the Rogers family going back 80 years. I tell my kids this and they look at me and say: "What are you talking about?" But it's true. During the birth of radio in the 1920s the *Star* would get all sorts of favours from its Liberal friends in government in Ottawa for its radio station CFCA and my father would not get any breaks. For example, the *Star* was given a full-time station and my father a half-time station; lots of deals like that happened behind the scenes.

When the Conservatives came into power in the first half of the 1930s, the *Star* applied for a power increase for the radio station but was turned down. The *Star* was so irritated it just turned in its radio licence and left the business. (The *Star*'s official reason for leaving radio is that it believed the government was squeezing out private broadcasters to create a government monopoly, according to its corporate website. History, of course, proved that version wrong.)

The sad thing about the *Star* is that it has been a big newspaper for a long, long time, but the people running it have never made it something greater. Each generation of leaders at the *Star* had so many opportunities to do this, but never did. Back in 1971, I offered them half my company, and they showed me the door before even talking price, which would not have been very much because I was so desperate.

Years later, in 1998, the *Star* was offered all of the Eaton shares of Baton Broadcasting, which held effective control of the CTV network. Again, the *Star* snubbed the offer. Then six years later the *Star* went out and bought 20 percent of CTV for not much less than it turned down for control. What for? What good is 20 percent?

Only days after the devastating CRTC decision, we set up a huge TV screen outside Toronto's city hall and broadcast the moon landing, on July 20, 1969. We launched our groundbreaking community television Channel 10 with a special on the two-hour opening of the new and exciting Ontario Science Centre in October 1969. One year later, our Toronto AM station won the exclusive radio rights for the popular Toronto Argonauts football games. On June 21, 1971, the anniversary of my father's birth, we had a huge party at Casa Loma to celebrate the rebranding of CHFI-AM to CFTR (one of the top stations in the market). The name was a play on my dad's CFRB—Canada's First Ted Rogers.

Behind the scenes, I knew things were grim, but I was still hopeful. John Graham and I took the necessary step of separating Rogers Broadcasting Ltd. from Rogers Cable TV with the hope of hanging onto the radio stations if the worst came to pass. There would be no guarantees we could hold onto radio, but we had to try.

On July 14, 1971, the day before the deadline and with money nowhere to be found, it looked as though I would be handing over the cable business and there would be a fire sale and Baton would be out at last. I called Dick Thomson, not to beg for money but just to say that I understood where things stood and wanted to thank him for all his help. Some of the other banks we dealt with never treated us as well as TD during the crisis. So many thoughts went through my head. Had I exhausted every possible avenue? Was this really the end of the line for my cable dream, maybe even my entire company? I wondered what my mother, in the late stages of her cancer battle, would think. Naturally, I thought of Loretta and our young children, Lisa, Edward and Melinda. (Martha would not be born until nine months after this crisis passed.)

The call with Dick was rather emotional. I do not give up easily. As a scrawny kid at school, I didn't win the boxing title by resigning myself to defeat. But now it looked like it was all over. Then Dick Thomson said, "Ted, there may be a way out. But it won't be easy."

I said, "I'm ready to listen."

"Okay," he said. "I will have Robin call you."

Robin Korthals then lined me up with Gordon Osler, chairman of UNAS Investments Limited, a venture capital company owned by TD Bank. The CRTC forbid banks from owning equity in cable companies because it could potentially put lenders in conflicts of interest with various cash-hungry cable operators. But subsidiaries like UNAS (United North Atlantic Securities) could own equity. UNAS presented us with its proposal the same day, July 14. I had to pay the Eatons and Bassetts $450,000 the next day, July 15. There was no negotiating with UNAS. Take it or leave it; that was my choice.

The terms of the deal were extraordinarily tough. UNAS would loan us $2.3 million for a period of three years with an interest rate of 15 percent, or double the prevailing prime rate. In addition, UNAS demanded an option to buy 5 percent of the company, or 5,000 shares, at $45 a share. Five percent for a total of $225,000 (5,000 shares multiplied by $45) was cheap when the company was worth at least $10 million, but at least I would retain control.

At 10 minutes to midnight on July 14, Loretta and I were in the lawyers' offices at the TD Centre, the same building where our head-end on the roof pulled in signals. We signed the deal, paid off John David Eaton and Big John Bassett and had money left over to keep running the company for at least another six months.

After signing the UNAS papers, we headed home after midnight with a new lease on life. My mother, Velma, who was by now quite ill with her throat cancer but still a director of the company, stayed awake in bed in her Glenayr Road house until we dropped by with the news. Though on her deathbed she was still active in the company's affairs. During this period, I remember having board of directors meetings around her sickbed because she was too weak to get out but insisted on being part of things. That night she seemed pleased and with the UNAS news, I was glad she was alive to see the deal happen.

As an addendum to the UNAS story, Gordon Osler retired from UNAS not long after our deal and a fellow from England named Bob Smith was brought in. One day I went down to his office with a big cheque and offered it to him for the options from the deal. I told him that although the options were worth much less than the $45 price I was nevertheless willing to buy them back. He turned me down flat and later told John A. Tory, who sat on his board, too, that "that Rogers fellow must know something" and that "his company is about to do very well." Tory, who was on our board, apparently responded, "I've been trying to tell you that." But it was all bullshit on my part.

It was around the same time that Loretta came up with one of her greatest quips. One day, I was struck by one of her beautiful paintings, and I said, "You're such a good painter. I wish I were an artist, too." She retorted, "But you are, Ted. You're one of the great bullshit artists."

Years after the UNAS deal, John Graham would say that we had often come close to the brink, but "never quite that close." As usual, he was right. We were by no means out of the woods. But the UNAS deal was tremendous for several reasons. Obviously, it saved the company from bankruptcy. But it also meant we could get back some of the personal collateral that had been pledged to the banks by Loretta, Toby Hull and my sister, Ann. It also injected enough cash for us to boost our subscribers past 60,000, a number that really increased our cash flow, making interest payments on the loans much easier—not to mention paying off all the creditors on time instead of pulling invoices from the hat.

After two long, hard years, I could start looking forward to the 1970s. Only about 15 percent of Canadian homes (about 1 million) had cable at this point, but the industry was growing at a clip of 25 percent per annum. We were charging $4.50 a month for the service and there were important new revenue streams coming on board, like the converter, which could double the number of channels into the home and boost our finances.

It was easy to see that Rogers Cable TV was at the forefront of a growth industry. Finally I could now truly say that the best was yet to come.

Chapter 11

MY FIVE ENTREPRENEURIAL RULES

After coming within a hair of getting wiped out, I was battered but unbowed. I believed in cable television, just as I had believed in FM radio. I knew the future of television involved specialized programming and that the relatively small number of over-the-air frequencies would create a future need for broadband cable to provide hundreds of different channels.

That fight for survival was a turning point in my life as an entrepreneur. More individual business battles were around the corner, but this one episode was greater than any single skirmish: it taught me so much about being an entrepreneur and ultimately about how to succeed.

Do I have any special insight into entrepreneurialism? Can what I learned then and over my entire life somehow help budding entrepreneurs? Have I found the "secret sauce" of entrepreneurialism? Those are heady questions, but over the years I have travelled through entrepreneurial valleys and climbed many peaks. Often I am asked, What is the secret to my success and how do I handle the enormous stress of being an entrepreneur when everything is on the line?

The answers do not fit into a nice little box tied up with a ribbon because situations and people are different. What worked for me may not work for someone else. But I shall do my best to address them from my perspective.

I have observed common traits among the successful entrepreneurs I have met along the way—Bill Gates and Warren Buffet to name just two. These qualities appear to be common in most, if not all of them: they are unpretentious, bright, hard-working, and quiet about their accomplishments. They tend not to have inherited their wealth.

I wouldn't call what I am about to tell you "secrets," but here are some of my own ideas on entrepreneurialism. But first I should mention that I have always looked for industries that are just starting to grow. The momentum of growth has made up for a lot of my errors and has carried my companies. Second, being an entrepreneur is not the career path for the faint of heart. It requires a healthy appetite for risk and a belly that can digest setbacks, even failure. I learned early that failure is a necessary component of success and an entrepreneur cannot let setbacks sideline him or her from objectives.

Over the course of my life I have followed five consistent concepts or strategies. I have boiled down each concept into one word:

Perseverance

Build

Listen

Partnerships

Customers

Perseverance is one of those words that is a lot easier said than done for many people.

I was fortunate, very fortunate. From the earliest age my mother drilled into me the need to work hard, never give up and get back what the family lost. At the age of eight or nine, I would fall asleep at boarding school thinking of ways to get back my father's radio station, CFRB. We came close to losing everything more than once, but we didn't. We had good people and I was lucky at times, but I also worked extremely hard.

It may be worth adding that perseverance is important in life, too, not just business. For example, just before I launched into the cable TV business, I quit smoking. Until then, I was puffing on three packs of Export A cigarettes a day. It was a great decision to quit. One day, I stopped and said to myself, "See if you can go all day without a cigarette." That worked. Then I tried it again the next day and the next day, until I never gave cigarettes more than a passing thought. Toby Hull teases me that the only reason I quit was because they brought in lower life insurance premiums for non-smokers around this time, in the 1960s. That may have played a role, but with my family history and my own health challenges, I just knew I had to quit.

I get so frustrated when people tell me they can't quit smoking. If they really wanted to, they would. If somebody said to them, "The hearse is coming with a casket at eight o'clock tomorrow morning unless you quit smoking right now," you know they would quit.

Turning back to business, over the years I have come to realize that I am often not the smartest person in the room. But I always want to be the best prepared person in the room. This comes from my legal training. In a courtroom, the best prepared side has the advantage. The same holds true for business. Solid and thorough preparation can trump just about anything.

Perseverance must be backed by faith and belief, not only in the underlying business, but in yourself. When times are dark, you must believe, roll up your sleeves and work, work, work. When times are good—as they are right now for my company—you must ring alarm bells because the sun does not shine every day. The rains can come more quickly than imagined.

You have to storm-proof your company. Believe me, I know from experience about getting battered around in a storm. You have to take some of the money you make in the good times and spend it on getting really locked in and solid as a rock. It could be spending wisely on research and development or marketing; or it could be building new engineering technologies and computer systems you'll need as you grow. You simply can't take your eye off the ball even if things are rolling along wonderfully.

The good times can be a killer for an entrepreneur who starts thinking, I'm pretty damn good. Sure, you've got to build people up and you want to thank them and all that. But you've got to guard against the leadership suffocating on its accolades or believing all its press clippings in the good times.

Being an entrepreneur is almost as much about giving things up as it is about getting things done. An entrepreneur does not enjoy as much family time as the average person. An entrepreneur does not play as much golf or engage in as many other leisure activities. A successful entrepreneur must constantly be thinking about the business and working toward objectives.

Having said that, as I get older I believe more and more in balance, and I freely admit my life could have used more of it. I have been strictly about work and family. I really have no hobbies, as Loretta does with her painting, though I suppose over the years you could say politics, music and the Sigma Chi fraternity have been imortant outside interests.

My life really comes down to two things: work and the time I spend with family and friends—Loretta, the kids, the grandchildren, my sister Ann, our family physician Bernie Gosevitz and his wife, Susan, John and Liz Tory, Toby Hull, Ron Besse and others.

Speaking of Ron Besse, I recall a funny incident involving him and Prince Philip, Duke of Edinburgh. The prince was in Nassau, Bahamas, on World Wildlife Fund business and was our houseguest in Lyford Cay. (The prince had known Loretta's parents, the Lord and Lady Martonmere, but this was in 1996, some years after their deaths.) We were sitting in the living room in great conversation and enjoying a drink. Ron Besse and the prince were drinking Scotch whisky and at one point Ron said, "I am going to have another one; can I get you one, too, Your Royal Highness?" Prince Philip thanked him, but said he preferred to pour his own drinks so that he always knew exactly how much he was consuming. Ron sat back down and said, "While you're up, Your Royal Highness, would you mind getting me one then?"

There was a short, awkward pause, followed by tremendous laughter. The prince went to the kitchen and came out with a tray full of drinks for everyone. It was quite something having the queen's husband serve us drinks! He is a lovely man with a marvellous sense of humour.

I've always believed that successful entrepreneurs must combine vision with passion and constantly strive for action. Driving forward and getting things done is essential, whether it's a multibillion-dollar deal to buy a company or simply upgrading the company's information technology system. Get it done and get it done as quickly as possible. I am not advocating that speed take the place of preparation and due diligence, but once a decision has been made, act on it and get it done. It is better to do 10 things really well and in a timely fashion than to try to do 50 things poorly and slowly.

Few things drive me as crazy as people putting decisions off for budget reasons; spreading a project out over time so that it doesn't look like such a hit all at once makes for stranded capital and can be a drag on the business. If something is not worth doing as fast as possible, it's not worth doing.

As you can tell, I love speed. When you launch new products and services, always try to be first onto the market. Yes, there may be hiccups, especially when technology is involved, but it is so important to get your business's stake in the ground and to be a leader not a follower.

Indeed, there is really only one product where we took our time getting to market and that was the Rogers Home Phone, our cable phone service, which has been a tremendous success, with 650,000 customers in its first two and half years. (We also have 335,000 traditional phone customers from an acquisition, bringing the total

Rogers Home Phone customers to about 1 million.) Why did we move more cautiously here? Simply put, our competitor had a 100-year head start so it was prudent for us to make sure the service was damn near bulletproof before we went to market.

As for my second point, I have always tried to build from scratch or cultivate other people's great ideas if they have chosen to undernourish them. Acquisitions and financial engineering have their place, but they set a higher return threshold. The best bang for the buck is most often gained by the person who develops the business from the early days.

The value of this stratagem has been proven by our track record in FM radio, cable television in both Canada and the U.S., wireless telephony, high-speed Internet to the home and more. We rescued our full-time ethnic TV station, now called OMNI, from the liquidator, just as we did with The Shopping Channel (TSC). We spent many years nourishing them until both became viable, dynamic and profitable enterprises.

As you're building, always keep the number one in the market in your cross-hairs. Avoid getting distracted by targeting number four or five. There's a reason those companies are not number one. Always aim high and look for vulnerability in the market leader.

Another advantage of building from scratch is that it provides the opportunity to "overbuild." In our business, we built cable and wireless networks with capacity far beyond what anyone at the time thought we would need. Services that would suck up bandwidth weren't even dreamt of at the time, but when they came along, we could handle them better than the competition. At Rogers, we have a 50-year history of doing this. Sometimes we're accused of being on the "bleeding edge," and there has been many a time when I got hell from bankers and shareholders for spending too much money on advanced networks and equipment. Or we'd get ripped in the business press with descriptions like "debt-laden Rogers" or "debt-riddled Rogers."

But look at what we've built and the value we have created for shareholders. If you had invested $1,000 in Rogers when the company converted to a publicly traded corporation in 1979 and just left it alone, it would be worth $126,000 at mid 2008. By comparison, if you took that same $1,000 and put it in an investment with a guaranteed annual return of 8 percent, it would be worth $8,965 over the same period of time. If you put the same $1,000 into the Toronto Stock Exchange composite index, it would do better, but still would earn only $16,602 over the same period, significantly less than $126,000 worth of Rogers stock.

Finding and developing a business model based on recurring revenue and subscriptions has its advantages. Though capital intensive, these types of business models make it more difficult for competitors to enter the market and the monthly income, or cash flow, can be leveraged for growth if you need to borrow money against it. It also keeps marketing costs down, because it is cheaper to keep customers than it is to constantly attract new ones.

Now for my next point: I have always tried to listen to people, especially to trusted advisors. I don't have all the answers, not by a long shot. There is an old saying that none of us is as smart as all of us. Other people have lots of great ideas but ideas can die on the vine if they are not harvested in a timely fashion. An entrepreneur must try to foster a culture where ideas are exchanged and explored. I've been so lucky to have a number of people in my life whom I've trusted completely and who have added so much to the progress of Rogers Communications. Those still with me include Phil Lind, Alan Horn, Nadir Mohamed, Bill Linton, Tony Viner, Rob Bruce, David Miller, my son Edward, daughter Melinda and others.

My daughters keep telling me we should have more women in senior positions and on the board of directors. I am a product of my times, and at age 75 it is pretty hard to teach an old dog new tricks. But they may have a point. We have three women on the board with Loretta and Melinda and Isabelle Marcoux, appointed in 2008. All are doing a fine job. But beyond issues of gender, when you build a team you look for integrity, intelligence and ambition in each and every member. There is a reason why I put integrity at the top of the list. So much flows from that one word. This company was built on that foundation, starting with the late John Graham and running through to this current team.

I cannot overstress the importance of integrity. If you hire someone without integrity you're better off if the person lacks intelligence and ambition too. Think about it. A smart and ambitious team member without integrity can wreak havoc. I have enough worries without having those sorts of people on our team.

I am proud that Rogers Communications is a "family company," with me as the head of the family. Now, with 29,000 employees in the family, it's impossible to listen to everyone, but I try to listen to anyone who has a great idea to improve the company. I like to chat with the employees who answer the phone, with customer service reps, with the wizards in engineering, and with anyone who has ideas. Like my dad, I talk to everybody and pick up an idea here and an idea there. I put that idea together with an idea I have and come up with something totally different.

Partnerships are essential for the entrepreneur. It is an entrepreneur's greatest flaw to think he or she can do everything alone. I'm sure that some readers are rolling their eyes hearing that from Ted Rogers. (When Ryerson University changed the name of its business school to the Ted Rogers School of Management, my good friend John H. Tory—son of John A.—said it should have been named the Ted Rogers School of Micromanagement.) Yes, I have been guilty too often over the years of thinking I could do everything myself, and that's what qualifies me to offer this advice. It's just not possible to do everything and trying to do so will limit the entrepreneur's potential. I have had several tremendous partnerships along the way, from Joel Aldred in the early days to AT&T and Microsoft in later years. And I have had some partnerships that were challenging, too.

An important point about partnerships: while they are beneficial, there has to be someone in charge. Partnerships don't work by committee. I don't always have to be in charge (witness my partnership with John Bassett) to make it successful, but I do prefer to have my hand on the tiller. Look out if you're in a partnership where two or three people *think* they're in charge. I have always respected my partners and believe that this increases the chances of being respected by them, too.

At the end of the day, it's all about the customers. In a play on Bill Clinton's campaign slogan in 1992, "It's the economy, stupid," I like to say, "It's the customer, stupid." Find a need and fill it has always been my slogan. There is no sense selling a product or service if it doesn't have a market. Fill a need and a market will be created, not the other way around. FM radio, cable television, wireless phones, high-speed Internet services, ethnic TV programming in the mother tongue of viewers, electronic shopping, all-news radio: they all fill a need for customers.

These days, the management consultants and the various "suits" out there would label what Rogers has done as "disruptive innovation," "paradigm shifts" and with other buzzwords. When Alexander Graham Bell invented the telephone, or when my father introduced the world to the plug-in radio, no doubt the big talkers of those eras said similar things. To me, you don't need big words and fancy charts to build a business. You need to know what customers wants and give it to them.

And it's not just major new products and services like high-definition TV or video to wireless phones, but little things, too; simple things like combining the wireless phone with the home phone when it comes to voice mail so that Rogers Wireless customers and Home Phone customers have just one voice mail to check for messages. This innovation helps to make people's lives just a little bit easier.

Twenty years ago, the *Globe and Mail*'s *Report on Business Magazine* quoted me as saying, "I'm not interested in technologies. I am interested in what they can do for you." I still believe that, even more so as technological advancements speed up. It all comes down to filling the customer's needs, how we can make his or her life a little better, a little more convenient.

When it comes to customers, I am also constantly sounding the alarm that we have to improve service—whether it's for people calling in with a problem with their Internet connection or their BlackBerry device or for customers who are confused by their bill. We're getting better, a lot better. But we are not perfect and I want us to be as close to perfect as possible.

Let me give you an example from my own company's past. The controversy over the so-called "negative option" (sometimes called "negative billing") was most definitely not a high-water mark for Rogers Cable back in 1994. I do not wish to dwell on the episode, especially since it has been well chronicled in many, many places. In a nutshell, we coupled new specialty channel services with popular existing services. Under this plan, customers got and were billed for these new Canadian channels unless they expressly said they did not want them, and because the channels were coupled (or bundled on the same tier) with existing services, if you cancelled the new services you could lose channels you already had.

For years, Rogers has been committed to promoting Canadian programming and Canadian channels, from initiatives like simultaneous commercial substitution that keeps advertising dollars in Canada to local community programming across our systems. Indeed, the CRTC has noted our success many times and encouraged us and other carriers to further promote Canadian programming.

The CRTC's view was that the new services needed a fixed amount of money each year to fulfill their business plans, which had been approved by the CRTC. So, if the new services achieved low penetration into Canadian homes, there would be regulatory pressure on us to pay them a higher wholesale fee per subscriber. In other words, there was an incentive to create high penetration for the new services in order to keep their wholesale fees reasonable on a per-subscriber basis. That is what led us to try to figure out ways to ensure high penetration by coupling them on the same tier with existing popular channels like CNN and Arts & Entertainment. But, in this particular case, we put too much emphasis on the country's broadcasting industry and forgot about the customer as we tried to promote Canadian programming and ensure the long-term success of new Canadian specialty channels. It was a mistake that was quickly rectified and has not been repeated, nor will it ever be repeated at Rogers.

Chapter 12

GO BIG OR GO HOME

I changed in the 1970s. Not at the core, but part of me changed in a number of ways.

Cable TV just got so big, so demanding of my time, that radio simply could not compete. Make no mistake, I will always be a radio broadcaster at heart, but my head was telling me bigger gains lay in cable. This was a period of rapid growth in the cable industry all across Canada. At Rogers, we played a significant role in helping to build the industry, with innovative community programming, new products like the TV converter that doubled the number of channels going into the home, and fighting for the Canadian broadcasting system with simultaneous substitution of commercials to keep advertising dollars in Canada.

Rogers Cable entered the decade with about 50,000 customers and the cable industry facing derision from the giants like Bell Canada. We exited the decade with 1.3 million Rogers subscribers and Bell threatening war with the entire cable industry. Along the way, we acquired two much bigger cable companies; one was an on-again, off-again courtship, and the other was one of the nastiest corporate fights I would ever experience.

We built an incredibly strong team of top management talent with Phil Lind, Bob Francis, Barry Ross, Bob Short, Keith Dancy, Jim Sward, Ron Turnpenny, Frank Verkaik and others. We bickered with bankers and faced a "work out squad" from the CIBC, whose number crunchers camped in our office for six months, bent on ultimately taking over and selling us off in pieces.

Mixing business with family, our board voted 9–1 for a plan that released some of the family collateral as pledges to the business. I was the only one who voted against it. With marvellous counsel from Loretta, I finally gave up my lifelong quest for radio station CFRB and sold the remaining Rogers family shares. Her father, Lord Martonmere, graciously joined our board of directors and we tapped into his knowledge and experience on a more formal basis.

In 1977, Loretta and I spent $177,000 to buy a winter home on Nassau in the Lyford Cay community, near her parents. Times remained financially difficult with the business, but I am glad we bought the oceanfront home. We have had so many wonderful times there with family and friends for more than 30 years. The house was built just after the First World War by a Wall Street financier, who owned it for about 50 years until his death, when it was turned over to his son. Fortunately for us, the son wasn't really interested in it and we purchased the property for a good price.

During this period, I lost my mother. Velma Melissa Rogers-Graham succumbed to cancer on November 5, 1971. My mother was my bridge to my father's dreams and the person who taught me so much, especially about persistence and never giving up. It was so painful to watch the disease ravage her. Thankfully, as the end approached she was able to get out of hospital and die in her own bed, as she so wished. She was mentally strong, right to the end.

A few months after her death, I approached the same age as my father had been when he died. I was nearly 39 years old. Naturally I thought about how much time I would have to complete my quest to return the Rogers name to prominence in communications and to ensure it would stay there after I was gone. Only four years earlier, just after Lisa's arrival, I had started succession planning by setting up the first two Rogers trusts, so that the family would retain control of what I had built in radio and cable.

Throughout this stage I also began to ponder more and more whether I should slow down. I suppose that was a natural thought for a father as he approached 40. Should I spend more time with Loretta and the kids and less time working? But cable was still so new and vulnerable to attacks from the phone companies and others. Radio was flourishing with 500,000 CHFI listeners and 1 million more listening to the new Top 40 format of CFTR. Could we really get to the next level if I didn't step on the accelerator? These were the sorts of thoughts I would jot down in my Daytimer.

The Canadian cable industry was experiencing tremendous growth in the 1970s. Canadian operators like André Chagnon in Quebec, Bill Stanley in the Maritimes, JR Shaw and Syd Welsh out west, and Ed Jarmain and Fred Metcalf in Ontario were just some of the pioneers who would help make Canada the most wired nation in the world. Canadian viewers love their television and cable provided the best reception for both Canadian and American programming.

In the 1970s cable subscriptions rose sharply. By 1977, only a decade after the beginning of Rogers Cable, the number of households subscribing to cable surpassed 50 percent across Canada. Cable penetration into Canadian homes continued to increase and spiked in the early 1990s at approximately 80 percent, with Rogers holding 85 percent in our licensed areas. (By 2006, cable at 58 percent, and direct-to-home satellite at 22 percent, served Canadian TV viewers. Today, Rogers' penetration is of the highest amongst big cable companies, at 64 percent, and revenue is still growing as we bundle Internet, Home Phone and wireless with our cable-TV service.)

The early days of cable TV were exciting times; any idea was worth trying. Phil Lind and his team in programming were coming up with so many ideas. Some seem pretty wacky today; others were simply way ahead of their time. They set up a "speaker's corner" at the corner of Yonge and Adelaide streets in downtown Toronto, where people could come and have their views broadcast on Rogers Channel 10. Moses Znaimer, the hip and progressive founder of Citytv, would later use the idea with great success.

We wanted always to be first and never to miss an opportunity. When an armed robber held 16 people hostage at a downtown Toronto bank around the corner from our Adelaide Street offices, we kept our community channel TV cameras at the scene for 11 straight hours. CBS News in New York aired some of our footage, as did the local networks.

Some of the other ideas from Phil and his team included putting a camera on a turntable on the roof of the TD Centre and airing panoramic views of Toronto with music from CHFI in the background; broadcasting municipal council meetings; creating alphanumeric channels for news headlines, stock prices, airport departures and arrivals, job classifieds, and even one that listed sale items at local grocery stores. Believe it or not, Phil Lind and Kip Moorecroft even came up with the idea one Christmas to broadcast a log burning in a fireplace to provide a yuletide feel for those without a hearth in the home. It is commonplace now, but then it was original. I would tease Phil and Kip that if an idea didn't work it was "Phil's Folly" or "Lind's Lemon." But we were trying, experimenting, all the time, with many of the ideas working.

Our ability to afford to experiment partly came about as a result of the TV signal converter. On March 15, 1973, Rogers Cable was the first to bring this product to Toronto, offering 19 channels initially, up from a 12-channel universe on basic cable. (Within 18 months we bumped up the number of channels to 23.) We charged $2.50 a month to rent the Jerrold converter box with its push buttons. Anyone under the age of 30 probably has no idea what I am talking about because cordless converters and remotes have been ubiquitous in television sets for 30 years or more. But back then, those Jerrold converters with the brown wire running from the TV set and snaking around the room were revolutionary.

In the first year, we thought we could get 10,000 customers to rent one. How wrong we were. Within three months, we already had 10,000 in the field and we were scrambling with suppliers to get more. By the end of 1973, only nine months after introduction, we had 35,000 customers renting converters out of a total of 115,000 customers.

We charged $4.50 a month for 12 channels on basic cable. Paying the extra $2.50 for the converter meant viewers could bring into their homes some popular channels not on basic, like WNED, Buffalo's Public Broadcasting Service (PBS) affiliate, and CHEX in Peterborough, which often carried Montreal Canadiens hockey games on Saturday night.

With this increased bandwidth (by 1978 our converter's capacity reached 36 channels), we had room for all sorts of new programming, which we filled with those alphanumeric services. Throughout the mid-1970s, Rogers was spending about $200,000 a year creating and buying programming, more than any other cable company in Canada. We had some great ideas, like movie channels devoted to the old classics and westerns, but they tended to get shut down by the CRTC after broadcasters complained that they went beyond the community programming mandate for cable and cut into their audiences. We also began buying foreign-language programming to sell to new Canadians so that they would sign up for cable service.

In the early days TV broadcasters cast a wary eye on cable. At one point, broadcasters planted the idea with the CRTC that cable should not be allowed to carry U.S. signals. For some reason, they felt this ostrich-like stance would help the Canadian broadcasting system. The chairman of the CRTC even mused in public that he liked the idea. I for one like to look for solutions, to get things done, not stick my head in the sand and hope the problem goes away.

In July 1972, I was elected the second chairman of the Canadian Cable Television Association, succeeding Ted Jarmain, son of cable pioneer Ed Jarmain. The CCTA had the idea to initiate "simultaneous program substitution," which would keep millions of advertising dollars in the Canadian system instead of these revenues leaking south of the border. I used my new position with the CCTA to further that cause. It works this way: when Canadian and American stations broadcast the same program at the same time, cable operators are required to substitute the Canadian program, together with all of its Canadian advertising, on the American channel. This system is still in place today.

I also moved to help Canadian broadcasters by randomly deleting commercials on Buffalo TV stations carried on Rogers Cable. I thought that this would discourage Canadian advertisers from running commercials in Buffalo because there was no guarantee Toronto viewers on Rogers would see the ads. I was attacked in some quarters and accused of "illegally" tampering with others' signals. The *Globe and Mail* mocked me as the "defender of the Canadian way of selling soap." But the issue was really about keeping Canada's broadcast system strong and thereby enriching our own cultural identity. It was the right thing to do and the Canadian government agreed with me. First, the CRTC helped with our legal bills when the Buffalo stations took us to court (and lost), and then Ottawa changed the tax rules so that Canadians buying advertising across the border could not deduct the cost as a business expense.

One other public fight marked my year-long tenure as head of the CCTA, and it would foreshadow our struggles with Bell Canada in the years ahead. It was something called "pole access." Because Bell's poles were on public rights of way, the phone company couldn't refuse to install cable for our industry. But it could make life difficult and expensive for cable companies. One small cable company run by a man named Omer Girard in Magog, in

Quebec's Eastern Townships, fought back against Bell. When the giant phone company threatened to terminate Girard's pole access, he took midnight photographs of Bell crews about to cut down his cable. The media had a heyday and, fortunately for cable operators, the incident just happened to be in the midst of a pole-access hearing in Ottawa. From then on, cable operators were guaranteed fair access to Bell's poles and Omer Girard would be forever known in the cable industry as the "Hero of Magog."

These skirmishes with American broadcasters and Bell Canada certainly put me in the public eye as chairman of the cable association, but I was also watching closely the goings-on behind the scenes at Rogers. I could ill afford to take my eye off the ball, because we were a little behind in our payments to the CIBC on a loan for a couple million dollars or so. It doesn't sound like that much money today, but back then it was significant. The bank didn't want to call in the loan too soon, because if we couldn't pay, the business could be destroyed before they'd get their money out. So, that's why they sent in an executive team, or "work out squad." The squad's job is to ask a lot of questions of a company's CEO, CFO and others, to get a firm understanding of the business. When they are satisfied that they know enough to run it, they call the loan, fire the CEO and CFO and take over the assets. They then run the business with the sole purpose of maximizing their chances of getting as much of their money back as possible. They have no long-term regard for the company or whether it might be a viable business that is just going through a tough patch.

The trick was to not let the number crunchers learn too much, which would buy us time to meet all the covenants of the loan. And that was no easy task because these guys were no dummies; they were sharp. One of them, Tony Melman, went on to have a tremendous career with Gerry Schwartz at his investment firm, Onex Corporation. Bob Francis, our CFO, and I were always running around, trying to keep them off balance. We weren't hiding information per se, but we made it hard to understand. As long as we made it so that they weren't totally sure they knew what the hell was going on, we were still in control and could look for a magic solution. It worked. After six months the bankers left and we were back on course. That was the only time any bank sent in a work out squad.

Another financial challenge, the so-called "Korthals Formula," also happened in the early 1970s. In September 1972, while most of the country was wrapped up in the hockey series against the Russians, I was working my way through a 50-page document outlining a new loan package from a consortium of banks headed by Toronto-Dominion. It was filled with a lot of tough conditions. As the value of the company rose, many of our loans were backed by the inherent worth of the business, but there was still $3 million in securities from Loretta's family trust on the hook as collateral. I wanted that removed because the value of the company was growing rapidly and I was uncomfortable having the family in hock to the banks. Robin Korthals came up with a formula that stated the family was only on the hook if the company exceeded 12 times its operating profit for the most recent three-month period.

At the board meeting, John Graham moved the motion to accept the terms. There had been lots of discussion, and I was adamant it should be rejected because it could put the company in a financial straitjacket. I had also pointed out that the banks were valuing our customers at only $75 each, which was way too low, at least half of their true value at the time. The directors voted 9–1 in favour of the new bank agreement; even Loretta accepted it. I was the lone dissenter. I thought they were nuts, but looking back at the success we have achieved, I suppose you can't argue with their decision.

We were now several years past that fateful CRTC decision that forced the Eatons and Bassetts out of Rogers Cable. It had been a hand-to-mouth existence but we were beginning to see a faint light at the end of the tunnel. Less than a year after near-disaster when no one but UNAS would lend us money, a gas utility offered $5 million for half the cable company in June 1972, which I quickly turned down. During 1973, Rogers Cable made its first profit before interest charges—$400,000 and not as much as hoped, but still not bad for a business that was only five years old. We had control, although the banks sometimes did their best to tell us what we could do. The CFTR transmitter site in Mississauga was increasing in value every day and was now worth 11 times what we paid for it nine years earlier, or about $6 million. The radio division was also growing and becoming more profitable.

It was around this time that I fell into intense reflection: I could rest on my accomplishments, ease up and enjoy the fruits of my labour, or I could push ever harder to ensure the family name would carry on long after I was gone. Money is nice, but ensuring a legacy is nicer. Besides, I liked being in a pressure cooker. Henry Parker, the deep thinker who was my father's friend and colleague, once told me, "The only creative thing is aggressive imagination in action." I couldn't just turn the tap off; there was too much to be done.

Some of the freedom to move ahead came in February 1975, when I sold the Rogers family's last 50,000 shares of Standard Broadcasting Limited, the company that owned CFRB. The sale fetched close to $500,000, but the significance of the deal was not the money but the symbolism that I was finally, truly letting go of that dream. Only a few years before, after four unsuccessful tries to buy back CFRB, Loretta had sat me down on the patio in our back-yard and told me to forget about my father's old radio station. "We have our own radio stations that you've built, with wonderful peo-ple working at them," she told me, adding that if I bought CFRB I would have to sell CFTR. "It's not fair to our people or to you to keep looking at the past. Look to the future." It was great advice.

Selling the Standard Broadcasting stock in 1975 coincided with our setting our sights on acquiring another cable company; either

Canadian Cablesystems Ltd. in Toronto or Premier Cablesystems Ltd. Though based in Vancouver, Premier also had significant cable holdings in Toronto.

Two things were apparent about the cable industry at this stage. The first was that consolidation, or clustering of operations, was essential for the long-term health of the cable industry. In Metropolitan Toronto alone, there were 10 different cable operators with 10 fleets of trucks, head-end antennas, community studios and staff. Second, Rogers was now in two-thirds of the homes within our licensed areas. That meant further growth would need to come through acquisition. As I said in the previous chapter, I have always tried to build from scratch or cultivate others' undernourished ideas, but now we were forced to buy other cable companies or prepare against getting swallowed up ourselves one day.

Though the financial situation had eased, we were certainly not flush with cash. Bob Francis, the chief financial officer, and I were often in the office on weekends. Sometimes our sons would tag along. We'd pay Edward and Bob's son, Andrew, a buck or two to clean up scattered piles of papers. Bob was an easygoing guy who laughed a lot and worked really hard. He joined Rogers in November 1975, after being recommended by an executive recruiter. He was very smart and personable, and the banks liked and trusted him. Our relationship was truly a partnership, and we held nothing back. He was a close, intimate advisor who didn't do anything without my being aware and vice-versa. Those were exciting times working with Bob, during the time of the CIBC work out squad, the big acquisitions and expansion into the United States.

I made the decision to step on the accelerator in 1977. In my Daytimer, I jotted down "need new mountains to climb." But I also made a cautious note about the cube root principle: "If you do twice as many deals you'll get into eight times as much trouble." Of course, I ignored my own advice. It wasn't the first, or last, time in my career that I would be juggling more than one ball.

Enter the two big cable rivals, Premier Cablesystems and Canadian Cablesystems (CCL), the two largest operators in Canada at the time. Premier had 650,000 subscribers and CCL had 430,000. At Rogers, we had 203,000 cable subscribers. These two "David and Goliath" episodes were both difficult, tough battles, but they differed in one significant respect: Premier was almost like a high school courtship, going on and off, time and again; but CCL was like a messy divorce with some of the nastiest accusations and innuendoes ever tossed at us.

We were accused by CCL of being "predatory" opportunists and "raiders" going against public policy and the public good to make a buck. It was all baloney. They presented a petition to the CRTC with names of cable subscribers, supposedly against our takeover, but they were the signatures of people who had not been briefed on the issues. As the *Toronto Star*, hardly a Rogers ally, reported: "It was the most caustic personal attack on one major operator by another in the annals of the CRTC."

At various times throughout the 1970s, I bought and sold shares of CCL and Premier on the stock market, typically through my family holding company RTL (Rogers Telecommunications Ltd.). Both CCL and Premier had been controlled, directly or indirectly, by big U.S. corporations until Ottawa restricted foreign ownership to 20 percent of voting shares in a cable company in 1969. With encouragement from Bob Smith at UNAS and Robin Korthals at the TD Bank, I was looking for investments in the cable industry. It was pretty clear back then that big cable companies were needed to support Canadian program production for our market and beyond, as well as to export technology and Canadian cable expertise, not to mention to get ready to compete against the telephone companies, with cable's bigger information pipeline into the home.

On four occasions, I thought I had a deal to take control of Premier. One memorable incident involved Phil Lind and me travelling to Vancouver to discuss the proposed purchase. We had a tentative agreement, but it was by no means a certainty. I had tel-exed 145 "thoughtful questions" that I had wanted to review with the Premier management team. Phil worried that this might be a bit excessive. While we were flying out, I struck up a conversation with a couple across the aisle. They were shepherding a Hawaiian band across Canada, and I came up with a creative idea. I thought it would provide an entertaining diversion to have the group per-form at the next day's meeting with Premier's management. They agreed to do it for $200. Unfortunately, Phil and I are not known for carrying a lot of cash and we were shy $150. Not to be deterred, I went around the plane and collected the remaining amount from fellow passengers, promising to pay everyone back, which I did after collecting names and addresses.

At the meeting, my assistant, Daphne Evans, was outside the boardroom, listening at the door for my cue when I said "What about Hawaii?" which was one of the cable systems operated by Premier, but not part of our tentative deal. When I said that, Daphne swung open the door and in came two hula dancers in grass skirts and a bare-chested fellow banging away on the bongo drums. Needless to say, they broke the ice and definitely proved to be the diversion that I had hoped for. There were certainly some surprised faces around the negotiating table, and in the end we got our deal, not right away, but some months later.

CCL was the opposite. In February 1977, on my way back from Vancouver after an unsuccessful bid to buy Premier, I received a phone message from Gary Van Nest, president of Triarch Corporation, a merchant banking firm controlled by Brascan Limited, which was then controlled by a man named Jake Moore. He wondered if I was interested in buying a 25.6 percent stake in CCL—the largest stake—which was owned by another Brascan subsidiary.

A few days later I invited Ted Jarmain to lunch. I liked Ted. He was smart; he had three university degrees. He was president of CCL, but his family owned only 8 percent of the stock. His boss, a guy named Tony Griffiths who was chairman and CEO, would probably oppose my taking a run at CCL, but Ted Jarmain could really help in front of the CRTC. I told him I would not buy Brascan's stake if he or his family was interested. He responded by saying he saw no evidence that a controlling shareholder could improve the profitability of the company. It has hardly the endorsement I was looking for so I let the Brascan offer simmer. Over the spring and summer, I remained interested in CCL. Then by the end of August, I was given an ultimatum on the Brascan block. I bought it Labour Day weekend for $17.2 million, or $16.75 a share.

This set off a whole chain of events and created lots of nitty-gritty details that gave the lawyers and corporate finance guys something to chew on. I received a call from Trevor Eyton, whom I had articled with at Tory's law firm almost 20 years earlier, and who was now working for Edper Investments Ltd., which was owned by Edward and Peter Bronfman. (Edper would take control of Brascan a year or two later.) Trevor told me he was aware of my CCL purchase from Brascan, and he was calling as a courtesy because Edper planned to diversify into cable and it too planned to buy CCL stock on the market. I told him that was a terrific idea.

Within a month, Edper had accumulated 24.2 percent of CCL. Our two blocks were obviously very powerful together, and we wanted three people each on the 15-person CCL board. We also agreed to a standard shotgun agreement that if either side wanted to sell their block, the other would be given first crack at buying it. (I had the same agreement with Joel Aldred when we bought CHFI radio back in 1960.) There is nothing surreptitious about such an agreement; it is standard business practice. But the agreement between us set the folks at CCL management spinning. You see, they were controlling the company even though they had only 9.3 percent of the stock. They were willing to fight for the status quo and an 18-month battle was in the works. It would take several public hearings and regulatory submissions to iron it out. The first began January 17, 1978, to determine whether the Rogers-Edper agreement constituted a change of control.

Leading up to the hearing, Ted Jarmain had written to me, saying: "I am increasingly confident that the CRTC is unlikely to allow control of this company to be acquired by some other entity against our wishes." This was the linchpin to our success. The CRTC has never taken kindly to anyone arrogantly presuming it will or will not rule one way or another. I tried to make peace with both Jarmain and CEO Tony Griffiths. There was no advantage to anyone in fighting. Loretta and I invited Tony and his entire family over for dinner; we could talk and the kids could play. We were rebuffed.

After a two-day hearing, the CRTC ruled there had been a change in control at CCL and that another hearing would be held to determine whether the deal was in the public interest.

Canada, with its widely dispersed population and proximity to the United States was and is more dependent on its communications networks than most countries. We were already seeing our leading role in cable slip by the end of the 1970s because our disparate group of small cable companies could not keep up with the innovation and advances coming from south of the border. Canada needed big, healthy cable companies.

The Bronfmans were tiring of the negative publicity splashed all over the media. Both Peter and Edward were honourable men, but I could sense that they did not like the spotlight. By April 1978, I had a feeling they were about to squeeze the trigger on the shotgun: they were either going to buy me out and let Griffiths and Jarmain run Canadian Cablesystems or get bought out by me and make a nice profit.

Our family was down in the Bahamas when I received word that the Edper folks wanted to meet with me as soon as possible. I knew it had to be about the shotgun. I flew back to Toronto to meet with Dick Thomson at the TD Bank and asked him how much he would back me should I need to buy Edper's share of

Canadian Cablesystems. He told me TD would go as high as $21 a share. I flew right back down to the Bahamas later that day. I didn't want anyone to know I was in Toronto meeting with TD. I was always short of cash in those days and I had to set myself up beforehand with the banks. I was dealing with really sharp guys who knew I was cash-strapped.

The next morning I called up Jack Cockwell, a brilliant guy from South Africa who worked with Trevor Eyton at Edper. I wasn't preparing for a war. I was pretty nonchalant and told him I was away with my family, but would be delighted to meet with him when I returned. Our deal was that one of us could set the price and the other could either sell or buy within 30 days. At our meeting upon my return to Toronto, Jack Cockwell was there, along with Trevor Eyton and Peter Bronfman. I was alone.

Cockwell started off by saying he wanted to change the decision period from 30 days to three days. I almost blew it. I said, "I don't need three days. I'll give you answer in 30 seconds." I was so foolish—he then realized there was a trap. He literally went running over to Peter, urging, "Don't proceed, don't proceed." Of course, Peter wanted out. He knew cable was my life and to him it was simply an investment. So he set the shotgun price at $18 per share. With Dick Thomson's $21-a-share backing in my pocket, it was a no-brainer at the $18 price. I said, "Done." The block cost $17.4 million and I was now in for $35 million for control of CCL, all of it borrowed money.

The next CRTC hearing began September 12, 1978, and it was a bloody affair with CCL management pulling out every nasty trick it could. Despite these tactics, I even told the CRTC I would like Ted Jarmain to stay on as president. Even with CCL's mud-slinging, we won approval. In large part, our victory was due to Jarmain's written admission that he expected the CRTC to bail out CCL management. New CRTC commissioner and later chairman Charles Dalfen seized on this during the hearing and made it clear the CRTC was not in the corporate protection racket. The CRTC approved the transfer of ownership on January 8, 1979.

Most of the key CCL players in management came over to us, including all 11 of the cable system managers, and two bright young MBAs: Colin Watson, CCL's vice-president of operations who would head up Rogers Cable for close to 20 years and remains a company director today; and Graham Savage, who rise to CFO and pioneer the high-yield corporate bond market in Canada.

It was a long and bitter fight for CCL, but it was over. And we used the reverse takeover to introduce Rogers cable and broadcasting to the public equity markets.

After the CCL approval and amalgamation, we didn't have time to celebrate and rest on our laurels. In the blink of an eye, the fourth and final opportunity to buy Premier landed in our lap. A management shuffle at the top resulted in long-time friend and Sigma Chi brother George Fierheller being named the new president of Premier in April 1979. I began buying shares of Premier on the stock market throughout the year. I found out that its chairman, Syd Welsh, was 66 and wanted to retire. The cards were on the table to make a move. George Fierheller acted as a conduit and had Welsh call me and we negotiated back and forth.

I also called William S. Paley, chairman of Columbia Broadcasting System Inc., to buy CBS's 18 percent stake. I was pleased he remembered doing radio deals with my father 50 years earlier. CBS sold its shares, and all told the deal cost us $78 million. On July 30, 1980, the CRTC approved the takeover of Premier by Rogers.

At the time, I gave a speech to the Toronto Society of Financial Analysts outlining my vision on the three scenarios for the future of cable in Canada: to maintain the status quo and watch Canada's broadcast system be threatened by satellite TV from the U.S.; to watch cable operators sell out to the telephone companies, an attractive option to everyone but consumers, who would have high prices without competition; and to establish big, strong cable companies to compete with local phone companies like Bell Canada. That's where I saw Rogers.

In only 18 months, Rogers Cable went from 200,000 subscribers and being the sixth-largest cable company nationally to 1.3 million customers and becoming the biggest company in Canada. We also inherited 73,000 Premier subscribers in Ireland. Our long-term debt ballooned from $2.5 million to $114 million. Interest rates were about to spike above 20 percent and we were entering the greatest period of inflation in modern times.

There was another opportunity south of the border. We had picked up some U.S. cable licences through the CCL and Premier acquisitions. Americans were playing catch up to Canada in a gold rush mentality but cable channels like Home Box Office (HBO) and Ted Turner's Cable News Network (CNN) were spurring rapid growth. We had the experience, the know-how and the gumption to compete and win against the Americans in their own ballpark. With our toe in the water in Syracuse, New York, thanks to an advanced cable system we took over from CCL, we couldn't let mounting debt and double-digit interest rates scare us away from that sort of opportunity. Besides, both CCL and Premier had untapped debt available on their books that we could leverage. And the Canadian government had altered Canadian tax laws in 1977 to allow business tax losses to be carried forward. We were about to enter yet another pressure-cooker period.

Chapter 13

AMERICAN BEACHHEAD

In the early 1980s, as Pierre Trudeau moved back into the Prime Minister's Office and Ronald Reagan moved into the White House, the cable industry across North America was changing dramatically. Rogers was again pushed very close to bankruptcy with double-digit inflation, interest rates spiking above 20 percent and the economy falling into the worst recession since the 1930s.

But for Rogers Communications this was also the era of an exciting (and ultimately profitable) foray into the U.S. cable market, the beginning of pay-TV and specialty channels in Canada and early battles with Bell Canada and other telephone companies.

I sometimes wonder how we made it through this period. We were building and acquiring some of the largest and most advanced cable systems in the United States and that took money—lots of it. Cable is a capital-intensive business at the best of times, let alone in the building phase and with double-digit interest rates. Not only did we survive, but for a time we were the *biggest cable operator in the world* with nearly 2 million subscribers in Canada, the U.S. and Ireland. No one had more between 1981 and 1982. As the U.S. cable industry grew exponentially throughout the 1980s and consolidation inevitably occurred, others surpassed Rogers internationally but being bigger than anyone else in the world at one point is something I still look upon with great pride.

This period also saw the Rogers management team really spread its wings, changing the corporate debt market in Canada with high-yield bonds and beating the Americans at their own game for cable franchises. It was a time when I became convinced that wireless telephony would be the future. In an episode that underlines the strength and independence of the Rogers board of directors, I was overruled when I wanted the company to invest in the cellular phone business in 1983. I went out and used my own money to get into the game. (I deal with the Cantel and Rogers Wireless story in more detail in a later chapter.)

And, of course, there was still radio. CFTR was challenging CHUM as the biggest station behind the perennial leader, CFRB, in the Toronto radio market. Despite overly restrictive CRTC policy on FM programming implemented in 1976, the 1980s were FM's years to become the dominant radio medium. This fulfilled the dream I held for more than 20 years. Rogers Radio Broadcasting Ltd. moved from being privately held by the family (89.7 percent) and employees (10.3 percent) to the public company then called Rogers Cablesystems Inc.

In 1985, independent radio valuations came in at prices ranging from a low of $32.6 million to a high of $55 million for CHFI, CFTR and three regional stations in southern Ontario. I was not party to any negotiations, and the board of Rogers Cablesystems approved the purchase at $41.5 million. The price was higher than I would have anticipated, but it was the right thing to do. The public company could better fund radio's growth (today Rogers has 52 radio stations across Canada), but more importantly, long-time employees were rewarded when their shares were liquidated. Remember, these employees believed in the company; many lent us money, and even put mortgages on their homes to help us out during the lean years. I hope they kept most of what they received in Rogers stock because the price went up 40 times during the decade following this sale. Indeed, in 1988, Rogers Cablesystems Inc. had the distinction of being the best-performing equity in North America, with a one-year appreciation of 262 percent.

The ongoing and interesting saga of the AM transmitters for 680 CFTR continued. We had fought so hard for this spectrum and spent $1 million over five years just to squeeze ourselves onto the dial in the early 1960s. The collection of transmitters was located west of Toronto, near Burnhamthorpe Road and Hurontario Street in Mississauga, the heart of the burgeoning suburb. A big shopping centre called Square One, Mississauga's municipal offices and high-rise apartments and condominiums began sprouting up. Construction was going on everywhere around the transmitters.

We had paid $477,500 for the 43 hectares of then farmland in 1964. By the early 1980s, this land was worth $8 million to $10 million and was too valuable to be home to radio transmitters. We knew we had to move, but something strange happened that forced us to move sooner than anticipated: the construction cranes and the new apartments, some 23 storeys high, were reflecting and amplifying our 680 signal in the easterly direction, which meant our signal was distorting and interfering with the 680 spectrum in Rochester, and even as far away as Boston. Our easterly signal was 30 times more powerful than it should have been due to this amplification. As a result, we had to power down from 25,000 watts to 5,000 watts during the daytime.

Engineers Ron Turnpenny and Gordon Elder said we'd have to move our transmitters south and beam north into Toronto. They joked about setting up some sort of contraption like an oil rig in the middle of Lake Ontario. Thankfully, George Ledingham, a director of Rogers Broadcasting and my unofficial real estate consultant, found four pieces of property side by side on the shore of Lake Ontario near Grimsby. It was pricey at $2.4 million for the nearly 50 hectares, but the property was only about 30 kilometres from Toronto, measuring straight across the lake. It was a perfect location, though the town's politicians didn't like the idea and the mayor fought us every step of the way. They thought the eight antennas would be an eyesore. (We also upset a nearby church because its recreation centre abutted the property. That was easy to solve; we promised to build the church a new recreation centre.) The politicians then hit us with a cease and desist order claiming we'd violated the town's bylaws. Our lawyers told us that the CRTC's approval of the plan superseded the local bylaws, which was good advice.

During the case, the local politicians and bureaucrats wouldn't even let us put up a temporary antenna to test the signal while things worked their way through court. It was in their interest to test, because if we could not get the engineering right and quality perfect we would have left, which is what they wanted. Instead, they claimed that if we put the antenna in the ground it was no longer a temporary, but rather a fixed, structure. John Graham came up with the brilliant idea to bring in a flatbed truck. He had found that a structure on wheels did not require a building permit. The temporary antenna went on the flatbed and the tests went well.

Shortly after the flatbed truck episode, the Ontario Supreme Court ruled in our favour, in 1984, and finally ended our six-year battle that cost a total of $8 million. At last, we had our new transmitters up and running. Nobody in the radio industry thought a Toronto station could broadcast from the south shore of Lake Ontario, but we showed it could be done.

We got our first taste of the U.S. cable market after the Canadian Cablesystems acquisition in 1979. CCL had a small but advanced cable system in Syracuse, with two-way interactive capabilities years before such technology was commonplace. It was a nice little system that opened our eyes to the opportunities south of the border. It was clear to us that our growth in Canada would be stunted for a while. After acquiring CCL and Premier, Rogers Cablesystems held 28 percent of the national cable market, and the regulator was not about to approve another takeover any-time soon.

In early 1980, Joe Clark's short-lived Progressive Conservative government was about to be pummelled by Trudeau and the Liberals. I liked Joe, and had known him since my involvement in the Progressive Conservative Student Federation in the 1950s. But he just lacked certain instincts that a politician and a prime minister needs. For example, the day his government fell in December 1979, he had a whole bunch of appointments sitting on his desk that only needed the prime minister's signature to be finalized. One was for me to be added to the board of Air Canada, then a Crown corporation. (I have never had a patronage appointment, nor did I particularly want one. In fact, the Air Canada appointment probably would have been a lot of work, especially when I was busy trying to keep my company from crashing. But as a lifelong Tory supporter, I would have taken on the task as requested.) One of his staff came rushing into his office in a panic. "Mr. Prime Minister, we don't have the numbers for tonight, we're going to lose the vote of confidence in Parliament," she said.

What did Joe do, according to what he told me three years after the incident, during a visit to the Bahamas? He said, "Damn" and then pushed aside all the papers to be signed. When he recounted this story, I said, "For goodness sakes, Joe, if it was a Liberal he'd have signed all the appointments and called for 12 more, maybe 100 more. Just bring them in by the dozens, the Liberal would say."

I was disappointed by Joe then and I have been terribly disappointed by his actions in opposing the merger of the two right-of-centre parties into the Conservative Party of Canada, under Stephen Harper. He and people like Sinclair Stevens, whom I used to respect, have been just plain wrong in their opposition to the union of the PCs and the Canadian Alliance. Stevens, a former Progressive Conservative cabinet minister, claimed the Progressive Conservative Party was illegally dissolved when the Tories merged

with the Canadian Alliance in 2003. He did not like the union of
the two right-of-centre parties and was widely quoted in media
as saying he found the merger of his party with the Canadian
Alliance "intolerable." One night in 2003, we had a horrible row
over the proposed merger at a big fundraising dinner I was chair-
ing at the metro Convention Centre in Toronto. It was a pretty
raucous meeting, with everyone getting his or her chance to air
opinions. Stevens got his two cents in and so did his buddies. At
one point, I went out to the washroom, and there was Stevens but-
tonholing some poor guy. As I walked past he turned to me to say
something, and I just said: "You're a goddamn traitor, you're a goddamn traitor. I have no time for you anymore and I am not even
going to shake your hand."

If guys like that had their way, we never would have been able to
force the Liberals out of government. (In fact, Sinclair Stevens went
all the way to the Supreme Court of Canada in his attempt to undo
the merger. Thankfully the court rejected his appeal in April 2006.)
The Liberals arrogantly refer to themselves as the "natural governing
party," and no wonder when you have guys like Clark and Stevens
shooting the Conservatives in the foot or stabbing us in the back.

In the 1980s, the cable market in the U.S. was behind Canada's, but
it was developing fast. Canadian cable got a leg up a decade earlier because viewers wanted high-quality reception of popular U.S.
programming like *Laugh-In*, *Get Smart*, *The Carol Burnett Show*
and others. In the U.S., there were so many big cities with powerful
over-the-air antennas and network transmitters across the country that American viewers didn't see the point in paying for cable.
In the U.S., the cable industry didn't really take off until pay-TV
channels like Home Box Office, Cinemax, Showtime and super-
channels like Ted Turner's WTBS and his all-news channel CNN
came along in the seventies and early eighties.

Both Phil Lind and Colin Watson were excited about the possibilities of untapped markets in the United States Licences, which the Americans called franchises, were issued by local governments in the U.S., not by the federal regulator, the Federal Communications Commission (FCC). At the time, towns and cities across America were opening up their areas and offering cable operators the chance to come in and bid on franchises. During this process, wild promises would be made by bidders of all stripes. It would start out with local programming pledges and then get into the ridiculous, with offers to help fund local pet projects like municipal building renovations and even civic tree-planting programs. There was a gold-rush mentality to get America wired up—and fast.

Phil Lind, chairman of our U.S. operations, and his team were terrific at winning franchises by highlighting our experience and quality service. They often had to battle against jingoistic attitudes held by many local councils; other bidders would paint us "foreigners." Regardless, we won dozens of franchises in places like Portland, Oregon; Minneapolis, Minnesota; and Orange County, California. We went up against Time, Cox, Warner, Storer and Westinghouse, and proved that a Canadian company could be their match.

After we secured a franchise, Colin Watson, our president of U.S. operations, and his team would go in and build and operate the systems. It was virtually all financed on bank loans with the help of local minority partners in each individual system. Cash was often very tight between the time of winning the franchise and getting it built and collecting the recurring monthly subscription fees.

We were getting noticed. I was on the cover of *Cable Vision*, a U.S. trade journal, in September, 1980 for an article entitled "Ted Rogers: The Brains Behind the Canadian Invasion," which was overly flattering, especially given the fabulous work by Phil, Colin and their teams.

In May 1981, a terrific opportunity arose. The tenth-largest cable company in America—called UA/Columbia Cablevision Inc.—

was in the middle of takeover battle. The company had 467,000 paying subscribers and its wires passed more than 1 million homes in 15 states, meaning that there was potential to double the number of subscribers. After reading about the company's situation in the *Wall Street Journal*, it seemed to me we had an opportunity to team up with the minority owner, to fend off the hostile takeover.

The minority owner was a company called United Artists Theatre Circuit Inc. (not to be confused with the movie studio United Artists). UATC held 28 percent of the cable company, and it was in turn controlled by two brothers named Robert and Marshall Naify of San Francisco. Phil and I flew to California and made a deal with the Naifys. Together, we would trump the other offer on the table and pick up the 72 percent of the cable company not owned by the Naifys. Our total bid cost C$215 million and Rogers paid C$185 million, which meant we had 51 percent and the Naifys 49 percent. Our loan came from a consortium of Canadian banks, led by TD; but it was only for one year. Our bid won. We would soon become the 51 percent owner of UA/Columbia Cablevision, once the deal closed later in 1981 after the necessary approvals. We thought we would have control, but with vetoes and other shareholder rules in place, we really didn't have control. Still, our deal meant that we now had two Rogers cable companies in the United States: one majority-owned with almost 500,000 monthly paying customers, and one wholly owned that was in the midst of constructing systems but had only 25,000 customers at the time. The plan was to merge them and leverage the recurring revenue of UA/Columbia to help finance the construction of all the other cable system franchises.

Unfortunately, the best laid plans do not always turn out as you hope. First, the UA/Columbia deal closed on November 19, 1981; interest rates had skyrocketed since we struck our deal with the Naifys. The prime rate was now 19 percent, up from 14 percent in May. Because we were paying for our investment entirely with bank loans the cost to us went up by more than 30 percent in a mere six months. And each time we'd broach the idea of merging the two U.S. Rogers cable operations, we were met with resistance from both the Naifys and management.

By fiscal year-end, August 31, 1982, we were again flirting with disaster. Rogers Cablesystems Inc.'s long-term debt jumped a whopping $400 million in one year to $566.7 million, from $163.6 million in 1981. Much of that was attributable to construction costs associated with the U.S. franchises and the loan to buy UA/Columbia Cablevision. The debt at this time was made up of bank loans, not bonds, and it cost $65 million in interest charges alone that year as the costs mounted. By this point, we had 94,000 paying customers in the U.S. franchises we won and were in the middle of building. That was terrific growth, but we needed even more cash flow to service the debt.

It was financially tight, to say the least. The banks were always applying pressure to issue common stock to raise money. But the shares were trading around $8 and I would have had to give up a lot of equity. Besides, the market was undervaluing Rogers Cablesystems Inc. at $8 a share. No entrepreneur likes to sell equity, but at this particular time doing so would have been throwing the baby out with the bathwater. There had to be alternatives.

Since the loan to get control of UA/Columbia was only for one year, we were constantly under pressure from the banks to clean up our balance sheet. Everything pointed to a short partnership. Severing the partnership would be our first survival move. As part of our agreement, we had a separation clause, and it became increasingly apparent it would be implemented by one of the sides. In essence, one party would divide up the assets and the other would choose which to take. It was just like any household where two siblings fight over the last piece of cake: the compromise is to have one cut it into two and the other pick his or her piece. The Naifys and their team made the cut. Strategically, they put the more mature systems with a higher number of paying customers (about 325,000) in one basket, likely figuring we would select this because of our need for cash flow to help pay for the under-construction U.S. franchises we held. These assets were in the northeast portion of the U.S., closer to Canada, which they also no doubt offered as an inducement. The other piece of UA/Columbia was a collection of cable systems in high-growth areas in the south and western parts of the U.S. There were fewer paying customers, about 300,000, but greater long-term potential. The crown jewel of this system was San Antonio, Texas, with 53,000 customers but with a potential of about 350,000 homes.

I guess it's no surprise that we picked the high-growth area, given our track record for building value and taking risks. And it was the right choice: we added about 175,000 customers in San Antonio within five years, and it was the keystone to a rich prize when we eventually retrenched and left the U.S. cable market.

In the spring of 1983, I was approaching my fiftieth birthday and the naysayers were out in full force. They had plenty of arrows in their quivers. Bay Street financial analysts wrote scathing reports and publicly asked just how long Rogers could stay afloat at 23 percent interest rates. Pay-TV and its promise of new revenue streams for cable operators had still not materialized in Canada because of a timid regulator fearful of the impact on the broadcasting system. We were in the process of severing our biggest U.S. cable operation while incurring high costs building out our licensed franchises.

In Canada, overall cable industry growth slowed to around 15 percent a year, from the 30 percent levels of the 1970s. Despite the fact customers were now receiving 25 to 30 channels, regulated basic cable rates were still only $8 (compared with $4.50 some 15 years earlier when only 12 channels were available). A new technology called the video cassette recorder (VCR) was exploding into the home market, and it was predicted that this would adversely affect cable revenue. Anything and everything negative about cable was trumpeted. On the surface, it did not look good. But I knew better.

In these kinds of situations, you can sit around and say woe is me or you can roll up your sleeves and get to work. I began by selling non-core assets, first jettisoning the Irish cable company with its 110,000 subscribers that Premier owned. Several MDS (Multipoint Distribution System, or wireless cable) holdings we had inherited were sold. We even sold a couple of small cable systems in the southwestern Ontario towns of Chatham and Leamington for $4 million. And we unloaded the 49 percent stake in Famous Players movie theatres in Canada that Canadian Cablesystems owned, albeit for less than its value because I hung on too long thinking I might get a shot at buying the whole thing.

I mustn't have been thinking clearly. Movie theatres were not my main business, or something I was passionate about and truly understood. I was fascinated by Charles Bluhdorn, the iconic entrepreneur who founded Gulf & Western, which owned the other 51 percent of Famous Players in Canada. I should have got out sooner, which would have saved me about $3 million. But we still got $47 million for Famous Players, some $12 million more than we paid for control of Canadian Cablesystems five years before.

An entrepreneur, I have always said, has to work hard, but he or she also has to be lucky. I believe in the old adage that the harder you work the luckier you get. In March 1983, I got lucky. A young financial wizard named Michael Milken of the Wall Street firm of Drexel Burnham Lambert was just beginning to really make a name for himself. And he was interested in helping Rogers raise money through high-yield bond issues, colloquially called junk bonds, though I dislike that term. Milken lived and worked out of Beverly Hills. He was brilliant, make no mistake. I was in awe of him. He changed the way companies like ours borrowed money. He could raise money like I had never seen and he had real style. He would attend seven dinners a night, eating a bit here and there and then moving on, making deals and schmoozing the entire time. There would always be beautiful women around and lots of nice music and good booze. He knew how to sell and how to raise money. In the presentations that he made to potential investors, he offered 50 years' worth of data showing that large established corporations defaulted just as often as smaller upstarts like Rogers.

Though he was the architect of the high-yield market, what Milken really did was free noninvestment-grade companies like Rogers at the time by offering an alternative to the banks with their high-interest floating rates. Milken never really got his due, maybe because he got caught up in securities violations that landed him in jail for a short time. But I admired him a lot, and I still do. Look at what he's doing today to raise money and awareness for cancer research as founder of the Prostate Cancer Foundation and an outspoken advocate for routine testing.

In 1983 when we were getting hammered by the banks with interest rates hovering around 20 percent, Milken sold US$181 million in high-yield bonds in the 13 to 14 percent range. We used the money to pay the banks, and we threw the first of several "paydown parties" at the exclusive Toronto Club in the heart of the city's financial district.

Graham Savage deserves credit here, too. He is the guy who ignited changes in the Canadian debt-finance market. Milken got us started with high-yield bonds and Graham expanded the program over the years. Others saw what Graham was doing at Rogers and they tried to emulate him. High-yield bonds took off in Canada in part because of Graham's pioneering work.

The banks were grateful, too. Our debt made them nervous and they loved getting our cheques with proceeds from a bond issue. Just weeks later for my fiftieth birthday, TD's Robin Korthals presented me with a framed loan document that breaks the stereotype of the humourless banker. It still hangs in my office and reads as follows:

We are pleased to inform you that the TD Bank on the occasion of your fiftieth birthday is prepared to make available the following line of credit for your personal use, subject to the terms and conditions generally as outlined below:

Borrower: Ted Rogers

Amount: $50 billion

Lender: TD Bank

Purpose: To help promote and prolong the state of good cheer and good health.

Availability: In amounts of $1 billion per year on demand subject to normal bank conditions, margin requirements and other security; interest rate to be negotiated in an amount consummate with risk.

Security:

One cottage

Other considerations as appropriate

Co-signature of Loretta Rogers with John Graham

Of course, Robin's certificate was all in good fun, but for the record, I don't think I will need the $50 billion. That's a *little* high. One of our financial people pulled together a document recently on the amount of money we have raised since 1979, and I can assure you that the debt portion is not much more than $30 billion—well short of $50 billion. That's correct: all the Rogers companies have cumulatively borrowed more than $30 billion since 1979. The equity raised over the same period has been about $4.5 billion. We've not defaulted on any loans, and any equity investors who held on without panicking have been rewarded handsomely.

In the early 1980s we weathered yet another financial storm. Money was tight, but was no longer constricting. Revenue was growing in Canada with new specialty channels TSN and MuchMusic launching in September 1984 and basic rate hikes in both Canada and the U.S. were around the corner. Our U.S. "baby" was growing quickly, and almost all the construction was complete by the fall of 1984. We were now in the position to market and attract lots more customers. Increased monthly cash flow would again keep the wolves at bay.

As we moved into 1984, we had seven clusters of cable subscribers centred in Toronto, Vancouver, Calgary, Minneapolis, San Antonio, Portland and southern California. (Syracuse would soon be sold to Seattle-based entrepreneur Craig McCaw, who would quickly jump from cable to the new growth industry: wireless phones.) In Canada, we had about 1.3 million cable TV customers and 400,000 in the United States, where the growth was furious. Lots of decisions were on the horizon, including one that would ultimately change the course of Rogers Communications forever.

Chapter 14

$110 MILLION GROCERIES

On Sunday afternoon April 10, 1988, I asked Phil Lind and Colin Watson over for a meeting at my home on Frybrook Road (they had nicknamed my home the "Frying Pan," and thought I was unaware of this). As soon as they sat down, I posed a question: Should we sell the U.S. cable operations? They each had a hunch I was thinking this way, but their jaws still dropped. Both argued persuasively for staying in the U.S.

Their arguments centred on several issues. We had built so much so quickly and had one of the finest reputations of any cable operator in the U.S. The market was exploding and rate hikes were in the offing. We were friendly with the likes of Ted Turner, Craig McCaw and the Roberts family of Comcast, which helped our cable business in Canada and the U.S. by sharing knowledge and innovation. We were competing and winning in the United States. More opportunities lay ahead.

I listened to my colleagues, but something was gnawing at me. Our debt stood at $1 billion. Wireless telephony was about to take off and Cantel had an insatiable thirst for cash. I had the simple feeling that we hadn't tapped all of the opportunities in our own country. Some may find this surprising, because Ted Rogers is a businessman who doesn't usually make decisions based on borders. To some extent, that may be true. But I do think of myself as a patriotic Canadian and I saw lots of opportunities at home. If there had been no more opportunities in Canada, that would have been different.

I had already consulted other trusted advisors like John Graham and John A. Tory. I had noted in my Daytimer that I had made my decision on April 9, the day before meeting with Phil and Colin, that we should sell the U.S. cable operations. But I just had to hear from them once more before making the decision final. Their arguments were good, but I was still convinced that selling was the right move. I told Phil and Colin we were going to pull back and sell the U.S. cable company—and that after we announced the news I would be heading to Wellesley Hospital in Toronto for an operation.

Again, they were taken aback. A week before, a routine medical exam had found an aneurysm that was 4.75 centimetres wide along an artery just below the kidney. My dad had died from a ruptured artery; I needed corrective surgery and was not prepared to put it off.

On April 20, 1988, we announced the U.S. cable assets were on the auction block. Our stock price soared $8.37 to $42 in one day. On May 11, I went into hospital and the three-hour operation was an unqualified success. It was a rough first night in the intensive care unit, and the next 48 hours were no bowl of cherries, either. But after 72 hours, I was off painkillers and on the road to recovery. Loretta brought a bottle of champagne to the hospital to celebrate. It tasted wonderful. "Euphoria today," I noted in my Daytimer.

Over the next six weeks, the outside world didn't notice my absence as I convalesced, much of the time at our Tobin Island cottage in Muskoka. I still held business meetings with senior people when I was home at Frybrook, and I popped into the office a couple times briefly to be seen.

But the recovery was tougher than I expected and I became even more reflective. In my diary I noted the most important principles for successful entrepreneurship: "Hard work, thorough preparation, detailed knowledge, careful planning, tight organization, strong leadership, controlled energy, good instincts, and an innate ability to deal." These all fit into the five overriding themes I mentioned in an earlier chapter and the last one, an innate ability to deal, would play a central role in the sale of the U.S. cable assets.

While I was recuperating, we had seven interested buyers kicking the tires of our U.S. cable company. In August 1988, we agreed to sell to Houston Industries Inc., the parent company of Houston Light & Power, the eighth-largest U.S. power utility. The price was US$1.26 billion, or US$2,400 per subscriber, a record at the time and three times the price per subscriber paid only three years earlier. The media loved this story and played it up as if we'd struck oil in Texas, which in a manner of speaking we had. But the best story was not so much the initial selling price but what transpired behind the scenes.

We had gone down to Houston to hammer out the final price after agreeing to a tentative deal. The people in Houston were very arrogant. The big shots didn't have handles on their doors. They had a button under their desks that opened and shut them. There was a movie around this time called *Local Hero* about a big Houston oil corporation; Burt Lancaster played the company president. He had buttons to open his doors, too. Maybe it was a Houston thing.

We agreed on a price but they had one remaining point of debate. I was sent to the big man's office, Houston Industries Inc. Chairman Don Jordan. His door opened with a push of a button and he was sitting behind a big desk. I could tell that I was nothing in his eyes. He looked at me and said, "We're paying a lot of money here. What if you lose 10,000 subscribers before the deal closes?"

I was taken aback. Yes, there was a long close because the deal had to be approved not only by the Federal Communications Commission but by local municipal councils where the 69 cable franchises were located in Texas, California, Oregon and Minnesota. The closing date was six months off, at the end of February 1989. I assured Jordan that we would not lose 10,000 subscribers and that we should just sign the deal. He was unconvinced, and insinuated that once he signed we would hightail it back to Canada and not care about how many customers might cancel. This was insulting. I told him we were professionals and had been running the highest-quality cable systems for more than 20 years, and it was not in our interest to lose any subscribers because we received the monthly revenue until the deal closed. He was undeterred and insisted he would not pay this price if we lost subscribers before closing. "We want an adjustment clause," he said.

I was getting angry, but then an idea came to me. "Okay, we'll give you an adjustment clause, but it has to work both ways. If we gain customers the price goes up. It can't be heads you win and tails you win." He agreed; we signed the deal and I left his office (after he pushed the button under his desk to open the door and let me out).

We went back to the Rogers office in Houston and started brainstorming ideas to increase the number of subscribers in time to close the deal. We dreamed up an idea to target the Latino population. In San Antonio, for example, there was a huge Spanish-speaking population and Rogers cable service was well liked there. In fact, Mayor Henry Cisneros, the country's first Hispanic mayor, had made me honorary mayor. We had 225,000 subscribers there and figured we could get more, with the right proposition.

We went on the Spanish-language television and radio stations to promote Rogers cable services. We booked a ton of airtime. We bought newspaper advertisements. We hired a Mexican actor to be our spokesman (in Spanish, of course), and he told audiences that Rogers would hook up new customers within four hours or give out $100 grocery vouchers when their new cable service was up and running. Of course, we knew we couldn't hook anybody up within four hours, but it didn't matter. Thousands of people ordered Rogers cable and we gave them all $100 grocery vouchers. For every order and $100 grocery voucher, we received $2,400 extra on the cable deal sale, so it was well worth it.

In the end, a total of 42,000 people in the San Antonio area ordered Rogers cable between August 1988 and February 1989, the closing of the deal, and our total number of subscribers increased to 558,000. With airtime, commercial production and grocery vouchers, we had expenses of about US$5 million but we increased the sale price by US$110 million to US$1.37 billion.

The Houston Light & Power executives thought we had played a dirty trick. But, as the Lord is my witness, I just wanted to sign the deal. They had insisted on that adjustment clause. They were so self-important that I was delighted to take all that extra money and get out of town. The Houston team was so mad that they refused to come to the closing; instead they sent their lawyers to sign the official papers. In the end, I learned to stay calm during all business deals, and never to take insults personally.

All told, over the nine years we were in the U.S. cable business, we invested US$350 million and came home with $1.37 billion, or a profit of about $1 billion. We ploughed this money into the wireless telephone industry in Canada, and into paying down debt. Much of that debt had accumulated the year before, when we bought back Rogers Communications Inc. shares to meet CRTC demands on foreign ownership restrictions. (In April 1986, the company name was changed to Rogers Communications Inc. to better reflect our growing interests beyond cable, in both broadcasting and wireless.)

In late 1987 and early 1988 we moved to buy back Rogers shares. The story boils down to this: American investors, who by their nature fear risk less than Canadian investors, loved our stock and were buying it up in droves, which threatened our cable and broadcast licences because the CRTC was saying we had too much foreign ownership in the company. In simple terms, we had to get back—or repatriate—stock that Americans owned, even if the equity in question consisted of non-voting Class B shares. We tried several tactics to make it a little harder for Americans to own our stock, such as requiring buyers to fill out citizenship forms and removing Rogers shares from the U.S. over-the-counter market, NASDAQ. This ticked off U.S. brokers more than anything else we did.

Rogers Communications Inc. has two classes of equity stock: A shares, which are voting shares, and B shares, which are non-voting. The Rogers family has always held the overwhelming majority of voting shares (and a good portion of non-voting), so control of the company was never close to being relinquished to foreigners. In 1987, our measures were working to reduce the number of foreign owners of equity. The number of non-Canadians holding stock was trending downward, but not quickly enough.

On September 30, 1987, 69.4 percent of the 22 million Class B non-voting shares were owned by people with addresses outside Canada. But 94.8 percent of the 4.6 million Class A voting shares were held by Canadians. In total, 58.3 percent of the total equity was owned by foreigners, yet control rested with Canadians.

We made a couple of offers at $25 a share, including one made shortly after the Black Monday stock market crash of October 19, 1987, when RCI shares fell to $15.75. We bought back 14.2 million shares and it cost us $360 million, a big reason why our debt jumped to $915 million in fiscal year 1988, up from $321 million the year before.

While all this was happening, a well known New York money manager named Mario Gabelli told the financial publication *Barron's* that Rogers was ripping off minority investors and doing "everything that they could do to hurt U.S. owners." His accusations centred on his pie-in-the-sky calculations that our stock was really worth $110, not the $25 we were offering, which was not true. The stock was trading at $17 or $18 at the time. Gabelli and Graham Savage, then our senior vice-president of investments, got into a very public spat, which of course *Barron's* just loved.

Gabelli has tremendous experience in our industry. He is also very smart. I have a great deal of respect for him, and I hope he has some for me, too. We still keep in touch, and I am proud of our friendship. But in this case, some years ago, he was wrong.

We also tangled with Gabelli on another issue around this time, centring on the sale of our U.S. cable assets. Before we sold—or even thought seriously about selling the whole kit and caboodle—we decided we should privatize our U.S. cable holdings, which we viewed as undervalued on the stock market. Talk about bad timing, it was just two weeks before Black Monday and we offered US$22.50 a share for the 20.9 percent minority stake we didn't own. We didn't recant after the market crashed. We continued with the offer and paid US$110 million for those shares.

Then when we sold the U.S. cable company nine months later we took more heat from Gabelli and his cohorts for supposedly underpaying minority shareholders and flipping the company to make a huge profit. Again Gabelli was wrong. When we bought out the minority shareholders we weren't even thinking of selling the entire U.S. cable company. As I said, both Phil Lind and Colin Watson fought hard to keep the U.S. operations—six months later. The fact is I thought we could sell off some of the small U.S. systems to get the banks off our backs and it would be easier by privatizing the company.

The reality is, that is exactly what we tried to do. For example, on November 12, 1987, we sold off a small system in Los Angeles County with 19,000 subscribers for US$28.9 million. We had to placate the banks all the time. We kept retreating, so to speak, on the orders of the banks. And we were also trying to finance wireless. It wasn't a very happy time, financially. This was not part of some plot to trick anyone. We were reacting to the circumstances as they arose.

Readers may be able to tell that I am getting worked up when I recall this period in the history of Rogers Communications, and perhaps now is the best time to address the issue of what the media call my "legendary temper." It is never easy for a person to admit his foibles, and if you knew me only by those old saws about my temper, you'd think me to be an evil sorcerer ready to unleash a fury of mayhem at any given moment.

Over the years, I admit, I have lost control of my temper and said and done things that I wish I had not. Looking back, some incidents seem humorous. On one occasion, Robin Korthals wanted new and onerous covenants for outstanding loans to the TD bank. I was infuriated because his demands would have put me and my company in a position where we simply could not manoeuvre quickly enough just when we needed to grow and expand. I hurled my keys across the table to him and shouted, "Here, you run the bloody company then!" and stormed out. Thank goodness John Graham was there to pick up the pieces. Robin, who would later serve on the board of directors of Rogers Communications Inc. for 10 years, jokes that I didn't toss him the keys to the business, but the keys to my convertible Chrysler LeBaron.

But at other times, the situation wasn't always so funny. And I know that now. I upset people, especially those working for me who didn't know me as well as John Graham, Phil Lind or Bob Francis did. I can honestly say, it was never personal. That's no excuse, but my loss of control usually was sparked by someone telling me why something couldn't be done instead of looking for ways to get it done.

I didn't bring my work frustrations home. In fact, my daughter Lisa says she can't remember me ever yelling at her. "And, boy, did I deserve it sometimes, especially as a teenager," she admits. Lisa, now in her early forties, went through a phase when she was about 15 where she would go to her room around nine o'clock, stuff things in her bed to make it appear she was asleep, then sneak out her window, climb down the side of the house, meet up with friends and stay out half the night, unbeknownst to Loretta and me. One night, I sat down on her bedside only to realize what was going on. I tacked a note to her pillow: "When the real dummy gets home, come see me. Dad." There was also the time when I called CFTR and had the announcer read this message over the air: "Will Lisa Rogers please call home right now." I was hoping she and her friends were listening to CFTR at whatever party they were at. This was long before wireless phones were in the hands of every teenager. Lisa was embarrassed, but I received kudos from both Melinda and Martha for showing some "coolness" by embarrassing their sister a little but not too much.

Getting back to my temper at work, I don't know why I would sometimes fly off the handle. But I certainly earned a reputation for shouting and slamming doors. There's no excuse for bad behaviour. Perhaps it goes back to being sent to boarding school at age seven and being caned for being a normal, mischievous kid. Maybe it was losing my father at age five and witnessing my mother's excessive drinking until I was 17, when she gave up the bottle. It could be that my drive to get the Rogers family back into communications has blinded me at times. I really don't know and I am not making excuses, I'm merely offering explanations.

But I have mellowed over the years. I am still relentless (as the title of this memoir attests), but I don't rant and rave the way I used to. I don't leave as many long voice messages in the middle of the night for my colleagues to receive in the morning. Sure, I still leave the odd voice mail, but not as many, and they're not as long.

I can offer two reasons for the change: the first is that Father Time is marching on, and the second is that John H. Tory, the best premier the province of Ontario never had, once severely reprimanded me for my temper. In 1999, about a year after John Graham died and Phil Lind suffered his stroke, the company was struggling with high debt levels and a low stock price. I had been under more intense pressure before, but this period was without the calming influence of either John or Phil. At the time, John H. Tory was president of the cable company. He and I were in my office when I told him that I had lost my temper that day. He told me then and there that I was losing my temper too often. Wrapping up meetings by saying how much I enjoyed the vigorous, spirited debate just wasn't enough to repair the damage my temper had caused, he warned me.

"You are a dear friend and I have to tell you something," John said. "You are an icon in these people's eyes. To be in a meeting with you is an honour and privilege for them, for all of us. But they are not in your so-called 'inner circle,' so they don't know you the way we do. They admire you and your accomplishments, and rightly so. You have achieved so many great things in your life and when you fly off the handle it lessens you right before them. You simply cannot treat people this way."

At first, I thought John was exaggerating. After all, it wasn't as if I was yelling at people all the time in an endless fit of rage. My resistance to his argument set him off. He got up and closed my office door and told me that in business losing one's temper just once is too often. It simply was not good for me, he said, or the company, and it was certainly not good for the person at the other end. He then raised his voice and even swore at me. John is not one to routinely use such language. The irony was quite something: he was yelling at me about my bad temper. But he made some valid points: I was treating good people unfairly; I was diminishing myself before them by not controlling my temper; and I was generating way too much stress and putting my own health at risk.

I went home and thought quite a bit that night. The next day, I came to work and thanked John for raising the issue. It is not easy for people to change who they are, but he was right: this behaviour was not conducive to running the company well. I have tried to change. I am still hard-driving, but I have succeeded in controlling my temper better. As I said, it is not easy to admit one's failings— to say nothing of publicly disclosing them in a book for the world to see—but there you have the true story about how Ted Rogers slew his "legendary temper."

Chapter 15

RIDING THE WIRELESS WAVE

When I went to the board of directors asking for $500,000 to invest in wireless telephones in 1983, every board member voted against me, even my wife. They forced me to put my own money on the line, which I did. I just knew wireless was the next big thing and I wasn't about to miss it.

Did I know just how big? Not a chance. Today, wireless generates about $3 billion per year in cash flow for Rogers Communications Inc., or about three-quarters of our EBITDA (earnings before interest, taxes, depreciation and amortization). It is wireless that transformed Rogers into an investment-grade corporation with plenty of growth. Wireless is the keystone of our "quadruple-play" strategy for customers—cable, high-speed Internet, Home Phone and wireless. Our collection of assets is unique pretty much anywhere in the world, certainly in North America.

Earlier in this book, I acknowledged that the Rogers board of directors might have been correct when they voted against me when I wanted to reject a tough financing package back in 1972. But I know that all 16 of the directors who voted against me on wireless would now agree that I was right. Had I not been stubborn enough to go wireless on my own (and later sell back the wireless holdings to the public company), Rogers Communications Inc. would not be the company it is today. Not even close.

For example, in the summer of 2008, the market capitalization of Rogers Communications was in the range of $25 billion. Of this value, about $1 billion applied to our media division, $6 billion to cable and a whopping $19 billion to wireless. (As the market cap fluctuates, the ratios are about the same, or growing on the wireless side.) I will always be a broadcaster at heart and a cable guy in mind, but wireless is a juggernaut. Often I am referred to as a "media mogul" or a "cable czar," but those monikers are outdated, if they ever were applicable, given the vulnerability of the company due to debt loads before wireless took off.

I was not the first to fully understand and grasp the potential of wireless. Just as with FM radio and cable TV, others had been thinking about wireless before I was. But once I saw and believed in its possibilities, I was committed because I just knew it was crazy being tethered to the wall with a wire on your telephone. Lifestyles were changing and technology could—and should—cut the cord.

In 1982, I was hearing and reading more and more about this new technology called cellular that harnessed the growing power of computers to use low-power transmitters that could "hand off" wireless phone calls seamlessly and fit thousands of callers in the same spectrum simultaneously. It was fascinating, Dick Tracy sort of stuff. Unlike with cable TV, Canada was behind the U.S. in its development of wireless. The U.S. was already in the process of auctioning off spectrum for cellular telephone companies. The Canadian government was taking more of a wait-and-see attitude. Ottawa decided it would award the various regional monopoly phone companies like Bell Canada, BCTel in British Columbia and Alberta Government Telephone (AGT) spectrum for free and then open up a bidding process for one competitor in 23 identified urban markets. This spectrum was also free, but we would have to earn it, unlike the telcos, who had simply been given theirs. The deadline for applications was February 28, 1983.

I floated the idea of cellular to Rogers management and was shot down. The executives cited the growing debt, the current deep recession and the 20 percent interest rates, as well as the fact that we had our hands full in the U.S. cable market. But I kept asking questions, finding out as much as I could about this new technology and whether it was for real.

Some thought cellular was a niche play at best and a fad at worst. After all, the big bulky handsets were priced around $2,000 and monthly charges were pegged at $200 or more. The first handsets looked like Second World War walkie-talkies and they had battery life of a mere one hour of talk time. The great technological breakthroughs since then make these cell phones sound about as advanced as a dinosaur, but they were a giant leap forward at the time.

In December 1982, on my way to our winter home in Lyford Cay, I had a layover in Miami. I made some calls, including one to Bob Buchan, a communications lawyer who did tremendous work for us during our takeover of Canadian Cablesystems. Unbeknownst to me at the time, his firm, Johnston & Buchan, had just begun building a file on cellular because Bob and his partner, Chris Johnston, were thinking wireless could have a future in telecommunications and they wanted to be ready should clients start coming through the door.

Coincidently, Buchan had recently had a meeting with the head of spectrum management at the Department of Communications, John de Mercado, who told Bob something that he would pass along to me: "Cellular is the future. It's where we're going. This is no fad—it's no hula hoop." Before cellular, there was this inefficient mobile phone technology that was more like a two-way dispatch system than anything; even if it did have a telephone handset. They were so expensive and waiting for a "free line" could take 30 minutes. The technology hogged so much spectrum, which prevented it from ever becoming mass market.

Buchan said I should talk to Charles Dalfen, a young lawyer starting his own practice aligned with Johnston & Buchan. Dalfen, the former CRTC commissioner, had impressed me with his penetrating questioning during the Canadian Cablesystems hearing. He was quickly becoming an expert on this new cellular technology. (He returned to the CRTC and served a five-year term as chairman beginning on January 1, 2002.) With Dalfen, Johnston & Buchan was preparing an application for a cellular licence for Marc Belzberg, a young financier and son of Sam Belzberg, who had built a fortune with his First City Financial Corp. of Vancouver. Joining the application almost right from the beginning was Philippe de Gaspé Beaubien, owner of the broadcasting and publishing company Telemedia Inc. They were looking for another partner. But they were both big Liberal supporters and my initial reaction was to pass.

About a month later at a cable show in San Antonio, I bumped into an engineering legend named Israel Switzer, who worked for years at Maclean Hunter Cable. He was now consulting to upstart U.S. long-distance competitor MCI Communications Corp. I knew and respected him a great deal. Israel asked me about cellular and what my plans were. I told him I was looking into it. He said he thought it was the future of telecommunications and urged me to get in before it was too late. I had to pay attention to a statement like that from a man of his stature. He focused my thinking, and I inquired whether there was still a spot open in the Belzberg-Beaubien consortium.

Two days later, February 4, 1983, I was on the phone from Nassau with Belzberg and Beaubien. We would split the initial $1 million start-up: I would get 25 percent and each of them 37.5 percent. Unlike Rogers Cable where the Bassetts and Eatons paid two-thirds of the capital for half the company, the shoe was on the other foot: I paid the same capital as my new partners, but received less equity. It didn't matter. I wanted in and the application deadline was only days away.

On Sunday, February 6, the application project team met in an office above the liquor store on Lake Shore Boulevard in Toronto. I was still in Nassau, but Bob Francis was in charge of the Rogers team. There were about 25 people there, including folks from NovAtel Communications Inc., a cellular systems manufacturer in Calgary owned by Nova Corp. and Alberta Government Telephone (AGT). They wanted our business and joined our group, bringing their engineering expertise. (Down the road, NovAtel's inability to deliver product put our business in peril and was one of many wedges that would develop between the three founding partners.) For three weeks, we all worked hard and handed in an application four centimetres thick and in both official languages that stressed our Canadian ownership and our affiliation with NovAtel, the only Canadian manufacturer of cellular systems and telephones. Naturally, we wanted to highlight our "Canadianness" since other applicants would be partnering with U.S. firms like Motorola. We faced several competing bids, including one from CNCP Cellular Communications, a partnership of the two big railways.

Two months later, seven applicants were invited to Ottawa for the next phase, which was to discuss their submissions informally with the Department of Communications. We were to meet the DOC committee of civil servants at nine o'clock one morning. I found Marc Belzberg and Philippe de Gaspé Beaubien eating breakfast together in the dining room of the Château Laurier Hotel, where we were staying.

"Come on, let's go get ourselves a licence," I said. We were all pretty confident. Our application was solid and stressed the benefits to Canada. Besides, I told them, our ownership team would appeal to the politicians: a Jewish guy from the West, a French-Canadian Catholic from Montreal and a WASP from Toronto. Our project team was headed by George Fierheller, a skilled leader accustomed to the corridors of government. George, whom I had known from my Trinity College days in the 1950s, started out as an IBM salesman who sold to the federal government when it was just beginning to get computerized. He co-founded a successful computer services firm called Systems Dimensions Ltd., sold it and moved to Vancouver in the 1970s and was hired as president and CEO of Premier Cablesystems Ltd. After we bought Premier, George became a vice-chairman of Rogers Cablesystems Inc. He knew both the Belzbergs and Beaubien and took on the Cantel project thinking it would take him away from Vancouver for a few weeks—it turned out to be a few years.

That summer in 1983, Francis Fox, the minister of communications, revised the process, saying there would be one national licence not several regional ones, and the winner must serve all 23 metropolitan areas and prove its Canadian ownership. This immediately knocked two regional players out of the bidding process and Fierheller brought them into our camp.

New submissions were due October 14, 1983, and Fox asked for another oral presentation on November 16. During our presentation, Beaubien led off by talking about how his family had been in Canada more than 200 years and how entrepreneurialism ran through every generation. I naturally mentioned my ancestors coming to Canada in 1801 and the genius of my father. Marc spoke about how the Belzbergs started in the furniture business just as Calgary was developing and then branched into real estate, insurance and oil and gas.

On December 14, 1983, Francis Fox announced that our consortium was the winner. In *Maclean's* magazine, Peter C. Newman called it the most significant government franchise since the licensing of the Canadian Pacific Railway. Now came the really tough part: building a national cellular telephone network—especially in a partnership with no one in charge.

We'd start with a preliminary budget of $1.5 million just to get going, but we knew it would cost hundreds of millions of dollars to build a coast-to-coast network. Our estimate was $200 million over the first five years, but that was wildly incorrect; the real figure would be more like $700 million. There were other immediate needs, seemingly all related to the local-monopoly phone companies we would be competing against in the 23 urban markets. We had experience in regulated environments and communications, but we were novices when it came to the games Bell Canada and the other telcos can play.

First, we needed a "no head start rule." In the U.S., the Federal Communications Commission had allowed the wireline phone companies to get into the cellular business first off, and they grabbed the early-adapters market of people, such as real estate agents. Thankfully, the Canadian government was committed to sustainable competition, and the phone companies were not allowed to unleash their wireless companies until July 1, 1985. Second, we needed fair rules on interconnection. Bell and the others wanted to treat us like a customer, not a telephone company. They wanted to charge us when a Cantel customer called a Bell customer and when a Bell customer called a Cantel customer. Bell has long been great at sucking and blowing together, and these interconnection charges could pull Cantel into the abyss pretty quickly. Third, we couldn't let Bell companies cross-subsidize their wireless operations. If, for example, the cost of wireless switching equipment was passed on to the wireline side, Bell companies could unfairly reduce wireless prices to consumers and undercut Cantel. Lastly, Bell was trying to charge us $1.50 for each phone number allotted to Cantel. In the U.S., the phone companies were charging wireless competitors between three cents and 30 cents. Fortunately, these issues were resolved and we had a chance to compete.

However, by mid-March 1984, we didn't have a management team, or even a CEO. The board of directors was not formally appointed until March 26. Fierheller was chairman. Beaubien, Belzberg and I all had three representatives on the board, and the two smaller regional partners had one each. A consultant's search turned up John McLennan as the top candidate for CEO. McLennan was by this time a private consultant, after making a pile of dough at Mitel Corp., the telecom equipment maker founded by

Terry Matthews and Michael Cowpland. John declined the CEO offer but joined the board of Cantel.

The president and CEO position then fell to Walter Steel, who had been president of AES Data Systems, a word-processing company. Steel was a good marketer, and he set up Cantel's strong dealer network, but he lasted less than a year, and McLennan stepped in to take over as interim president through the launch on July 1, 1985.

With my engineering bent, I was delighted Cantel hired Nick Kauser as vice-president, engineering. He was the brother of Stephen Kauser, a merchant banker and one of Beaubien's appointments to the Cantel board of directors. Nick had international experience and great ideas. He was a "can do" type of guy. With all the ownership squabbling and slowdowns, I asked him if he could get Cantel's system up and running in only a year to meet the Canada Day deadline. He said, "Do we have any other choice?"

His determination impressed me. When we had problems housing the cell sites, Nick came up with the idea of putting them in protective steel casings and planting them at ground level or wherever we could get the best deal to house them. The specially designed steel containers cost $17,750 each, but once we acquired a site, the equipment for each cell's base station—the transmitting, receiving and signalling—could be placed already assembled within the container on the site. In 1990, Nick left Cantel to join Craig McCaw at McCaw Communications in the United States. I was sorry to lose him and I made sure Craig knew that every chance I had. (Nick would return to the Cantel board of directors as an AT&T Corp. representative several years later, after the U.S. phone giant bought a minority stake. AT&T had bought McCaw Communications for US$12.6 billion in 1993.)

In the summer of 1984, Cantel could not raise the money it needed to operate. Even though we had promised the government we would be Canadian owned, nobody else in Canada was willing to invest. No one seemed to believe our story and our predictions of explosive growth. And we were conservative in our estimates! We budgeted for 110,000 subscribers by August 31, 1990, and we would reach 266,000 by that point—two and half times more than predicted. Still, in 1984 no one believed in our story and we were turned down by CNCP, Hydro-Québec, Caisse de dépôt et placement du Québec, Maclean Hunter and many other companies that were offered a chance into the cellular business at the ground floor.

We were forced to find an investor in the United States, Ameritech Information Technologies Corp., one of the seven regional "baby Bells" from the breakup of AT&T. Ottawa was not happy, given all our promises of Canadian ownership in our application. There were lots of strings attached in this deal, but in a nutshell, Ameritech invested $21 million for 19.9 percent equity and 15.6 percent of voting shares. This money was essential to keep us going.

Around this time it became apparent that NovAtel in Calgary could not deliver what we needed, so we moved to the Swedish-based L. M. Ericsson for the switches and other equipment. Ottawa was none too pleased. Marcel Masse, the new communications minister under my old friend from the "Youth for Diefenbaker" years, Prime Minister Brian Mulroney, threatened to pull our licence. Thankfully, Ericsson promised to build a research and development operation in this country, which created 2,000 jobs in Montreal and became a great benefit to Canada over the years.

At the beginning of 1985, we were busy at Rogers with so many things, from selling our prized Syracuse cable system to building out our Canadian cable systems' channel capacity to keeping the bankers at bay. For those reasons, Cantel may not have received the attention it deserved. But I was now more convinced than ever that this partnership could not last. There were simply too many cooks in the kitchen. Someone had to be in charge. Maybe it was this frustration. Maybe it was the stress of making sure the Cantel system would actually work when we turned it on July 1. Maybe it was financial stresses, or family concerns with four teenagers now living in my house. I don't know why, but I had a "silent" heart attack just days before the July 1 launch.

At the Cantel celebration on Canada Day, Toronto mayor Art Eggleton made the first cellular telephone call across the Cantel system to Montreal Mayor Jean Drapeau. At this point, I still didn't even know that I had suffered a heart attack. But I was certainly feeling better now that Cantel was launched.

As Cantel's fiscal year ended August 31, 1985, storm clouds were getting darker, bigger and heading directly for us. The launch was tremendously successful with more than 3,000 customers in the first two months, but money was a problem. Financing was still not in place and Cantel had eaten through the working capital of $15 million that Ameritech had provided. We were also under order from the Conservative government to increase our Canadian equity by December 31 or forfeit the additional $6.2 million from Ameritech.

In the fall of 1985, John McLennan and George Fierheller switched jobs; John became chairman and George president and CEO of Cantel. We dropped the price of a private placement stock, offering from $8 to $7 per share, and still couldn't get any Canadian investors to step forward.

Cantel needed $15 million. Despite so many other things going on, I decided to make a bid on December 11, 1985. My private family company, Rogers Telecommunications Ltd. (RTL), would put up the entire $15 million in exchange for equity that would give me "working control" of just under 50 percent but with about two-thirds of the votes. Alan Horn, then a young tax accountant at Thorne Riddell and an advisor to both RTL and RCI (he is now the chairman of RCI), warned me that I was stretching the family assets razor-thin with this offer.

As was typical, there was wrangling back and forth amongst the owners of Cantel, and nothing was achieved regarding the ownership question for two months. On February 12, 1986, Philippe de Gaspé Beaubien made a $16-million bid to trump my offer. Just four days later, our financial team was at my Nassau home going over this manoeuvre and other business when CFO Bob Francis died suddenly.

Bob was overweight and on some sort of medication to help him diet. One night, he went out for a drive and had a flat tire that he changed himself. When he returned to the house he told us what happened and then went to bed, saying that he was feeling weak. The next morning, we were all around the breakfast table, except for Bob. I went to his room, opened the door and confronted what was obviously an ominous situation. Graham Savage came in and we knew that Bob had died. It was a great loss to the company and to me personally. He was only 50 years old.

These were difficult days, to say the least. But on February 24, I came back with a $21-million counter-offer for Cantel, and $2 million cash to Beaubien and Belzberg for a portion of their holdings. With the offer, I wrote this letter to the founding partners:

> In my discussions, I have found agreement in principle from all of us that the company would benefit from having one controlling shareholder in order to provide leadership and direction. I have spent 25 years in a capital-intensive telecommunications environment in the cable television business, and my team and I feel comfortable meeting the challenges—both regulatory and marketing—which lie ahead for Cantel. Our first order of business would be to regain the engineering momentum which built this company, to ensure that our coverage, quality of technical excellence and service remain superior to Bell.
>
> Sincerely, Ted

On May 6, 1986—the forty-seventh anniversary of my father's death—we signed the documents to make official the new ownership structure for Cantel. A few days later, RTL sold 37 percent equity and 66 percent of the votes to the newly named Rogers Communications Inc. for $30 million, or the same price per share that RTL had paid. Under the deal, RTL maintained some ownership of Cantel, approximately 12 percent, down from the 20 percent RTL owned before it attained control.

It was the right time to move control of Cantel to the public Rogers Communications Inc., but I was also obligated to do so because of a cagey but brilliant move by RCI director Gordon Gray back in 1983, when the board turned me down for money to get into cellular. At the same board meeting, Gray, who had helped build the Royal LePage real estate company into a powerhouse, linked Cantel to an option the company had given me to buy a substantial amount of Rogers Class A shares. I didn't have the cash to buy the shares and time was running out on the option. Gray proposed extending the option period on the A shares in return for my granting the company an option on buying Cantel shares down the road.

Though Rogers had acquired working control of Cantel Inc., we did not have absolute control. At the board level, Marc Belzberg was constantly agitating to go public and promoting other ideas that I believed were not in the best interests of the company at this early growth stage. As a founding partner, he balked at putting more money into the cash-starved company. This went on for about two and a half years, until we had the money from the U.S. cable sale to buy out all the minority owners of Cantel.

Some of the ownership feuding became public at the time and has certainly been made public over the years. Without treading over well-worn carpet, this is what ultimately shook out. In the spring of 1988 Ameritech accepted $106 million—about four times what it invested four years earlier. In the fall of 1988, Beaubien agreed to $50 a share for a total of $146.4 million. Then Belzberg finally accepted $59.99 a share—with the $10 difference going to charity—for $235 million. Both were huge returns on their investments over the five years.

RTL sold its remaining Cantel shares to Rogers Communications for $58 each, or $267.2 million. RTL took $25 million in cash and the rest in RCI shares. The final 3 percent of outstanding Cantel shares, held by employees and dealers, remained. The investment firm RBC Dominion Securities was hired to provide an independent evaluation and the range came in at $92 to $105 per share in early 1989. The RCI board agreed to pay the remaining Cantel shareholders $98.50 per share cash and that cost another $24.5 million.

All told, it cost RCI more than $600 million to buy all of Cantel and another $700 million in accumulated debt to build the national network over the first five years. Those are big numbers. Cantel quickly became RCI's biggest cash gobbler, accounting for 60 percent of capital expenditures during 1989 and 1990, and it was the main reason why long-term debt jumped from $755 million to $1.9 billion over a mere 16-month period that ended December 31, 1990, when we aligned our year-end to the calendar year-end.

As the economy softened in the early 1990s I was often compared with Robert Campeau, the Ottawa real estate entrepreneur who overextended himself with leveraged buyouts of two major U.S. retailing chains. But I was different; Rogers was different. We were investing in things we knew, with great upside potential, like wireless. As I told the *Globe and Mail* at the time, people were expecting me to be blown out and that line of thought is the "Canadian way." I detest that negative way of thinking and the implication that Canadians cannot be as good as American, British or any other entrepreneurs. That sort of talk didn't scare me; it made me work harder.

Stepping back and looking at the big picture, I judge that the entire wireless industry has been an incredible economic stimulant to Canada, not only boosting worker productivity across all industries but with direct investment of about $25 billion of capital expenditures since that first cellular call in 1985. Each year, Rogers Wireless spends about $1 billion on capital expenditures and our competitors are spending similar amounts. (There has also been more than half a billion dollars sent to Ottawa in spectrum fees, too, with much more to come after the new-spectrum auctions in 2008.)

Of course, these annual capital expenditure investments constantly got us into hot water with the banks, not so much today, but a lot back in the early days of wireless and as we were ramping up our cable systems for future services that are here today. They'd look at our budgets and say, "Why are you spending so much on capital expenditures? Ted, you spend twice as much as anybody else."

I would push back, "I guess you're right, but look at what we've built and what we are building." They would ask me about the free cash flow, and I would tease them: "There's nothing free. What's this free stuff you're talking about? How do I get some of that free stuff?" This would go on for years whenever bankers looked at our budgets, but they didn't interfere much. It was serious, but it was good-natured fun, too.

Wireless went from 17,000 customers in Canada its first year to 17 million only 20 years later. Wireless phones, like automobiles and personal computers, are one of the greatest lifestyle innovations over the last 100 years. With the benefit of hindsight, one might think the birth of wireless in Canada was natural and easy. But it was not. There were plenty of naysayers in the early days and capital was scarce.

By 1990, wireless was out of its fragile early stages. But it was not yet entrenched in society, let alone having its potential realized or truly valued by the suits on Bay and Wall streets, investors and customers.

As for Rogers Communications, with Cantel finally and fully under its wing and the U.S. cable business sold, we embarked on buying Canadian assets that were either undervalued or fit into our ultimate goal of providing customers with an array of communications services: media, cable and telephone. During 1989–90, we increased our holdings in the Home Shopping Network and CFMT, the multilingual television station. We invested in pay-TV and pay-per-view through a minority stake in Astral Bellevue Pathé Inc., because we knew the CRTC would not let the largest cable-TV company control a pay-TV system. We acquired our first cable system in the National Capital Region of Ottawa-Hull. (Skyline Cablevision Ltd. was our first cable system acquisition in Canada since 1980.) We took a minority stake in Cancom (Canadian Satellite Communications Inc.), the distributor of TV and radio signals to smaller regional cable companies throughout Canada. We bought 11 radio stations formerly owned by Selkirk Communications Inc., to increase our presence in western Canada. We took control of a B.C. cable system that we had inherited a minority stake in when we acquired Premier in 1980. We spent about $40 million buying back a string of Cantel service centres.

And we forked over $288.7 million to buy 40 percent of CNCP Telecommunications, soon to be renamed Unitel Inc., which wanted to challenge the Bell monopolies and open up long-distance calling to competition. I think you'll agree from reading this that I am not a person who typically has regrets. I don't let them gnaw at me. There is only one past but so many future opportunities. What's done is done. But if I knew then what I know now, especially with RCI's debt reaching $1.9 billion at the end of 1990, we would have done many things differently with Unitel and probably saved Rogers Communications hundreds of millions of dollars.

Chapter 16

A BLOODY DISASTER

D isaster, bloody disaster. I can't think of a better way to describe our foray into the long-distance telephone wars with our minority ownership in Unitel Communications Inc. It cost Rogers Communications a fortune when it was all said and done. Even worse, so many of the pitfalls were avoidable.

After taking over Cantel we had wireless and cable-TV services, but we lacked the wireline phone service we needed to be able to offer customers if we wanted to be a full-service communications network. Back then, I referred to it as a "second force" that would enable us to compete, really compete, against the monopoly phone companies.

CNCP Telecommunications (Unitel's original name) was a natural ally, in that it had a nationwide microwave relay system that could be used to carry voice calls across Canada. If the government really wanted long-distance competition, CNCP had the facilities to compete. It also had the ability to carry plenty of long-haul Cantel phone calls from centres like Montreal, Toronto, Calgary and Vancouver. In other words, we'd take a wireless long-distance call off the wireless network, route it through Unitel's national network and then simultaneously deliver that call to a faraway place. The plan had the potential of saving network infrastructure costs for Cantel.

In December 1988, John A. Tory set up a meeting with Bill Stinson, chairman and CEO of Canadian Pacific and also a friend of John's. CP had just bought out CN and owned all of CNCP Telecommunications. We had a pleasant lunch at the CP-owned Royal York Hotel in Toronto. John even warned Stinson that I might get under his skin as a partner at times because I liked to get right into the action and manage things. Stinson was unfazed. Being a minority owner was fine with me at first because I ultimately wanted to buy the whole company anyway. Over the next few months, we talked and courted some more, and then in April 1989 we announced that Rogers Communications would buy 40 percent of CNCP. (A final price would be determined later that summer of $288.7 million.)

At the press conference announcing the partnership, I vowed to put an end to the "Soviet-style" monopoly of Bell Canada. I took some heat for comparing the Bell executives in their Beaver Hall offices in Montreal to the fur-hat guys in the Kremlin. (The Soviet Union was breaking up and the Berlin Wall would come crumbling down a few months later, in November 1989.) Terence Corcoran wrote in the *Globe and Mail* that "Ted Rogers is a wonderful man, brimming with enthusiasm, vision, drive, tenacity, hustle, smarts and other essential virtues of the entrepreneurial spirit. But the 55-year-old head of Rogers Communications Inc. is also capable of producing more than his share of self-serving malarkey when the occasion demands."

Bell liked to refer to itself as a "natural monopoly" in front of the CRTC, and accuse me of attacking its monopoly while protecting my so-called cable territory that others could not enter. But the fact is that while we were the only cable company operating in our licensed areas, TV viewers could still receive programming via over-the-air antennas and satellite dishes. If you wanted phone service in Bell's area, it had to come from Bell. Not only that, cable never had that "golden egg" called the guaranteed rate of return whereby government rules permitted phone companies to raise their rates the more they spent.

In 1985, CNCP tried to open the lucrative public long-distance voice market to competition but was rebuffed by the CRTC because it could not show it could make money. Instead, its business was restricted to public data (telegrams and telexes) and private data and voice (running intercity networks for big corporations and interoffice networks for governments). Unitel was the seventh-largest telecommunications company in Canada with annual revenues of $318 million, but it was puny compared with the likes of Bell Canada.

With the court-ordered breakup of AT&T and long-distance competition in the U.S. well under way by the mid-1980s, it was only a matter of time before the benefits of competition would arrive in Canada for public long-distance voice, a market with annual revenues of about $7 billion. Competition in other countries brought lower prices and new services and products. The Canadian public was itching for competition.

At Rogers, we had started calling ourselves "Canada's national communications company" after taking control of Cantel in 1986, and an alliance with CNCP would remove any doubt about that claim. All the ducks were in a row. We were ready for battle. The stock market liked the deal and predicted $10 to $15 gains in our stock price if we could break into the long-distance market and grab just 20 percent of the business. I really believed this partnership combined the best of Canada's corporate tradition with the history and continuity of CP and the innovation and entrepreneurship of Rogers. And then we got a look underneath the kimono of CNCP.

The company was still engaged in out-of-date communications services like telegrams. The culture of the company was old and tired. Everything seemed to move at a snail's pace, with committee meetings on just about everything. Some people even slept on the job. (I have nothing against napping. I even have a daybed in a small room off my office where I grab the odd nap. But I am 75 years old and I control the company, for heaven's sake.) At CNCP, there were reports of people in their thirties and forties sleeping in their offices during business hours; one guy would even regularly nod off in meetings.

The place needed a dramatic shakeup. The shareholders' agreement between us and CP called for representation on the board of directors based on exact proportion to our equity stakes. In other words, CP had the hammer on all votes. I was appointed chairman and I had some ideas for turning this company around, from dropping old product lines and picking up new ones, to changing the reporting structure of management, and investing more in microwave and fibre optic transmission facilities. I've been accused of coming in like a bull in a china shop, but the place lacked leadership and decisiveness.

We were in a real eye-opener when we saw CNCP's second CRTC application to enter the long-distance voice business. It was scrambled and in serious trouble. Phil Lind just about had a bird when he saw it. CNCP had announced its plans to refile in January 1989, months before Rogers bought into the company, and one year later there still wasn't even a business plan to present to the CRTC. It was disheartening, to put it mildly.

The business plan was a central component, and it was missing. To be successful, CNCP had to prove to the CRTC that its application made financial sense; that it would be able to generate sufficient long-distance revenues; that it would have enough money to help subsidize local phone rates so they didn't soar out of control; and that the company could be profitable so that it could survive in the long term.

Local rates were at the heart of the issue. Bell and the other monopolies across Canada argued it was only their high profit margins on long-distance that kept the price of local service reasonable.

They argued that if long-distance prices fell then local rates would have to rise. Whether that was true or not (the Bell accountants were skilled at fiddling with the numbers) is not the point. The point is that the team at CNCP—this late in the game in January 1990—did not fully grasp the heart of the matter and that could doom the application to failure. Phil and the team he compiled certainly understood this and, if not for his leadership and skill, long-distance competition in Canada may not have arrived when it did, in 1992.

By February 1990, the long-distance application was months overdue and both the media and regulator were asking questions. (There was a Supreme Court of Canada decision around this time that added to the delay, but CNCP's application still should have been filed sooner.) Even with Phil Lind's tireless work, I was becoming increasingly worried. After all, he was only one person among 3,100 CNCP employees all across Canada, and turning around this company was going to be like turning around the *Queen Mary.* In what turned out to be a prescient letter to directors of RCI, on April 23, 1990, I wrote: "CNCP entering long-distance voice without detailed planning and on-time/on-budget implementation could wipe out our investment."

On May 10, George Harvey, the affable president of CNCP Telecommunications, announced the name change to Unitel Communications Inc., and a week later we filed the application, which was written by our friends at the law firm of Johnston & Buchan in Ottawa. For the next year or so leading up to a CRTC hearing, Phil Lind orchestrated a masterful campaign to convince the public, the politicians and the regulators that long-distance competition was good for everyone—except perhaps the monopoly telephone companies that were raking in money by overcharging Canadian households and businesses. He presided over the contents and production of a brochure entitled *The Winners Are Everybody* in which Unitel promised to invest $1.5 billion to expand and enhance its network and pay its fair share to keep local rates affordable. It was mailed to 30,000 influential people across Canada.

Phil chatted up politicians of all levels and created an army of public speakers willing to hit the road to deliver pro-competition speeches across the country to chambers of commerce, service clubs or any organization in need of a speaker. No organization was too small or too out of the way to address in this grassroots campaign. Phil set the theme for all these speeches so that our message was clear and in sync. Like a submarine, he'd occasionally surface and appear in newspapers, magazines and other media outlets preaching the virtues of long-distance competition.

Meanwhile, back at Rogers, Graham Savage and I were doing our level best to raise money and keep the banks at bay (again). As I said in the previous chapter, Bay Street and the media tried to ascribe the "Campeau Factor" to us. One brokerage house issued a report in July 1990 asking the question: "Can Rogers meet its financial obligations?" There was a reporter working for the *Toronto Star* who was relentless in his columns day after day about Rogers' huge debt load or Unitel losing $1 million a day and sucking much-needed cash out of Ted.

I didn't like this talk. But facts were facts. We were at the maximum borrowing limit for our credit lines from the banks for Cantel and cable, and it looked as if another recession was in the offing. A couple of CRTC decisions limiting basic cable rate increases hurt our finances and our stock price. Michael Milken's junk-bond operation at Drexel Burnham Lambert blew up, taking the investment bank into bankruptcy and hurting anyone trying to tap the debt market. It wasn't the right time to sell equity in Cantel because the markets still didn't appreciate its true worth. Things were tough. So tough, in fact, that I had to go to Montreal and ask Bill Stinson for a loan of $135 million in 1991, using our Unitel shares as collateral. Our relationship with CP was not good, but it wasn't yet as bad as it would get. He lent me the money.

Making one of my many cold calls from our cluttered CHFI offices at 13 Adelaide Street East in Toronto in the 1960s.

Rogers Cable has always believed in community television. It spends more money on programming than any other cable company. Any idea was worth trying in the early days.

Loretta and me, with our children at the family cottage on Tobin Island in Muskoka: (from left to right) Martha, Edward, Melinda and Lisa.

Keith Dancy (left) headed our radio operations when I was spending much of my time building the cable business. Young Edward looks on as we discuss some of his grandfather's radio inventions.

At my winter home in the Bahamas with Rogers Cable's executive team in the early 1980s: (from left to right) Dave Friesen, Bob Francis, Nick Hamilton-Piercy, Phil Lind, me and Colin Watson.

George Fierheller (centre), president of Premier Cablevision Ltd. and a Sigma Chi fraternity brother who would be instrumental in the early days of wireless for Rogers, and Colin Watson (right), president of Rogers Cable, after we finally landed Premier in 1980.

When we started Rogers Cable, Dick Thomson was TD Bank's chief general manager. He and his colleague Robin Korthals saw the tremendous value of cable TV long before other lenders. Between 1977 and 1997, Dick rose to president and then chief executive officer.

V. Tony Hauser Photographer Inc.

HAVE YOU GOT THE SOLUTION
OR
ARE YOU STILL PART OF THE PROBLEM

Nothing drives me crazier than highly paid professionals telling me why things can't be done instead of looking for solutions to problems.

Angelo Drossos (right), the owner of the San Antonio Spurs basketball team, was angry when Phil Lind (left) and I were late for a meeting (and behind in our payments), but he felt better after I gave him a $1 million dollar payment in cold, hard cash.

In my right hand I'm holding an early model of a cellphone and, in my left, the alternating current radio tube that my father invented.

At the announcement of final regulatory approval of Rogers' $3.1 billion takeover of Maclean Hunter Ltd., Ron Osborne, president of Maclean Hunter, stands alone and away from the Rogers management team. Ron was hired by rival BCE Inc. a couple of weeks later.

In September 2000, Rogers Communications Inc. bought the Toronto Blue Jays and kept the franchise in Canada. Paul Godfrey, president of the team, and then–Toronto mayor Mel Lastman were on hand for the big announcement.

To help promote flu shots, Dr. Bernie Gosevitz sticks it to me. To my far right is George Smitherman, then–Ontario health minister, and on my immediate right is former premier David Peterson, who sits on the Rogers board of directors.

Loretta and me at a cable industry event with my friend Ted Turner and his then-wife, Jane Fonda. In the late 1990s, Ted Turner stretched our friendship to the limit when he gave a speech in Toronto urging cable companies and broadcasters to sell out before the big telephone companies controlled everything in the industry.

In my office with my son, Edward, and daughter Melinda, who work with me at Rogers.

Financially speaking, I could hardly stand up at the time and I think he pretty much had to lend it to us. He came through, and I was thankful for that.

On a personal note, it was around this time in the spring of 1991 that I became an officer of the Order of Canada. As a proud Canadian, I was delighted to receive such an honour. Prime Minister Brian Mulroney also asked me to join the Senate, which I respectfully declined because I simply had too much work ahead of me with Rogers Communications and this albatross called Unitel.

We made it through another financial crisis and now came the CRTC hearing into long-distance competition. I've seen it written that no one has appeared more often before the regulator than I have. I don't know if that is true or not, but I know I've been doing it for a long time, all the way back to the Fowler Commission in 1956 when I was 23 years old. Back then I was one of the folks who urged the government to set up an independent regulator, which it did, the Board of Broadcast Governors, the forerunner of the CRTC. Looking back at all those appearances I made before the regulator, I can tell you that the three days of cross-examination from the phone companies' lawyers in April 1991 at the CRTC hearing room in Hull, Quebec, was probably the most intense grilling I have ever faced.

The commissioners asked scores of questions. Was I truly committed to Unitel? Did RCI have the financial resources to stick with Unitel through the lean early years? Was Unitel simply going to be used as a complement to my cable and cellular businesses? Did I really believe long-distance competition would not raise local rates? How could I justify railing against the monopoly phone companies when no other cable company was allowed to operate in my licensed areas?

I was indeed committed. According to the transcript from the hearing, here is how I answered the monopoly question on April 22, 1991:

We don't dispute that in the CRTC "sense" cable is regulated as a monopoly. But I think if you compare it with the telephone company, if you want to make a telephone call, you have to deal with the phone company or interconnect with it. With cable, you still have 25 percent of (the population of) this country picking up television signals over the air that are free. We have video stores that are a tremendous business. We have satellite to the home, which is increasingly competitive and, in the 1990s, perhaps the one that will be a very, very real competitor to cable. I accept it [cable] is a monopoly for regulatory reasons, but it is not a monopoly in the same sense as the telephone company. People can disconnect and still get essentially all the over-the-air stations that they now get.

As Unitel's principal shareholders, Bill Stinson and I sat beside each other at the hearing. We worked pretty well together and it was one of the last times that we would collaborate. Our application was successful, and the CRTC ruled in June 1992 that Canada's long-distance market was open to competition.

But it was a Pyrrhic victory. The rules were not conducive to fostering sustainable long-term competition for a facilities-based company like Unitel. The CRTC invited too many players to enter the long-distance market, which attracted less than upstanding business people and in turn confused consumers, which played right into Bell's hands. Plus there were still just too many internal problems with Unitel.

At Rogers, we were up to our eyes in debt of more than $2 billion and paying almost $300 million annually in interest charges—more than $700,000 a day over the course of a year. In the two years since the U.S. cable assets were sold, RCI spent $2.5 billion on capital expenditures and acquisitions. The new watchword around our offices was "restraint." I make this point to explain two things:

we didn't have a lot of wiggle room and we had to aggressively change how Unitel did business before it was too late. Otherwise there was no hope of competing against Ma Bell and her sisters.

We sold nearly 20 percent of Cantel to the market and raised $273 million. I was disappointed because we had hoped to raise $450 million, but the low price reinforced my belief that the markets still did not see the real value of wireless. Still, there was some good news. First, even at that price the value of Cantel was now $1.5 billion—significantly more than the $1.5 million the three founding partners invested in 1983, only eight years before. Second, I used part of the proceeds to pay off the $135 million loan to Bill Stinson and CP. I did not enjoy being in hock to a partner, particularly one where the divisions were growing deeper by the day.

It was desperate at this point, but there was still time to salvage Unitel. We really needed a new and intelligent network platform that would allow Unitel to offer different kinds of long-distance products, so that the competition with Bell would be about more than simply price. Such a system was rare and existed in North America only at AT&T, MCI and Sprint. We needed an alliance. CP would have to reduce its 60 percent stake, and we would do the same with our 40 percent.

At first, we looked to MCI. The brash, entrepreneurial culture of this new titan company appealed to me as something Unitel really needed. Phil Lind thought AT&T would be a better fit because it was still the top dog and why not go with the best? The decision was made for us when MCI aligned with Bell Canada and its related regional phone companies.

As this was going on in early 1992, my family holding company, RTL, sold $75 million worth of RCI stock to clear up debts that RTL owed the banks and for estate planning reasons. The media made a big deal of the sale but it really was that simple. Little did I know, but there would soon be pressing reasons to get my estate in order.

In Nassau, I visited Dr. Dean Tseretopoulos, a brilliant heart specialist, and he found the numerous reports from other doctors confusing. He ordered an angiogram, which revealed damage at the base of my heart. I then flew to the Mayo Clinic in Rochester, Minnesota, where it was determined I would need a quadruple bypass operation due to blockages in several arteries.

Emergency surgery was not required, so I went home and tended to some business and personal matters. I reviewed my will and announced that RCI chairman John Graham and vice-chairman Gar Emerson would run the business in my absence. At my Frybrook Road home, I went through many personal items, sorting through memorabilia, updating the family tree, having some old home movies transferred to videotape, and putting together a few family photograph albums.

I returned to the Mayo and the operation took place on August 12, 1992, exactly two months after the landmark long-distance ruling. Loretta was there when I awoke. So were my children, and John Graham and his second wife, Tasha, and my old friends Toby Hull and Dr. Bernie Gosevitz. The first telephone call I received was from Prime Minister Brian Mulroney.

During convalescence, I really focused on what I wanted to do next, especially how I wanted to run the business. I decided I should spend less time on corporate administration and more on strategic decisions.

By the New Year, we had a deal with AT&T. The U.S. giant would take 20 percent of Unitel in exchange for an intelligent network (IN) platform and associated services. The deal was valued at $150 million. In return, CP would drop to 48 percent and Rogers to 32 percent. It became a three-headed monster. You might think that I would have learned from my Cantel experience to stay away from three-way partnerships with no one in charge.

To be honest, we got along fine with AT&T, and getting to know them was the best thing that came out of this Unitel fiasco because AT&T would be a valuable partner on the wireless side in years to come. But the problem was that no one was running Unitel and there were all these crazy veto powers at the board level. Both AT&T and Rogers tried to get things done but CP would always interfere. At one point, I confronted Bill Stinson about this and he just snapped. He spoke to me in a way probably nobody ever has, almost totally out of control. He was so mad he almost climbed out of his skin. (He might enjoy reading the part of this book about how I learned to control my temper better.)

He yelled, "You want to run this thing?"

I shot back, "Yeah, you're not running it. You know somebody's gotta run it. The goddamn thing is going to go bankrupt."

It was a terrible shouting match. The air was blue. He was a little senior to me and his company was very, very big, especially in comparison with Rogers at the time. I had to bear that in mind. It was a very unpleasant situation. As I saw it, he didn't seem that interested in Unitel, although he was certainly ready to disagree with AT&T and me.

One time, I went to the Royal York Hotel to meet with him. CP owned the hotel then and Stinson worked from his own special suite when he was in Toronto. On the wall he had a screen with a computer program running that showed where all the trains were across Canada, and he kept looking at it, mumbling that this train should be here and that train should be there and annoying the hell out of me. I kept asking him to turn it off so we could talk about Unitel. He always accused me of interfering, but Rome was burning. Unitel was bleeding $1 million a day. And he was watching trains. I never understood why he just didn't get out of Unitel and let AT&T and Rogers run it. We might have had a chance against Bell. But it wasn't to be until too late.

There were cash calls time and again. We tossed in again and again, even let AT&T ante up for us once, reducing our stake to below 30 percent. Each time we were asked for more money the debate at the RCI board would become more and more vigorous, with people rightly asking the point of tossing good money after bad, and with CP determined to let Unitel run off the rails.

Finally, in January 1995, CP decided it wanted out. We had an option to buy its stake for $210 million plus our share of the $650 million in debt the company had racked up. Rogers was already in for half a billion dollars and picking up the option would push us well over the billion-dollar mark. Unlike Cantel, Unitel was not in a new business with tremendous potential. In fact, some would argue the opposite: long-distance prices were falling fast.

The Rogers board of directors decided to pull the plug. It was a tough decision. I voted along with the board. I would probably have stayed in longer, but I wasn't prepared to go against the board on this one. We had already spent—and lost—$500 million. Besides, we had just received approval for the largest takeover in Canadian media history. There were much bigger fish to fry.

In late April 1995, a consortium of banks took over Unitel along with AT&T, and the ownership became AT&T at 33 percent; Scotiabank, 28 percent; TD Bank, 23 percent; and Royal Bank, 16 percent. The banks were not happy with us. We were in their doghouse for a couple of years for pulling the plug and leaving them hanging. But we had no choice.

Unitel would morph into AT&T Canada and then align with MetroNet Communications Corp. and ultimately line up with Manitoba Telecom Services Inc. to create today's MTS Allstream. The banks—the biggest users of long-distance, next to government—would save hundreds of millions of dollars in long-distance charges over the years because Unitel opened the door to competition. All businesses and consumers would benefit.

We didn't do so badly in the end. After losing $500 million on Unitel, we went out and built a little telecommunications company called Rogers Network Services (later Rogers Telecom) that offered speed and bandwidth to downtown Toronto businesses. In 1998, we sold it to MetroNet for $600 million cash and MetroNet stock worth $400 million, which more than doubled within two years.

But Unitel will always stick in my craw as the worst business disaster of my life. Having said that, every entrepreneur has to learn from his or her failures. At age 60, I certainly did—proving you can teach an old dog new tricks. The biggest lesson I learned from Unitel is that you've always got to have someone in charge in business, making decisions and not delaying. But I couldn't afford to dwell on problems or kick myself for falling into that trap—especially with what lay ahead.

Chapter 17

PAINTING CANADIAN DREAMS

The $3.1 billion acquisition of Maclean Hunter Ltd. was one of the three most difficult business deals of my life. Getting the 680 AM frequency in the early days was both an engineering marvel and a regulatory battle. Taking over Canadian Cablesystems Ltd. was straightforward business but fraught with underhanded, desperate moves made against us by management on the other side. Maclean Hunter was different altogether. The company put up a sound defence to our takeover (although I've always preferred to call it a "strategic merger"), and we were lucky enough to come out on top. Chivalry and humour played their parts. I am not saying there weren't bruised egos and hurt feelings. There were. But it was a chess match among gentlemen, unlike the schoolyard brawl that was Canadian Cablesytems.

Who in the world would ever have thought Rogers Communications—the little engine that perennially seemed so close to running off the rails into bankruptcy—could take out one of the icons of Corporate Canada in the largest media deal in the country's history to that point?

Before so-called "convergence" was a buzzword, Maclean Hunter was a true multimedia company with wonderfully diversified assets: in 1994 it owned more than 200 consumer and trade magazines and periodicals, from *Canadian Grocer*, which the company was built upon beginning in 1887 to *Maclean's* and *Chatelaine;*

20 radio stations; Calgary TV station CFCN and an interest in the national CTV television network; and the *Sun* newspaper chain with dailies in Toronto, Calgary, Edmonton and Ottawa, the *Financial Post* and smaller community papers scattered around Canada. And, of course, it was Canada's fourth-largest cable company behind Rogers, Vidéotron and Shaw.

The Maclean Hunter takeover story has been well chronicled, but there are a few behind-the-scenes tidbits that may add to the lore. There were some brilliant tactical manoeuvres on both sides, but particularly by our Gar Emerson. His job, ironically, was to get around the "poison pill" traps that he himself set up at Maclean Hunter five years before to guard against a possible takeover.

To fully understand the story and the strategies in play, you have to look at the context of the times. In 1993, media mergers and communications consolidation were going on full tilt in the United States and Europe. Huge companies like Time Warner, News Corp., Disney, Viacom and Bertelsmann were acquiring big and small companies in the race to produce content, whether for TV, films, magazines, newspapers or other media.

Carriers were active too: AT&T Corp. bought McCaw Cellular Communications Co., the largest wireless company in the U.S., for US$12.6 billion and regional "baby Bell" phone company Bell Atlantic Corp. was trying to buy the world's biggest cable company, John Malone's Tele-Communications, Inc. (TCI). That US$33-billion mega-merger collapsed in early 1994 after both companies' stock prices tumbled, but Bell Atlantic chairman Raymond Smith vowed to transform his phone company into a communications and entertainment conglomerate. "The merger with TCI was a means to an end, not the end itself. Our intention to be a video provider predated our attempt to merge with TCI," Mr. Smith said at the time.

The point is, big things were happening, except perhaps in Canada. There didn't appear to be any Canadian Time Warners on the horizon or any blockbuster deals. The new Liberal government of Jean Chrétien promised "a strategy for an information highway." And we all know what it means when a government makes pronouncements like that: more talk, more study, less action. In the hackneyed phrase of the day, Canada was at risk of becoming roadkill on the information superhighway.

In December 1993 I took the time to really study a map of Canada's cable systems. I noticed that virtually all of the Maclean Hunter cable systems in Ontario abutted ours at Rogers. This was a revelation to a 60-year-old guy like me who was not about to sit back, put his feet up and slow down. I wondered why I hadn't noticed this before. (Perhaps with Cantel, Unitel and the banks always on my tail, I simply didn't have time to pay attention.) In all, Maclean Hunter had 700,000 Canadian cable subscribers and Rogers was in the range of 1.7 million. (MH also had 534,000 cable subscribers in New Jersey, Michigan and Florida. Given Rogers' U.S. cable experience, I knew how valuable they could be to sell off and help finance the deal.) I couldn't help but think about all the efficiencies that could be gained by putting our Canadian cable assets together. It was the cable that churned out money for Maclean Hunter; printing and publishing still produced more than half the $2-billion in annual revenue, but it was cable that created 81 percent of its operating income.

When I added in the media consolidation frenzy across the border and around the world, it seemed to me that Canada needed bigger, stronger media companies. After 35 years in business (and 70 years since my father brought Canada and the world the plug-in radio), I was not about to let these international giants suffocate us. Without blinking, they could easily pluck advertising revenues out of Canada greater than the entire publishing revenue of Maclean Hunter. This was a new world. The Internet was moving into the mainstream. We didn't know then how all the content would be delivered (and we're still figuring things out today), but everyone seemed to agree that the old protectionist policies of Canadian governments would not be enough to withstand the media onslaught from abroad.

Canada was falling behind and we had to persuade the politicians and the public that big, strong cable companies could provide an alternative to the foreign multimedia conglomerates at the gates. With 95 percent of Canadian homes passed by high-speed broadband cable, it seemed logical to me that cable was the distributor best suited to protect and promote Canadian voices and ideas. The government and the regulator just had to allow cable to become bigger so the industry could become more efficient. Some might say this argument is self-serving, but it's what I believe. I am a proud Canadian and our culture and identity are worth fighting for and protecting. I like Americans, but I don't want to *be* American.

The other interesting point about the story is that Maclean Hunter's roots were entrepreneurial, but it had fallen into being a stodgy, bureaucratic company that was controlled in essence by management through a web of corporate holdings. It was all very confusing, but I knew that injecting our entrepreneurial zeal into the culture would bring the company back to its roots.

John Bayne Maclean started the company in 1887 when he quit a dead-end job at the Toronto *Globe* and started *Canadian Grocer*. Maclean Hunter was a wonderful entrepreneurial story as it grew and flourished. There are even historical links between Maclean Hunter and Rogers. Maclean took on a partner named Horace Hunter, and control passed to Hunter on the death of Maclean in 1950. Hunter's son, Don Hunter, was a great personal friend of John Graham. Indeed, Don Hunter was John's best man when he married my mother in 1941.

John Graham was Don Hunter's personal lawyer for many, many years. In 1961, Don took over as Maclean Hunter chairman on the passing of his father, Horace. Until this point, MH was in printing and publishing only. But Don took the company into broadcasting (Maclean Hunter competed against us for the CFTO licence) and eventually into cable. He had a great team of cable pioneers, including Fred Metcalf, whose cable company in southwestern Ontario Maclean Hunter bought, and Israel Switzer, who worked with Fred and was one of the engineers who told me to get into cellular phones.

Don Hunter was a neighbour of mine, both in Forest Hill and in Muskoka. He was a tremendous guy. We would chat over the fence or have lunch at the cottage and talk cable, exchanging and comparing business plans and ideas. He was a big man with a big laugh. He was special.

Another Don—Don Campbell—was president of Maclean Hunter at the time when Don Hunter, who was chairman, found out, in 1975, he had inoperable cancer. (One day in 1976, we went for lunch at the Hunter cottage and Don was very, very sick with brain cancer. He was in another room, lying as if already dead on a sofa. It was very sad. It had been less than four years since I had seen cancer do the same thing to my mother so it was not easy to see him like this.) Don Hunter gave up control of Maclean Hunter and sold his family's shares to a company called Maclean Hunter Holdings Limited. In essence, the shares in this company were owned by the operating company, Maclean Hunter Limited. Therefore, the controlling shares were in a holding company with no other assets that was owned by the operating company. The intent, I suppose, was to guard against a takeover but in reality it meant the management had control because the operating company (management) owned the company that had the controlling votes.

As the years wore on, Maclean Hunter management dealt with and rebuffed just one takeover attempt by an outside party, in 1988. That incident must have rattled management enough to make them look into the need for a "poison pill" to discourage, if not prevent, an unwanted takeover. The holding company just wasn't enough of a defence.

In 1989, they hired Garfield Emerson, a brilliant lawyer with Davies, Ward & Beck, a law firm Maclean Hunter had used since the early 1960s. Gar was perhaps the premier securities lawyer in Canada, and he had worked on the 1975 Maclean Hunter Holdings Limited deal. This new poison pill—or "shareholders' rights protection plan"—that he devised in 1989 was complicated and tough to get around. In essence, if the Maclean Hunter board deemed that an unfriendly bid had been launched, the directors could unleash up to 45 million new shares, or 25 percent of the public float, that current shareholders could buy at half-price. The effect was to dilute the stock and make the takeover more expensive and less attractive to a buyer. But, and this was important, the poison pill would not be triggered if the directors of Maclean Hunter deemed a takeover bid to be a "permitted bid." We had to approach this entire process so the MH directors would not trigger the shareholders' rights protection plan. Crafting the MH poison pill in 1989 was one of the last assignments Gar Emerson undertook for Maclean Hunter, because in January 1990 he became president of Rothschild Canada Inc., a new joint venture of the British and French banking families.

Gar, by the way, was and is married to my first cousin, Melissa Taylor, on my mother's side of the family. I have known him for years. In 1993, he accepted the position of chairman of Rogers Communications Inc. when the legendary John Graham retired and became chairman emeritus.

Exiting the early 1990s recession, Rogers Communications had come a long way since needing an emergency temporary loan of $135 million from Canadian Pacific Ltd. in 1991, just to make ends meet. All told, Graham Savage had raised $1.8 billion in 1991, $1.5 billion in 1992 and another $750 million in 1993, with most of it being debt, mainly from U.S. markets. Graham demonstrated that RCI could realistically cover the payments by structuring and compartmentalizing the debt in various operating companies and relying on growing cash flows. This was, by and large, a different kind of debt, too, that pushed payments farther out into the future when cash flows would be greater still. These debentures and other debt instruments gave us freedom from the bankers' covenants and repayment schedules.

By early 1994 RCI had eliminated all bank debt by transferring it to other debt instruments. As anyone who has paid off a mortgage knows, banks love you then; they give you their highest credit rating and want you to borrow more and more from them. The banks' favour couldn't come at a better time because we'd soon need a $2 billion bridge loan.

As the economy improved and RCI regained its footing, the family holding company, RTL, naturally found itself in better shape. For the first time, we had significant cash on hand after selling 7 million Class B non-voting shares into a buoyant stock market, in 1993. I remember Alan Horn teasing me that he was now in an odd position of managing money instead of debt. Alan by this point was RTL's full-time president, after leaving his accounting firm of Peat Marwick, where RTL had been his biggest client.

We decided that with cash sitting in RTL we should diversify beyond Rogers Communications and start investing in other communications companies in Canada and the United States. One of Alan's central investment tenets is to invest in areas one knows about and understands. I agreed wholeheartedly. We bought some Baton Broadcasting Ltd. stock for old time's sake. We bought some U.S. cable company stock. And we bought some Maclean Hunter.

Around Christmas 1993, I talked to Gar Emerson about my idea to take a run at Maclean Hunter. His initial reaction was positive and he said that he could design a legal manoeuvre to overcome the poison pill strategy that he'd built in the first place. He immediately put his staff to work analyzing every nook and cranny of Maclean Hunter's shareholders' rights protection plan and defensive capabilities. Gar assigned the project the code name

"Kona," after the Hawaiian island he and my cousin and their family were heading to for a vacation after Christmas.

Early in 1994, only Gar and my wife, Loretta, knew about my Maclean Hunter idea. Before heading south at the beginning of January, I told Phil Lind, now a vice-chairman of RCI. He liked the plan, though he cautioned that it would have to be properly presented to the public to have a chance of CRTC approval, because if the takeover was successful Rogers would have double the number of cable subscribers as the next-biggest cable company and be in one-third of all cabled homes in Canada.

When Loretta and I returned to Toronto a week later, I told Alan Horn I wanted to buy up to 10 percent of Maclean Hunter's stock on the open market through RTL. That worked out to about 16 million shares, and such a big purchase was sure to attract attention. We decided not to use our usual agents because if they were the buyers, the market would know I was behind the purchase. So I called Lawrence Bloomberg, president of First Marathon Securities Corp., a house known for moving big blocks of Maclean Hunter stock.

At 8 a.m. on January 12, Alan and I visited Lawrence Bloomberg at his house near Casa Loma, a short drive south of my home. I told him I realized Maclean Hunter had a tough poison pill, but I still wanted to buy up to 10 percent of the company as discreetly as possible, at prices up to $13 a share. Alan and I then went to the office and I told John Graham my plan. Almost as soon as he gave his approval, the phone rang. It was Lawrence Bloomberg saying there was no shortage of Maclean Hunter shares in the $12.75 to $13 range. By day's end, RTL had bought 3.5 million shares. Fortunately, there was a high trading volume in RCI stock that day, too, which kept us under the radar. The business press commented that there seemed to be a renewed interest in cable stocks.

Around this time, Maclean Hunter issued a statement that it was studying its options on what to do with its U.S. cable assets.

As I said, the U.S. cable market was in a consolidation phase and Maclean Hunter's cable was worth around $1.5 billion—but it was worth more to Rogers than to Maclean Hunter, because if we bought the company we would not have to pay capital gains tax on the U.S. assets. Maclean Hunter was in the process of asking Revenue Canada for a "purchase butterfly"—a special dispensation to avoid hundreds of millions of dollars in capital gains tax if it sold the U.S. cable assets. We were betting the government would not allow Maclean Hunter to avoid the capital gains.

On January 25, Graham Savage, our chief financial officer, closed a $300 million financing package and I called him over to my office. "You better sit down. I have something to tell you." He was exhausted, but I could tell the idea and the action revved him up. The next day, I called Maclean Hunter president and CEO Ron Osborne, and asked for a meeting with him and Chairman Don Campbell at 7:30 a.m. Friday, January 28, at their offices. There was a Maclean Hunter board meeting scheduled for 8:30 that morning.

The day before the meeting, Graham Savage, Gar Emerson and I started working on ideas for a $2 billion bank financing deal to carry us through the sale and regulatory approval of the U.S. cable assets, which could take six months or more. We decided to offer the bank consortium lead to Scotiabank, which had become Cantel's lead banker. TD Bank, which had been so great to us over the years, had what we thought was a conflict: both Don Campbell of Maclean Hunter and I were TD board members at the time.

The next morning, Gar and I headed to our meeting with Campbell at the Maclean Hunter building on Bay Street. A snowstorm prevented both Phil Lind and Ron Osborne from attending. Phil was in Montreal the night before when the airport was closed due to snow. He managed to get the last bus to Toronto, but unfortunately it got stuck in a snowbank in Kingston. Ron was in Calgary because his flight was cancelled since no planes were landing in Toronto, but at least he could participate via telephone.

We were met by Don Campbell at the elevator and we proceeded to his office. I informed him that RTL had acquired 15 million Maclean Hunter shares on the open market, just fewer than
10 percent. We proposed a "strategic merger," outlining all the
rational business reasons for doing so. Campbell responded by saying
our proposal was not a merger, but a takeover. On the phone from
his Calgary hotel room, Osborne was more reserved but said there
was no detailed plan or specific offer, merely a preliminary approach.
Soon afterwards, Ron would publicly refer to it as a "phantom offer,"
playing on the title of a popular stage musical of the time, *Phantom
of the Opera*. (Indeed, on February 11 at a charity event, Ron Osborne
gave me a spoof poster: "*The Phantom of the Offer*, a comic opera by
Rogers and Emerstein." It was hilarious and we'd have more fun later
with the spoof.) Campbell escorted us out of that initial meeting,
and he headed to the Maclean Hunter board meeting where he no
doubt informed the directors of what happened and the battle began
in earnest.

We headed to meetings at the CIBC and Bank of Montreal,
where Graham Savage joined us. I remember one episode during
all this shuffling back and forth where a senior banker at CIBC
had to be pulled off a ski slope in Switzerland to give his okay to
be part of the financing package. Later that afternoon I had a visit
from Dick Thomson, chairman and CEO of the TD Bank. I do
not need to restate how great my respect and fondness are for this
man. Rogers Communications likely never would have been able
to scale the heights without his support over the years.

Dick was angry, angrier than I had ever seen him. He did not
like the fact that Scotiabank was the lead bank. But we were in an
equivocal position: both Don Campbell and I were on the board
of directors of the TD Bank, and both counted Dick as a close
friend. As the lead bank, Scotiabank was "exclusive" to RCI, which
meant it agreed to refrain from helping to finance any takeover
defence Maclean Hunter might mount. I told Dick why we went

with Scotiabank in the lead and urged him not to press the point, warning that he would surely offend Don Campbell, his most senior director and a friend. If he insisted, I would have no choice but to accept his wishes. He insisted. We called Peter Godsoe, Scotiabank's chairman and CEO who was gracious not only on this deal, but also over the coming years, and was instrumental in developing the great business relationship between Scotiabank and Rogers. Now retired as Scotiabank's CEO, Peter sits on the Rogers board. On this occasion he agreed to share the lead with TD, although Dick did not want an exclusive, so TD could also lend to Maclean Hunter, if needed. Dick Thomson understood the Maclean Hunter deal better than anyone; he saw the efficiencies and the real business reasons. Still, I warned him once more that he could lose a friend over his decision. He said it was business and he wanted the co-lead.

Dick Thomson did lose Don Campbell as a friend. For the next year, Campbell remained on the TD board, but said very little at meetings and did not stand for re-election at the next TD annual general meeting in January 1995.

The next evening, January 31, I bumped into Ron Osborne at the Metro Toronto Board of Trade's annual black-tie dinner, and I mentioned that Phil Lind had been in Ottawa to apprise the CRTC of a possible strategic merger between Rogers and Maclean Hunter. Ron had a strange look on his face, almost as if he didn't really believe our overtures of Friday morning. The next day I began framing an offer that would be made to Maclean Hunter shareholders. Two securities firms would be advising us: ScotiaMcLeod Inc., whose chief executive officer, David Wilson, was a director of RCI, and Burns Fry Limited and its vice-chairman Peter Eby. Back in 1989, Peter had worked with Gar Emerson on creating and implementing the Maclean Hunter poison pill.

Maclean Hunter hired Tony Fell, chairman of RBC Dominion Securities Inc., and Ed King, chairman of Wood Gundy, two very formidable opponents. They asked us to delay making the offer. I said I would do that only if Maclean Hunter promised to refrain from looking for other possible bidders, so-called white knights. They said they could not promise so I said we'd be making an offer soon. It was Tuesday, February 1, and the closing price of Maclean Hunter was $13.38 a share.

There is no hard and fast rule about what premium one should put on a takeover bid, but 20 percent above the last closing tends to get shareholders' attention. Twenty percent above $13.38 would have been $16.05 a share. There were almost 180 million shares outstanding, so the deal would be $2.88 billion at $16.05 per share. There was still the question of the 36.4 million control shares in the subsidiary called Maclean Hunter Holdings Limited that were owned by the operating company, Maclean Hunter Ltd. If we were obliged to buy those shares, it would add $600 million to the price tag. We were confident—or at least hopeful—we would not have to buy them.

The next morning, Ron Osborne and Maclean Hunter issued a preemptive strike by making a public announcement of our plans and saying that they were told that a takeover proposal was forthcoming. Osborne is one smart guy. Born in England, he was a Cambridge University graduate who arrived in Canada to work as an accountant at Clarkson Gordon, before it became Ernst and Young. Maclean Hunter hired Osborne as its chief financial officer in 1981, and in only five years he was promoted to chief executive at age 40. He knew the preemptive strike would drive the stock price up and make our premium small or non-existent.

Phil Lind was in Ottawa meeting with CRTC chairman Keith Spicer and vice-chairman Fern Belisle to keep them up to date about our plans. Gar got me out of the shower to tell me about Maclean Hunter's move and I immediately called Lind. We decided we had to call a news conference immediately. It was planned for 4 p.m. that day at Unitel's auditorium, which was big enough to house the

throng of expected media. Jan Innes, then Unitel VP communications, who now holds the same role at RCI, did a tremendous job
handling all the arrangements on such short notice.

We had less than six hours to prepare our public relations campaign for a unified Maclean Hunter and Rogers Communications.
On the plane back from Ottawa, Phil Lind crafted the basis of my
opening remarks and came up with the well-known phrase "We need
companies that can tell Canadian stories and paint Canadian dreams."
The theme was two-pronged: that Canada must have big multimedia companies to battle the foreign information-entertainment
conglomerates and that building the national information highway
should not be left to the telephone company monopolies.

The news naturally spurred even greater trading in media stocks
on the Toronto Stock Exchange, with Maclean Hunter climbing
$1.63 to $15.38. We deferred announcing a formal price we would
offer until after the RCI board met two days later. But as we saw
the price of Maclean Hunter stock continue to rise, we figured we
would wait about a week and see what happened. We didn't have
anything to lose: by Friday, February 4—one week after our initial
meeting with Maclean Hunter—the stock had climbed from $13.38
to $17, well beyond our premium.

At a lunchtime speech on Friday, February 11, to a group of
investment analysts and institutional money managers, I revealed
the terms of the offer: $17 cash, or 40 percent above the median
stock market price of Maclean Hunter over the preceding five
years. We even offered Maclean Hunter shareholders a "participating right" to a little more money if Rogers could sell the U.S.
cable assets for more than $1.5 billion. It was an outrageously high
price, I told reporters afterwards. Nothing could persuade me to
go any higher than that, "not even my wife," I joked. We made the
so-called phantom offer after we received a positive ruling from
the Ontario Securities Commission that meant Rogers did not
have to buy the 36 million shares of Maclean Hunter Holdings

Limited (the control shares owned by the operating company) as part of the overall offer to takeover the company.

We had now been in the full glare of the media spotlight for 10 days, and the intense heat would continue for almost another month as both sides jockeyed for position. I was even featured in the *Wall Street Journal* with my old friend Ted Turner of Cable News Network fame under a headline that read, "Two Dreamers, One Dream: To Be Media Kings."

There were many battles to fight and both sides were pulling out all the stops. Because of foreign ownership restrictions, Maclean Hunter had to look for a higher bidder in Canada. Bell Canada wasn't possible because it was barred from owning broadcasting licences at the time. Paul Desmarais' Power Corporation of Canada was rumoured in the press to be talking with Osborne but a counter-bid never surfaced.

I got wind that JR Shaw of Shaw Communications, the third-largest cable company, was in discussions with Maclean Hunter as well. This was troubling, if true. At one point, JR's son, Jim Shaw, who would soon take over the mantle as Shaw's chief executive, told the media they'd be interested in Maclean Hunter or at least the cable and broadcast parts of the company.

With expiry of our offer pegged for March 15, 1994, Osborne stepped up defensive tactics and threatened to break up the company and sell off pieces to increase shareholder value. He opened up data rooms for prospective bidders to go over Maclean Hunter's books, but prevented Rogers people from entering unless we abandoned our takeover. Maclean Hunter directors issued an information circular on February 23 calling our offer "inadequate," but the board still did not call for the poison pill, which was great news.

As events unfolded, Gar chaired all the meetings on our side. If I were to compare the negotiations to the circus, he was the ringleader. It was his to run. He was captain and the rest of us just did what we were supposed to do. One thing that Gar turned up was that Maclean Hunter did not have directors and officers liability insurance. This can be a tell-tale sign of corporate arrogance—a board may figure it won't be sued by shareholders or anyone else. But not all directors have the same resources to defend a suit if one is launched. In Maclean Hunter's case, we saw this as an opening; seven of the ten directors were independent and we focused on them.

Gar came up with a strategy of serving the directors with legal writs personally. We wanted the directors to really think about what they were voting to do or not do. Our success depended on not triggering the poison pill and unlocking some 45 million extra shares into the equation. Gar believed it more effective to have the writs delivered by people who were as ferocious looking as possible. It was February and some of the board members were in Florida so at 8 o'clock in the morning, we had six-foot-six-inch giants serve writs on them. One of the directors felt it wasn't worth the gamble because he didn't have the wealth or the insurance, so he resigned from the board. The writ-serving was a brilliant tactic of Gar's.

On the topic of Gar, I would like to address an issue that was raised in the 2007 book *High Wire Act: Ted Rogers and the Empire That Debt Built* by Caroline Van Hasselt, a story that was later picked up in some media. I have been accused of forcing Gar Emerson to step down as chairman of RCI over a single episode in 2006. The book, and subsequent media reports, accuse me of forcing Gar to resign because he had somehow discovered some corporate governance infraction that I wanted swept under the carpet. The accusation is untrue. I am not going to rehash an episode that was not much fun for either of us, except to say that people can have different perceptions and recollections when they recount how certain events unfolded. Gar was a terrific asset to the company over the years. He was invaluable on so many files, especially when it came to the Maclean Hunter takeover, and to say his departure was due to one single incident involving the audit committee of the RCI board is simplistic at best.

But back to Maclean Hunter in 1994. Our side won big when Liberal finance minister Paul Martin's first budget in mid-February eliminated the use of the so-called "purchase butterfly" as a way for corporations to avoid capital gains taxes. If Maclean Hunter sold its cable assets it would attract capital gains taxes in the hundreds of millions of dollars. Around this time, there was also a tempest in the teapot when a *Globe and Mail* reporter called me and I told him we would walk away if we could simply buy the Maclean Hunter Canadian cable assets. This was in response to a question about Osborne threatening to break up the company and sell off the pieces. I probably was too candid, but I was responding to questions about Osborne's sabre-rattling about his various defensive measures. I was not saying that all I wanted was the Canadian cable systems of Maclean Hunter. Of course, Osborne went to town in the media, accusing me of all sorts of nasty things and of being untruthful about our intention to create a powerful multimedia company when really it all boiled down to the Canadian cable systems, which wasn't true.

That fact is that our offer was for the entire company, not simply the Canadian cable. We wanted to grow the Canadian operations, especially on the content side. Regrettably, we had to later sell the *Sun* newspaper chain, but we've proven our commitment when it comes to the magazine business. Since 1994, we have invested heavily in the magazines division and brought the titles back to the lustre they had in earlier days when Maclean Hunter was run by entrepreneurs like John Bayne Maclean and Horace and Don Hunter. Just look at our flagship magazine, *Maclean's*. It is relevant again and, I might add, a must-read for news junkies. Across the publishing division, revenues have increased 50 percent since the takeover, we have invested tens of millions of dollars in acquisitions and new magazine launches and we employ more than 1,000 writers, editors and designers who publish 80,000 magazine pages per year. As owner, I have taken a great personal sense of responsibility when it comes to the magazines and I have shaken hands with almost every member of the staff. Magazine publishing is a tough business economically, but we've poured capital into it.

On March 3, 1994, after a wireless conference in San Diego, I offered TD Bank's vice-chairman Bill Brock a ride home in my Challenger jet. (Lieutenants Lind, Watson, Savage, Tory Jr. and others dubbed the aircraft "Quiz Air" because I always grilled whoever sat next to me during flights.) Brock offered me some good advice: after a month of public wrangling and legal manoeuvres, isn't it about time you had a private chat with Maclean Hunter chairman Don Campbell? As soon as we landed, I invited Don to my house the next evening, March 4. By then, I was hopeful of having some big news that could end this public corporate chess game once and for all.

On March 3, I was to have dinner with JR Shaw at the Toronto Club on Wellington Street in downtown Toronto in a private dining room; no lawyers, no financial advisors, nobody but us. I've always liked JR. He was raised in the same town in southwestern Ontario where my mother came from, Woodstock. Like me, he was a cable entrepreneur. He built Shaw Communications from scratch after moving to Alberta in the 1960s. We were roughly the same age and started our cable companies at the same time. His operations were centred in western Canada but Shaw had assets in Ontario, too. I foresaw a cable map with Shaw dominating the west, Rogers in Ontario and Vidéotron in Quebec. Though we were both large players in Canadian cable and we often worked together to strengthen the industry, there was no doubt in my mind that JR put his company first, just as I did with mine. There would be no breaks expected and none given. But I wanted to get him to step aside from Maclean Hunter.

We arrived in an oak-panelled dining room with a big table covered with a white linen tablecloth. It was strange with him at one end and me at the other end. I didn't feel comfortable negotiating when we were so far apart physically, but we got the job done. I proposed an asset swap so he could consolidate in the west, and Rogers would consolidate in Ontario. This would then mean he would avoid riding in with a bid for Maclean Hunter. In a nutshell, subject to Rogers' successful takeover of Maclean Hunter, we traded our cable systems in Victoria, Calgary and Thunder Bay for Shaw's systems in parts of Toronto, Woodstock, St. Thomas, Strathroy and Tillsonburg. Shaw gained 145,000 subscribers and paid us cash for the value of the difference. In addition, Shaw bought Maclean Hunter's Toronto FM station CFNY.

Once the Shaw issues were resolved, I thought Campbell and Osborne would have no alternative but to accept our $17 offer. On Friday evening, Campbell arrived at my house around eight o'clock and we talked. He was noncommittal but left saying the Maclean Hunter board would be meeting the next day to discuss the offer. The board instructed Osborne to meet with me on Sunday. He arrived at Frybrook and we talked and talked for two hours. He was insistent that I had to raise my offer beyond the $17. I was just as insistent that I could not and would not renegotiate with the banks. We broke off and said we'd sleep on it and have lunch the next day.

We had the lunch but still neither side would bend. After a month of fighting, Osborne needed a "sweetener," I knew that. But I wasn't about to go back to the banks—especially since $17 was already a 40 percent premium. I was exhausted and after lunch I walked down Front Street and checked into the Crowne Marriott Hotel, where I had a much-needed afternoon nap.

Osborne awoke me with an idea: Bob Furse, his chief financial officer, was suggesting that Maclean Hunter declare a special 75-cent dividend to shareholders and then the board would recommend the Rogers offer. This would give Osborne and the Maclean Hunter board the sweetener they needed, and the special dividend would be rolled into the overall debt that Rogers would be responsible for after the takeover was completed. I told Ron I could do that, but at 50 cents, not 75 cents, and there would be no participating right on the sale of the U.S. cable. (It would turn out the U.S. cable would sell for less than the $1.5 billion anyway because, by coincidence, the Federal Communications Commission had ordered a rollback on cable rates in the U.S., reducing value on cable stocks.) Ron said he would check with the board and get back to me.

That Monday evening, March 7, I was hosting the traditional board of directors dinner held on the eve of the Rogers annual general meeting. I took Ron Osborne's call in a phone booth in the foyer of the Toronto Club. The offer—with the new 50-cent special dividend—would be recommended by the Maclean Hunter board.

The next day, about 300 people attended the Rogers Communications AGM at the Art Gallery of Ontario. With all those reporters and cameras, we just had to do something special. At high noon, the hauntingly familiar music from Andrew Lloyd Webber's *Phantom of the Opera* filled the room and the Phantom's voice boomed out: "My dear Maclean Hunter, resist no longer. Allow your shareholders to accept the offer."

While this was going on, Gar and I signed the official papers for the $3.1 billion deal, which the lawyers worked through the night on. The signing occurred at the podium and no one noticed. I then spoke for about 20 minutes before announcing that Maclean Hunter's board had approved the final settlement just moments before the meeting. The room broke into applause, a standing ovation. It was one of the happiest moments of my life. Loretta and I kissed and hugged.

We still needed approval from both the CRTC in Canada, and the FCC and numerous town councils with regard to the U.S. cable assets in Michigan, New Jersey and Florida. The FCC provided two challenges which, looking back, don't seem big, but one could have killed the overall deal and the other could have mucked up the cable assets sale to Comcast Corp. for US$1.27 billion.

In the first case, when the takeover changed from "hostile" to "friendly" with the Maclean Hunter board's approval, the FCC's timetable changed and the deal no longer became a priority in Washington. Without our receiving a timely ruling, everything would have collapsed. Thankfully, we received dispensation at the eleventh hour—with only minutes left before things would unravel—and the deal went through. There was also a hurdle in closing the deal with Comcast because some microwave licence did not get properly filed and transferred. Again, at the last second, we got the FCC to amend things and grant approval. The lesson here was that had we lacked experience in the U.S. cable industry and regulatory environment, and had Phil Lind's team not had the contacts in Washington, things could have turned out very differently.

Ultimately, the CRTC, after a lengthy hearing, granted its approval of the takeover on December 19, 1994.

Had we not won this battle, I still think that we would have won out sooner or later. That may sound a little arrogant, but acquiring Maclean Hunter was the right move and I really wanted it. (I am determined—the only acquisition that I really wanted and did not get was CFRB radio station.) Though the merger made so much sense, some of the asset sales that were forced upon us to shed debt were regrettable. In 1998 we sold a Maclean Hunter–owned printing company called Davis & Henderson Ltd., which printed invoices and cheques, for $53.5 million. We were all convinced a printer like that was going the way of the dodo. Shortly afterwards, the company went up in value about six times to somewhere in the neighbourhood of $300 million. I always say you can't live with regrets, but that one I wish I could do over again.

The last time I saw Don Campbell was shortly after the merger was completed. At the time, John Graham told me there was a painting hanging in Don's old Maclean Hunter office that he loved and John thoughtfully suggested that we wrap it up and present it to him. John set up a lunch at the Toronto Club and Don was very appreciative of the gift.

Everyone at Rogers wanted to celebrate the victory, but there wasn't time. There was just too much going on. Besides, Bay Street and the media weren't about to give us much time to work out all the benefits of the merger before pouncing.

Chapter 18

BAY STREET PUNCHING BAG (AGAIN)

I t didn't take long to go from hero to goat after the Maclean
Hunter acquisition. The fickle folks on Bay Street went from
calling me the "Cable King" to constantly using adjectives like
debt-laden, debt-soaked or *debt-ridden* in front of my name or the
company's name. "Debt-soaked Rogers"—that was about the worst.
They loved using that one.

This helped to drive our stock to record lows. The media picked
at and analyzed every piece of Rogers news six ways from Sunday.

The financial community and leaders in the business community
conveyed their continuing belief that Rogers Communications was
over-leveraged and that Ted had just spent far too much money on
fulfilling his dreams, making the company a very risky investment.
This was a load of crap. We had been building over many, many
years to get to where we were. In all fairness, back in the late 1990s
I didn't know how enormously successful the company would be
today, but I sure as hell knew that we would succeed and that these
people would be proven wrong.

It really started to tick me off, but what could I do? As always
during tough times, I simply worked harder. And these were tough
times, but not the toughest. I didn't lose any sleep during this
period, as I did when we almost went bankrupt in the early '70s
and again in the early '80s. I am not being flippant here, but I really
believed things were not as bad as everyone kept saying. I know

some people thought I was whistling as I walked past the grave-yard, but I really wasn't. It seemed that during this period no one would believe me when I said, "The best is yet to come." But I had travelled this road before, and although there were a lot of bumps it was no dead end.

Sure, Cantel was drumming up huge loses while we spent billions of dollars on the country's only national cellular network. We'd made a misstep with cable customers on introducing new specialty channels; the Bell monopolies with their war chests were at the gates; several key Rogers executives turned to other opportunities and left the team; personal tragedies struck; and our stock dropped so low that RCI was taken off the key indices on the Toronto Stock Exchange, triggering money managers' automatic sell orders.

Yes, it was cause for concern, but I've always just kept driving and having faith that the good Lord would somehow pull us through and help us turn things around. I've always had that optimism and passion. Passion is key. If you don't have passion for what you're doing then you're going to be unhappy, and I don't think you'll be anywhere near as successful. Passion, when mixed with action, overcomes not everything, but almost everything. (I saw cancer strike at my mother three times and each time I still thought she could pull it off. She fought so hard, but didn't beat it. But if you have the faith that you can do something, it's more often you can do it. That's the passion.)

We got off to a rocky start in 1995 due to the marketing snafu (negative-option billing) related to the new specialty channels, but we changed course quickly. "We now know we made a mistake and we apologize to our customers," cable president Colin Watson told reporters at Vancouver news conference carried live on television on January 5.

Despite all the challenges, 1995 held its share of positives, too: we closed the deal to sell the U.S. cable assets of Maclean Hunter to Comcast Corp. and paid off our $2 billion bridge loan. Once again, a last-minute regulatory hitch developed that almost sunk the deal. Fortunately, our U.S. cable experience and the contacts Phil Lind and his team had cultivated helped tremendously. My son, Edward, who was working at Comcast at the time getting some cable training, was also helpful.

Edward had wanted a job away from Rogers, to get his feet wet. So I phoned Ralph Roberts, chairman of Comcast and a long-time friend from years together in the cable business, and I asked him and his son, Brian, who was by then president, to give Edward every lousy job they could. I wanted him to really see the cable business from the inside out. After Edward was there about six weeks, he phoned home and told Loretta, "I just cannot understand it, just cannot understand it—I haven't had a Saturday night off yet. Nobody else has had to work every Saturday night." After hanging up, Loretta came to me and asked what was going on, and I told her. Mothers are protective of their children, but I explained that the job was good for him. He worked hard and he learned a lot. In 1996, Edward came back to Canada and started his career as a vice-president in Cantel's paging area. Today, he continues to work hard as president of Rogers Cable and I am proud of his accomplishments; I am proud of all my children.

Also in 1995, we launched North America's first high-speed Internet service to the home when we unveiled The Wave in Newmarket, Ontario, where my ancestors had settled some 200 years earlier. Colin Watson and his team at cable were really pushing high-speed Internet access. You have to remember that these were early days: terms like *email* and *World Wide Web* were not part of the everyday lexicon.

A year earlier in a speech at the industry's CableLabs conference in Phoenix Colin had predicted that the personal computer would outstrip the television as the vehicle to take users onto the not-yet-hackneyed "information superhighway." He was the first person in the North American cable industry to make such a bold prediction. At the time, fewer than one quarter of homes had a PC and I wasn't yet sold. But as I have said, I am not always the first on board (witness FM radio, cable TV and wireless), but when I do recognize a trend, I am committed and go full-bore. In many ways, Colin's prediction was similar to mine in 1960 when only 5 percent of radios could receive the superior quality of FM, yet we bought CHFI and helped build the FM radio industry.

The other good news from 1995 was the continued growth of wireless. Cantel reached the milestone of 1 million customers, doubling its subscriber base in only 30 months. This was an industry on the cusp of explosion. So we had two lines of business—high-speed Internet and wireless—that we knew would one day turn Rogers Communications into an investment-grade company. But to reach that harvest period, we'd need to sow seeds that would cost billions of dollars, investing in our networks.

Our debt began to really mount, topping $5 billion and creeping to five or six times our cash flow. In plain terms, it was like having a $500,000 mortgage on your home with $100,000 of annual disposable income. You could be of the mindset that you'll work hard and get more disposable income or you could fret about being leveraged too highly because you have little room to move should an emergency occur. Over the years, our companies have borrowed more than $30 billion cumulatively, so this situation wasn't the end of the world for me, but I was being urged to rein in spending at a time when I could see so many opportunities with high-speed Internet and wireless.

The "over-leveraged" and "debt-soaked" monikers were now all the rage. And some of the executive team began to leave. Cantel President David Gergacz went back to the U.S. in August 1995. Colin Watson departed in April 1996 to take the CEO's helm at Spar Aerospace Ltd. and he was followed by a cable vice-president named Dave Masotti, who was part of Colin's Internet team and is a very bright and innovative guy. Around this time Scott Colbran, who headed Maclean Hunter's Canadian cable systems, also left. The financial analysts and the media were treating Rogers as a "sinking ship" story, which, of course, it wasn't. We were prepared to bail water, but we were not sinking.

Did the naysayers ever have a heyday in August 1996, when Graham Savage decided to leave! He and I got into an argument about covenants on a high-yield bond issue and one thing led to another. Graham Savage showed more emotion than most other CFOs. He is a very smart and astute guy. He wanted to make a lot of money quickly and he wanted some guarantees and I just couldn't give them to him. So he left and his departure showed me once again the class of Dick Thomson at the TD Bank. By this time, Dick was chairman and CEO of the bank and getting close to retirement. Graham Savage resigned unhappily and publicly and it adversely affected the stock. I was running the cable company away from the downtown head office of RCI at the time and I got a call from Dick, a true foul-weather friend if ever there was one.

"Looks like you're in a lot of trouble," he said. "I am coming up to see you."

He came up to the cable offices (the first time he'd ever been inside a cable operator's offices despite lending the industry billions of dollars), and laid it out for me: he would arrange a press conference where I could explain things, his people would help us script it out and offer impartial third-party advice on what I should say. Dick was such a big help. In life, you don't forget friends like that who know what to do when you need help.

Graham Savage and I have since made amends. Some years later, he had a heart problem and I sent him flowers and a note and he reacted positively. We now see each other periodically. Graham Savage is a principled man who really knows his way around numbers. It may be worth mentioning that he was one of the people brought onto the board of Hollinger International Inc. to clean up the mess. He did a good job and the story is that Conrad Black, long before his current jail term, told Graham, "I'm going to take your house or I am going to throw you out of your home." Whether the story is true, I don't know, but it is widely told in some circles.

Graham Savage's departure from Rogers opened the door for Alan Horn to step in as chief financial officer, moving over from the family company, Rogers Telecommunications Ltd. Alan is a tremendous man who at first was underestimated by the financial analysts and the media. If I had to pick our best-ever CFO, I would be hard pressed to choose between Alan and Bob Francis. And that is no slight toward Graham Savage and our current CFO, Bill Linton, who is also terrific.

In October 1996 we continued our debt reduction program by closing the deal and sold our 63 percent stake in the Toronto Sun Publishing Corp. with its chain of tabloid newspapers in Toronto, Edmonton, Calgary and Ottawa, a host of community newspapers in Canada and Florida, and canoe.ca (Canadian Online Explorer), a groundbreaking Internet news and information website. The buyers were a consortium led by Sun management and financed by private investors like big pension and mutual funds. I may sound like a broken record, but I try not to live with regrets. We had gotten Sun Publishing as part of the Maclean Hunter deal and Rogers raised $259 million in cash with this sale. Two years later, Quebecor Inc. came in and bought Sun Media Corp. for $983 million by topping a hostile takeover bid from Torstar Corp. That was quite a two-year return on investment for my friends like Paul Godfrey, CEO of Sun Media, and the Ontario Teachers' Pension Plan and mutual funds Trimark and Talvest.

In 1996, Rogers once again partnered with AT&T Corp., this time on the wireless side with Cantel. As I said earlier, one of the few good things to come of the Unitel disaster was our working relationship with AT&T. This new wireless venture was really a marketing deal: we changed the company name from Cantel to

Cantel AT&T. We paid a little for using the AT&T name and offered some warrants to AT&T to buy a little equity in Cantel, about 1 million shares. (Seeds were being sown for future equity participation in Cantel.)

Even though little money changed hands, it was a big deal for AT&T chairman Bob Allen to come to Toronto in November 1996 to make the announcement with me. This was the first time in history AT&T had shared its brand, and it was just two years after it spent $12.6 billion to buy McCaw Cellular Communications Inc., so everyone knew AT&T was committed to wireless. AT&T's endorsement gave us a shot in the arm and through Cantel we were willing to help—to a degree—AT&T Canada (formerly Unitel) take another crack at the big monopoly phone companies with a co-branded wireless offering.

And then our luck changed. In 1997, the cable industry was out of favour all over North America and we were caught in the down-draft with our stock price dropping throughout the year to well below $10, less than half its value two years earlier at the time of Maclean Hunter. Wireless was still gobbling up capital expenditure money for building and upgrading the network to digital. To make matters worse, U.S. media and cable kings Ted Turner and John Malone of Tele-Communications Inc. (he coined the phrase "500-channel universe") did not help matters by highlighting the tough times ahead for cable in the battle with the giant telephone companies. Ted Turner—who had sold Turner Broadcasting System Inc. to Time Warner months before—even came to Toronto in 1997 and publicly urged others in cable and broadcasting to sell while they still could get a decent price. That may have been the low point in a tough year, but there was also a significant high point and it involved Microsoft's Bill Gates and leading players in North American cable.

In April 1997, a bunch of us from CableLabs, an industry association group for swapping ideas and helping each other, were meeting with Gates and others from Microsoft in Redmond, Washington. Comcast president Brian Roberts was our designated spokesman and he started talking about the big, fat cable pipe to consumers' homes that could deliver the Internet far better than the phone companies and their twisted-pair copper wires. Remember, we were still years away from mass penetration of high-speed Internet into the home. Gates saw what was coming and how his software could drive development, so he was naturally interested in what Brian was saying.

At dinner, Roberts gestured to the other cable guys present, including TCI chairman John Malone, Time Warner Cable Chairman Joseph Collins and me from Canada, and said: "Bill, just buy 10 percent of everyone here, because that would rally cable stocks, overcome Wall Street's skittishness about the heavy capital spending required and end computer hardware manufacturers' reluctance to fully commit." In essence, such an investment would pave the information superhighway.

Bill Gates made the usual sort of "let me look into it" remark, but about a month later there was this big announcement that he'd invested $1 billion in Brian's company, Comcast. I phoned Brian and said, "Where's my share? Here you are, a spokesman for all of our businesses saying how good it would be for Bill Gates to invest in cable, and you take all the money." Brian just laughed and said that some folks from Microsoft had followed up with him a few days after his pitch to Gates about whether he was serious about selling 10 percent of Comcast, which he ensured them he was. And things just went from there.

At age 64, I had broken one of my own rules that I had been preaching for years: always follow up on initiatives. I should have followed up with Microsoft and Gates immediately, and I didn't. But I got $600 million from Gates two years later in convertible debentures—I always needed money in those days. I remember making the announcement on a conference call because I'd just had an aneurysm repaired in my abdomen and I couldn't stand up. Nobody on the call knew I was lying flat on my back and talking loudly into the speaker phone. At the time of writing this book, Microsoft was still the registered holder of 25.3 million shares of Rogers non-voting B shares, or 4 percent of total outstanding shares, although there are many ways to liquidate shares while remaining the registered owner.

Despite Microsoft's much-need endorsement of cable in 1997, it was a difficult year. Rogers Communications took a record loss of $539 million and our debt approached $6 billion. But then real sadness and more trouble occurred in the New Year.

John Webb Graham died on January 9, 1998, at age 85. It was a big loss for the family. From his teaching me how to keep meticulous financial records when I was a 12-year-old boy to his acting as a calming influence throughout my entire business life, John was indeed much more than a stepfather to me. He was a second father. After my mother died, he married Tasha, with whom the family remains close. John was a religious man and a canon in the Anglican Church.

I remember one time when he and I found ourselves in a less than elegant religious situation that we both enjoyed immensely. I am what you might call an irregular churchgoer, unlike John. I attend a very high Anglican church that is near my home and has a beautiful-sounding choir, but I'm personally more comfortable at a more modest service. I would probably be more at ease in the United Church but I've never changed denominations because I worry about being disloyal.

I was in California for an operation with John Graham one time. There was a church nearby with an 11 a.m. service and I suggested we go. We walked in and it turned out to be a Baptist church that was neither formal nor fancy. They had buglers and horn players and people walking up and down the aisles. We took communion by going up on the stage where wine was being poured and people were holding hands and praying together. At one point, someone shouted out: "Is anybody sick or going to have an operation?"

I said, "Yes, I am going to have an operation."

So they bowed their heads and said, "Let's all pray for Ted's operation," and a woman did some sort of a dance around John Graham. I just couldn't believe it. Here's John, a canon in the Anglican Church, standing there while some stranger dances around him praising the Lord, but he seemed okay with it. There was so much positive energy in that church. Years later, I tried to go back but I couldn't find the church.

Less than two weeks after John Graham's death, Rogers Communications Inc. stock hit rock bottom at $4.80 a share. A few weeks later, even after it gained a bit, RCI stock was pulled from the benchmark indices on the Toronto Stock Exchange because our market capitalization was so low we fell below required thresholds. This created even more downward pressure on the stock because many big portfolio managers were automatically forced to sell Rogers stock. (The rules allowed them to hold only stocks in the benchmark indices.) As I've said, in tough times we hold on tight, work hard and look for an opportunity. Luckily, one came along.

In May 1998, we sold Rogers Telecom, the local phone company we began building after exiting Unitel, to MetroNet Communications Corp., for $600 million in cash and 12.5 million MetroNet shares valued at $400 million. Rogers Telecom had connected more than a thousand office buildings and condominiums in cities in our territories with 3,400 kilometres of fibre optic cables to deliver high-speed voice and data. Within a year, MetroNet and AT&T Canada merged and our MetroNet shares doubled in price, producing an ultimate $1 billion net gain after losing $500 million on Unitel only four years before. I was more than an interested observer in that union.

The Rogers Telecom sale was the right move. We weren't going to beat Bell in local phone service in those days because the technology simply wasn't yet available to challenge the monopoly telco that had been around more than 100 years. Instead, we had to focus on reducing debt. The biggest battles—in wireless, high-speed Internet and home phone service—lay ahead.

During this rocky period, bad news often followed on the heels of good. Phil Lind had a stroke on July 1, Canada Day, at age 54. Fortunately, he was not alone and a friend called 911 immediately or he would have died. It is difficult to describe the impact of his illness on me, especially only six months after John Graham had died. Two very calming influences on my business life were now missing. Phil and I had worked together for almost 30 years. He was there through thick and thin, good times and bad. We were not always on the same side of every issue but often enough we were. He suffered paralysis on the right side and had trouble speaking during the early stages of recovery. He still doesn't have full use of his right arm and leg.

Almost a year after the stroke, Phil returned to work but his office was empty a lot of the time. Eventually, I sat down with him and said, "Look, Phil, I'd love you to come back to work really and not just on paper, because you make a huge contribution. But if you feel you can't do that, then you should resign and we'll treat you well financially. You deserve the best." His response was, "No, I want to work." And I am so glad he decided to stay. People love to deal with him and everyone at Rogers is inspired by his courage, given everything he has gone through.

As the millennium was coming to an end, things began to really improve at RCI. Phil returned to work. John H. Tory took over as president of Rogers Cable after a couple of other presidents didn't work out. My daughter, Melinda, who of my children is the most like me, poor girl, was now working for the family firm in the areas of strategy, acquisitions and partnerships. Edward was moving up the ranks over the three years since his return to Canada from Comcast. (Lisa and Martha would both choose other paths.)

Most important, the financial community was starting to "get it"—both the inherent bandwidth advantages cable had over phone companies and the meshing together of the Rogers assets of cable, wireless and media. RCI stock moved from less than $5 in January 1998, to almost $40 by the autumn of 1999. (These numbers are based on prices before the stock split two for one in 2006.)

In July 1999, as I said earlier, Bill Gates made his first investment into a Canadian cable company when Microsoft put $600 million into Rogers. And then in August, AT&T and British Telecom (BT) bought 33 percent of Cantel AT&T for $1.4 billion. This was a significant investment for many reasons, not least of which was the endorsement from these two telecom giants as they made bets in markets beyond their home countries. We were thrilled to be their Canadian partner. We used the cash to reduce debt and beef up the network. BT was also a positive influence in our deciding to move to the GSM (Global System Mobile) wireless platform. There's no sense in getting bogged down in technical details, but suffice it to say the entire world—except North America—had embraced GSM as the wireless platform.

Moving to GSM while our competitors stayed with the CDMA (Code Division Multiple Access) platform gave us a remarkable competitive advantage, because all of the hot new phones and wireless data devices were being made first for GSM. Not only that, but when visitors with GSM devices came to Canada, we automatically received roaming fees from them and when Canadians travelled to Europe, the Far East or elsewhere, only Rogers phones worked overseas. The importance of this move to GSM cannot be overstated.

Naturally, since we had two new partners, speculation arose that this was a long-term plan on my part to sell out to the American and British giants once Ottawa eased foreign ownership restrictions. Where these so-called experts get their ideas and opinions is beyond me. I had no intention of selling Rogers' core assets like wireless and cable. I spent my entire life compiling wonderful assets—and worked my ass off doing it—to bring the Rogers name back into the forefront of Canadian communications. For years and years I had told this to anyone who would listen.

The Rogers family will never sell as long as I am alive—and hopefully not until long after I am gone either. What would we do with more money? We have enough. My personal wealth—the bulk of it—is all tied to our ownership of Rogers Communications, so it's in "paper," but we have plenty of real money to live well. If someone offered us two, three, four times the market value for our stock I would decline. What would I do with all that money? Buy a new toaster? Buy another car? How many cars do you need?

Now, a worse scenario, a more difficult decision, would be if the company were failing and somebody made an offer that could turn it around, and the controlling shareholders were difficult and refused to sell. That's a very tough one. But that's also why we're working so hard now, bringing Rogers Communications to investment grade, ringing alarm bells to be ready when the rains come.

For us, 1999 was a good year and as the twenty-first century approached, things were getting better and better.

Again, I have my great friend and family physician, Dr. Bernie Gosevitz, to thank for my being able to see the new century. In December 1999, I was in Los Angeles on business and feeling unwell. I phoned Bernie back in Toronto and he ordered me to head to a medical facility immediately. He had a hunch based on the symptoms I was describing on the phone. At the clinic a nurse asked if I had any health insurance. I told her I was Canadian and in Los Angeles visiting. "But is there a cash discount?" I asked. She went away, asked a superior and came back saying she could give me 40 percent off the $1,600 worth of tests. "Done," I said, unintentionally doing my best Big John Bassett impersonation.

Thank goodness I listened to Bernie and got over there right away; they found a vein in my neck that was 90 to 95 percent blocked that could very soon cause a stroke. It was the week before Christmas and Bernie got me into the Mayo Clinic for treatment work a few days later, on December 27. From a health standpoint, the 1990s were tough, beginning with the 1992 quadruple heart bypass and including various procedures to repair aneurysms, remove facial skin cancers and deal with my degenerating eyesight due to glaucoma, and ending with removing the blockage in the vein in my neck.

But what are you going to do? Mope around the house? Not a chance, especially with a blockbuster event about to happen that would be the catalyst for the greatest business success of my life. Within a few short years, the once "debt-soaked" Rogers Communications Inc. would be an investment-grade company paying dividends, generating free cash flow and operating profits. Once and for all, I was about to prove the naysayers wrong.

Chapter 19

MAKING THE (INVESTMENT) GRADE

A couple weeks after the repair work at the Mayo Clinic, I was back in California at the annual Salomon Smith Barney media and telecom conference in Palm Springs. On the morning of January 11, 2000, it was announced that "new economy" America Online Inc. was buying (or merging with) "old economy" media titan Time Warner Inc. in a stunning US$165 billion deal.

This announcement occurred just before the dot-com bubble burst and it ignited so many changes in not only the communications sector but in all industries globally. As is so often the case, the herd stampeded in one direction. It seemed everybody in business was looking for high-tech, "new economy" solutions to reach customers. And Rogers Communications, with its high-speed broadband to the home, was best positioned in our markets to link buyers and sellers in the new economy. We would just have to grow quickly to battle the colossus Bell Canada with its $50 billion in assets, $16 billion in annual revenue and 21 million customer connections through wireline and wireless phones, (slower) Internet service and satellite TV.

Bell's home turf is Ontario and Quebec, although by 2000 it was starting to attract customers elsewhere in Canada, particularly through its satellite provider ExpressVu. To ratchet up the battle with Ma Bell, we needed to cover her home territory. We were strong in Ontario, with about two-thirds of the cabled homes, but that was far short of Bell's near 100 percent penetration into the province's homes. As for Quebec, we were nowhere, except for some media holdings such as L'actualité and other popular magazines. I came up with a two-pronged plan to mirror Bell's territory in Ontario and Quebec and beat her with superior bandwidth, immediately in Internet and cable-TV service and coming soon with home phone service. Bundling in wireless phone service would create the holy grail—or "quadruple play"—of communications services for customers.

Part of the plan succeeded, but the biggest part didn't. And, in hindsight, that was an incredible stroke of good fortune because the greatest success of my business life could not have occurred four years later had this two-pronged plan in 2000 been wholly successful. We simply would have been stretched too thin.

It is ironic: all my life I never operated with a grandiose plan but rather identified trends and technologies (FM radio, cable and wireless) and then seized opportunities as they presented themselves. This time I came up with a big plan and its failure opened the door to the ultimate opportunity that would turn Rogers Communications into an investment-grade company and ensure that the Rogers name remains at the forefront of Canadian communications for years to come—the fulfillment of my lifelong dream. I've always said successful entrepreneurs have to get lucky along the way, and we sure were when our plan got trumped in the first place, triggering other winning conditions.

Whether the AOL acquisition would ultimately work or not, the event changed the rules. Convergence was now in play; old economy or new economy, it didn't matter. This was the symbol, a "legitimizer," that the online world was truly for real, that online had entered the mainstream. People across North America and around the world would begin to do things differently, from how they communicated with friends and family to shopping, working, even entertainment activities. The online world would not eliminate the demand for shopping malls, grocery stores or movie theatres, but it would offer broader consumer choice. In short, it was changing our daily lives. The AOL–Time Warner deal didn't cause this change, but it was a stamp of approval that got people thinking. I started planning how to battle Bell in this changing world. The only option I saw at the time was to consolidate in Ontario and enter the Quebec market.

The Ontario part of the plan was easier. We traded our British Columbia cable systems to Shaw Communications for its holdings in Ontario and New Brunswick. We swapped about $4 billion worth of assets, with Rogers releasing 623,000 subscribers to Shaw and getting back 600,000 from Shaw in March 2000. We fortified Ontario and entered a new province to fight a Bell subsidiary, NBTel (now called Aliant). Since there was a difference of 23,000 subscribers, Shaw paid us cash for those to make the deal balanced.

On February 7, we had announced our Quebec plans: after two weeks of intense negotiations, Rogers was to merge with Groupe Vidéotron, the dominant cable company in the province with about 1.6 million subscribers. Vidéotron's controlling shareholder, founder and chairman André Chagnon, insisted on shares, not cash, because he and his son, Claude, who was president, wanted to remain active in the new entity. It was also tax efficient for them. We offered 0.925 Rogers shares for each Vidéotron share. The Chagnon family was firmly behind us, but minority shareholder Caisse de dépôt et placement du Québec, the giant pension fund, was against a cable company from English Canada taking over Vidéotron.

We went in with our eyes wide open about the possible ramifications of a Toronto company taking over a Quebec company, but it was such a perfect fit that I thought we could get around the politics. André Chagnon was a cable pioneer who started the company in 1963, when I was in radio but not yet cable. Like me, André was passionate about taking on Bell and he probably also carried some scars from the early days when Bell mocked us in the cable business. In 2000, Vidéotron was probably the most advanced cable company in Canada, if not the world, when it came to cable telephony. Together we created one of North America's largest contiguous cable companies and a force with half the assets of Bell Canada but big enough to really compete because of our advanced broadband networks.

To cut to the chase, the nationalist fervour of Quebeckers was greater than anticipated, resulting in a six-month battle that we lost. Quebecor Inc., headed by Pierre Karl Péladeau and backed by the Caisse, trumped our bid with a $4.9 billion all-cash offer. Quebecor overpaid, but I was still disappointed, although the $241-million breakup fee paid to us was rather soothing.

On September 18, I received rousing applause from the financial community at a Canadian Club luncheon in Toronto when I quoted American media mogul Barry Diller: "They won. We lost. Next!" Then I announced we'd bought the cable assets of Cable Atlantic Inc., the Newfoundland company controlled by Danny Williams, who would go on to become the province's premier. The Cable Atlantic acquisition cost $232 million for the 75,000 cable customers.

We were acquiring and moving forward. For example, as we were losing Vidéotron, Rogers Communications bought the Toronto Blue Jays to ensure the team would not move to the United States. But I would be lying if I said that losing Vidéotron did not sting. It did. But I would also be lying if I said it wasn't a blessing in disguise. We just didn't know it at the time.

In June 2000, Nadir Mohamed, senior vice-president of marketing and sales at Telus Communications, flew to Toronto to meet Charlie Hoffman, our wireless president at the time, and me. Charlie, whose family remained in the United States after he joined Rogers Wireless as president, was tired of the commuting back and forth to New Jersey and wanted to move home. One

Sunday morning, he brought Nadir to my home and, of course, our golden retrievers (we always seem to have a pair) made a big fuss greeting and jumping up at him. They are harmless but are not the best behaved dogs. Melinda's theory on our dogs is that because there are always so many people coming and going through the Rogers house, the dogs hear so many different commands that they pay attention to no one. Anyway, I found out later that Nadir is scared of dogs so I didn't make the best first impression.

But I liked Nadir right away. He was born in Tanzania and his family originally came from India. He had entrepreneurial role models in his life, including grandparents who ran a lumber business in Tanzania. He also spent years at boarding school, as I did. He and his family came to Canada about 30 years before I met him.

Entrepreneurs, as I have said, tend to be emotional and relationship-oriented people. We make decisions quickly and take to people (or not) quickly, too. I liked Nadir right from the start and wanted him to take over from Charlie. I am so glad he accepted and joined Rogers Wireless in August 2000 as president and chief operating officer. He was promoted to CEO of wireless in July 2001. Over the years, Nadir has played a big role in the success of this company, in particular his planning and plotting the Fido acquisition. Under his leadership, Rogers Wireless flourished with 13 consecutive quarters of double-digit network revenue growth, 14 consecutive quarters of double-digit operating profit growth, and improved free cash flow from negative $800 million in 2001 to over $270 million positive in 2004.

In May 2005, Nadir was named president and chief operating officer of the Communications Group, which encompasses the cable and wireless groups of Rogers, the lion's share of the company. He also sits as a director of Rogers Communications. We had a nice ceremony that day in May 2005 at the board. We invited

Nadir's wife, Shabin, to attend the board meeting. Both Nadir and Shabin are wonderful people and that's important at a family company like Rogers.

Robin Korthals, formerly of the TD Bank who also served on the Rogers board for 10 years, tells me Nadir and I are a terrific combination because Nadir is so strong on operations and marshalling incremental change, which complements my sweeping reforms from my entrepreneurial perspective and makes the entire organization stronger. I don't know why exactly, but certainly our partnership is working well.

Not long ago, I was at a wedding reception and the bartender, a young fellow, said to me: "Well, we won today."

I looked at him and said, "Won what?"

"The Blue Jays won, Mr. Rogers."

"Oh," I said. "Tremendous."

I didn't know him at all, but I guess he recognized me, and made the connection with the Blue Jays. Rogers Communications bought the Toronto Blue Jays on September 1, 2000, for US$112 million, or about $175 million Canadian in those days.

I have to be careful how I say this, but I am not really a sports fan. In school, I was active in cross-country running, boxing and soccer, but I didn't go to many professional games. My dad died when I was young and John Graham was away in Europe during the war when I was a youngster, so I didn't get the usual opportunities of going to a lot of Leaf games and things like that. My mom took me occasionally, but not often. There was no TV in those days broadcasting sports teams.

I think most sports fans will tell you their allegiances are imprinted on them from an early age. I didn't have that opportunity. But I think I can describe myself as somebody who is getting more and more interested in sports, both from a business stand-

Loretta and me with JR Shaw and his son Jim, chief executive officer of Shaw Communications Inc. JR, now Shaw's chairman, and I started in the cable business around the same time in the 1960s, he in Alberta and me in Ontario, and like the Rogers empire, Shaw has grown into a top-tier cable company.

Loretta and me with my old friend, former prime minister Brian Mulroney. We met in 1956 when we worked together in a youth group to help get John Diefenbaker elected. I often tease Brian about what a great gofer he was at the 1956 Progressive Conservative convention when the Chief finally won the leadership after two failed attempts.

John A. Tory and his wife, Liz, have been lifelong friends. John has served on the Rogers board since 1964, when it was a small, fledgling company.

John H. Tory (centre) is the son of John A. and Liz Tory, and he has worked for both former Ontario premier William G. Davis (left), as his principal secretary, and for me, as president of Rogers cable, among other executive positions. John H. is now the leader of the Progressive Conservative Party of Ontario.

Phil Lind, so instrumental in building Rogers Cable in the U.S. in the 1980s, was with me in October 2002 in Denver, when I was inducted into the Cable Hall of Fame. I am the sole Canadian to be so honoured to date.

My son, Edward Samuel Rogers III, is the president of Rogers Cable.

J.P. Moczulski/National Post

Even rivals can share a laugh. Michael Sabia, former CEO of BCE Inc., was with me at an industry conference in Toronto in June 2007.

I am always ringing alarm bells with my executives, but in this photo I am ringing the opening bell on March 2, 2006, at the New York Stock Exchange to mark 10 years of Rogers stock being available on that exchange. Pictured here are (left to right) Rogers executives Bill Linton and Phil Lind, CEO of the NYSE John Thain, me, and Rogers executives Alan Horn and Bruce Mann.

Alan Horn (left), formerly RCI chief financial officer, moved up in 2006 to become chairman. Nadir Mohamed, pictured beside me, is president and chief operating officer of the Rogers Communications Group, which encompasses both wireless and cable, the lion's share of the corporation.

Bill Linton (left) stepped into the CFO's office after Alan Horn became chairman. Tony Viner (right) is president of the Rogers media division, which encompasses 52 radio stations, about a dozen television properties, the largest collection of magazines in Canada and the Toronto Blue Jays, as well as the building they play in, now called the Rogers Centre.

Me with my sister, Ann Graham.

Peter Bregg

A proud father surrounded by my three daughters (from left to right), Lisa, Melinda and Martha, at my seventy-fifth birthday party. Held at the Rogers Centre on May 27, 2008, it was quite an event, with 7,000 Rogers employees attending.

On a Jet Ski in the Bahamas a few years ago.

Toby Hull has been a great friend for some 65 years, since our days at Upper Canada College. He was my best man and continues to serve on the Rogers board of directors.

In February 2008, Ralph Wilson (centre), owner of the NFL's Buffalo Bills, joined me and Larry Tanenbaum (right), chairman of Maple Leaf Sports and Entertainment and a neighbour of mine, in announcing a series of eight NFL games to be played at the Rogers Centre in Toronto.

In May 2007, Loretta and I made a significant donation to Ryerson University in Toronto. With us at the announcement are (from left to right) G. Raymond Chan, Ryerson's chancellor; Ron Besse, a Rogers board member and former Ryerson governor; and Dr. Ken Jones, dean of the newly named Ted Rogers School of Management at Ryerson.

At my formal birthday party on May 24, 2008; 300 family and friends attended. Harry Connick Jr., standing beside Loretta, performed that evening, as did Paul Anka and Harry Belafonte (not shown). Also in the picture are (from left to right) Edward's wife, Suzanne; Edward; Lisa; Melinda's husband, Eric Hixon; Melinda and Martha.

Thanking the thousands of Rogers employees who came to the Rogers Centre to wish me a happy seventy-fifth birthday on May 27, 2008. That's not a hospital bracelet I'm wearing but a wristband that all Rogers employees, even the president and controlling shareholder, had to wear to get into the event.

point, in that I mean a branding standpoint, and just as a fan. I go to every one of the Blue Jays home openers and some other games, where I get to meet and shake the hands of a lot of wonderful fans. And my sister, Ann Graham, is a diehard Blue Jays fan.

Certainly, our experience with the Blue Jays has been positive. Yes, we've lost money. I am not going to give a specific number but it would be around $300 million plus the initial investment. Don't get me wrong: $300 million is a lot of money. But I take a broader view. We would have paid the same money just for the equivalent branding opportunity. Every year, Rogers Communications spends over $100 million in marketing its brand and products and the Blue Jays are right in the middle of our most important customer base in southern Ontario, so the team is a huge branding opportunity for us. Besides, *Forbes* magazine in 2008 put a value of $344 million on the Blue Jays and that is about double what we paid in September 2000. So if we sold the team tomorrow—which we have no intention of doing—we'd make back our losses and really be ahead of the game when branding is factored into the equation.

We also bought the SkyDome for $25 million and renamed it the Rogers Centre and invested another $25 million or so in renovations. There is no question: the team and the building have really helped Rogers' presence in and around Toronto. The Rogers Centre is mentioned all the time in newspaper reports and radio and television clips, and not just for sports but also for other events held there. It was Phil Lind who pushed us into this purchase and I have no regrets. I would never tease him about the Blue Jays being another of "Phil's Follies" or "Lind's Lemons." I am glad the late, great Albert Gnat, who served on the Rogers board for 25 years and was a fabulous lawyer at Lang Michener, also pushed for us to buy the team. Albert really believed that getting the Jays would be good for both the city and the company. He was right. Sadly, Albert died in April 2004 after a six-month battle with cancer.

In terms of the Blue Jays, I don't know what I'd do differently. We want another World Series Championship but it's difficult when you're in the same division with the New York Yankees and the Boston Red Sox and they spend more than $200 million a year on players and we spend up to $100 million and are in the middle of the pack when it comes to players' salaries in baseball.

I think it has gone as well as it could so far and I am happy with the results. We've lost money but we've gained great recognition for our company and our products. I'm not saying every Blue Jays fan would select a Rogers phone over a Bell phone, but I think they'd give it a little more thought than they would have before we owned the team. Rogers is a good corporate citizen. A lot of people don't care about sports and that is fine. But I think having a Major League Baseball team in Toronto is good for the city and the country, for civic pride and in business terms for restaurants and hotels.

Owning the Rogers Centre has also created the opportunity to bring the National Football League and the Buffalo Bills to Toronto for eight games over five years, beginning in 2008. We're in a partnership on this with Larry Tanenbaum, who lives directly across the street from me on Frybrook and who is chairman of Maple Leaf Sports and Entertainment, owner of the Leafs hockey team and Raptors basketball team. We'll start with eight games and then who knows? Canadians love the NFL and having live action in Toronto will be great and a boost to the Toronto Argonauts and the Canadian Football League. Argo season-ticket holders will get first access to great seats, and increasing the excitement about football in the market can only help the Argos.

We have a history of helping domestic businesses while bringing in foreign product. Remember, when cable was new the Canadian broadcasters thought we were going to kill their business by bringing in U.S. programs to areas that couldn't pick up U.S. signals clearly with antennas. But history has shown we have helped

Canadian broadcasters with things like simultaneous substitution of commercials. At Rogers, we even went to court in the 1970s to keep Canadian advertising dollars here instead of them flowing to American TV stations. It's not a perfect analogy with the CFL, but I think the football league will benefit just as the Canadian broadcasters have.

I should address the media brouhaha that erupted after a press conference in February 2008 to announce the deal with the Buffalo Bills. Of course, the *Toronto Star* led the charge and took great delight in mocking me for supposedly making fun of taxpayers who funded the bulk of the $600 million SkyDome construction costs while Rogers bought the building for $25 million. It was never my intention to make it sound as if we got a deal from taxpayers. In fact, we bought the SkyDome in 2004 from an American consortium that bought it for $80 million from someone else who bought it from the Ontario government for $151 million. Believe me, I would never insult taxpayers.

––––––––––

I'd like to briefly mention Michael Armstrong, chairman and CEO of AT&T Corp. from 1997 to 2002. He is a big man with a firm handshake who looks every bit the chief executive. He and I shared the same dream to build full-service powerhouse communications companies. In 1998, he spent about $100 billion acquiring cable companies, including $48 billion for John Malone's Tele-Communications Inc. (TCI), the biggest cable company in the U.S., in a bold move to reestablish AT&T as an end-to-end carrier.

Unfortunately for him, the dot-com bust, high debt, endless regulatory squabbles and a falling AT&T stock price killed his dream and he broke up this new AT&T into four units at the end of 2000: broadband/cable, wireless, business and residential. A year later, Ralph and Brian Roberts at Comcast shrewdly picked up the cable assets for $50.5 billion, or about half what they cost AT&T.

It was also Michael who got Rogers into @home, a third-party Internet company whose servers would handle the Internet traffic of our customers and other cable companies. At Home was owned by a consortium of cable companies, with AT&T broadband in the lead. It was a horrible failure that infuriated Rogers customers with technical problems and it cost me a few million dollars personally as the stock plummeted into the abyss.

Still, I liked Mike. You could talk to him. He was approachable. His predecessor, Bob Allen, could have thought of himself as the Pope; at least that was the way his staff seemed to treat him. But Mike wasn't like that. I remember going to a dinner in New York honouring him and a few other business leaders during his waning days at the helm of AT&T. I couldn't believe it: there was only one couple from AT&T in attendance at the dinner honouring the company's chairman and CEO. He was a marked man, I guess. After the dinner I told him that I would remain loyal to him and I could see a tear come to his eye.

If I had to pick one event that has created our prosperity and caused Bell's woes it would have to be Microcell, better known by its marketing name of Fido. Bell failed to buy Microcell Solutions Inc. when it had the opportunity and our ability to work around many roadblocks (including those put up by our minority partner AT&T trying to prevent us from buying it) robbed Bell of an opportunity to better balance its portfolio. At the same time we just happened to buy when the growth curve went up for wireless like the blade of a hockey stick. Am I so smart that I could see this would happen so soon after our purchase? Of course not. The timing was serendipitous, but we also knew we wanted more wireless because we could see the growth coming, particularly in data networks, with devices like the BlackBerry.

For two years, starting in 2002, we kept our eyes on Microcell.

We knew it was struggling to make money but we could see it seemed to have innovative ideas all the time and it was using the same technology platform, GSM, as Rogers, while Bell and Telus continued on CDMA. Nadir Mohamed and Bob Berner, his chief technology officer, kept close tabs on Microcell during this period. They developed strategies and tactics over a two-year game of chess. Even near the end, we could have been checkmated by Bell, or to a lesser extent by Telus, but we were lucky.

In the beginning, some in Rogers management (and much of the RCI board) were against our going after Microcell. We'd all lost our bonuses because wireless was draining the coffers with network building and falling prices. People were leery of buying more wireless. They thought it was just too big of a bet, especially since we still weren't over the effects of the late 1990s debt load. Some directors thought we would be better off concentrating on the cable side. But then, as we got into it deeper and deeper, meeting after meeting, more people started believing in the idea. Nadir would turn up numbers that showed the long-term benefits and gains.

Board member John A. Tory, often a voice of restraint when it comes to my spending, was a great supporter. We knew what we were planning would cost in the billions of dollars, but John A. saw the advantage wireless had over cable at this stage: cable keeps eating up capital whereas wireless, once you get all the radio towers built and network in place, generates free cash flow, huge amounts of it. And the wireless marketplace had much more growth potential, not just in sheer numbers of people but in revenue-generating services, from downloading songs to wireless email.

We had a huge impediment in the way of our plan: AT&T, which owned 33 percent of wireless after buying British Telecom's share in 2001, sat on the Rogers Wireless board with veto power over any acquisition above $500 million. This board was separate and distinct from the RCI board. I tried hard to convince them of the merits of the Microcell plan, but I could not. They held that hammer over us. They would say things like, "Look, you're going to lose half the Microcell customers because that's what always happens. It happened to us when we picked up MCI; we lost half the customers. That's just the way it goes. Your numbers are all wrong." I didn't want to say the obvious like, "Who the hell do you think you're talking to—a bunch of rubes in Canada? We all work our asses off and we've been at this for quite a while." Maybe I did say something similar to that a few times. Anyway, AT&T would not relinquish the veto. Mike Armstrong was gone by this time. I could deal with him. But these guys were different. We had to buy them out before we could even move on Microcell. Of course, AT&T played hardball with us and wouldn't sell. It wanted every last cent and kept asking for numbers way above market value.

Then, along came Telus Corp. to launch a hostile $1.1 billion bid for Microcell on May 13, 2004. Now we faced a dilemma: pay the extortionate prices AT&T demanded or play cat-and-mouse for as long as we could before getting into the fray as a potential "white knight" buyer for Microcell, but risk losing before we even got into the ring. Again, we lucked out in several ways. First, Telus didn't move quickly and left its bid out there too long by extending it three times. I like to work fast and push things along, but in this case, we were relieved by the slow pace because we needed as much time as possible.

We also caught a break with Bell, which could have walked in and snapped up Microcell, but chose not to. Bell's CEO at the time, Michael Sabia, a very bright and good man, told me later that his people were against it. He didn't have the information I had at hand after keeping Microcell in our crosshairs. I don't want to sound too negative, but the larger a company gets, the longer it can take to get things done and the CEO may have to rely too heavily on underlings who are reluctant to follow his lead. This may have been the case with Bell. Whatever the reason, it must haunt Bell that it didn't swoop in, buy Fido and operate on both technology platforms, its CDMA and Microcell's GSM. That way Bell could have picked up some of the GSM roaming fees that have been so lucrative to Rogers and at the same time begun moving its own customers to GSM, because that technology has become the world platform, much like the home video recorder market in the 1980s went to VHS over Sony's Beta technology. We picked the winner (GSM) and Bell and Telus did not.

In terms of Microcell, thankfully Telus gave us the time and Bell didn't pounce. We had already been lucky when we lost on Vidéotron four years before because the RCI board had enough misgivings about Microcell and would never have let us proceed with Fido had we been successful with Vidéotron. We were also fortunate that my old friend Craig McCaw had just spent $50 million investing in Microcell because of its stake in Inukshuk Wireless Inc., a fledgling venture to provide fixed wireless broadband Internet services to rural areas. McCaw entered Microcell just days before the Telus bid. Besides our friendship, he wanted an ally to protect this wireless broadband venture, which was his passion at the time. That summer, the government also removed the cap on the spectrum that companies could hold, which made Microcell even more valuable to us. (I have always believed in holding as much spectrum as I could get.) There were a lot of factors pointing to Rogers in this endeavour, but we were a long way from winning.

The entire deal—adding up to almost $3.5 billion—came down to one week in September 2004. We negotiated a deal with AT&T, paying $1.8 billion cash for its stake in Rogers Wireless on Friday, September 10, at $36.37 a share with assurances from AT&T Wireless CEO John Zeglis that his board would approve it on Monday, which it did.

A few weeks earlier Nadir had called Microcell president and CEO André Tremblay and booked a dinner meeting in Montreal for Monday with him and his chairman, André Bureau, a former CRTC chairman I had known for years. We also set up meetings in Ottawa on Monday during the day to inform the CRTC, the Competition Bureau and Industry Canada about our plans regarding Microcell. We had a nice dinner in Montreal and told the two Andrés that we intended to keep Fido intact, both the brand and the workforce, and to grow the entire Rogers wireless business. There was no formal offer at this point. Nadir and I went home and then returned to Montreal on Friday with the formal all-cash offer: $35 a share compared with Telus's $29; or $1.4 billion to $1.1 billion. By Sunday we had a deal, with the Microcell board approving and recommending it to shareholders. In less than a week, we spent a lot of money, got rid of a partner of eight years, added 1.4 million new customers and turned a competitor of about eight years into a partner.

We cleaned up the entire deal in November when we bought up the remaining Rogers Wireless shares held by the public (about 11 percent) and privatized wireless under the RCI umbrella. This cost us almost $900 million and we financed it by issuing RCI Class B shares, which diluted the Rogers family holdings to around one-quarter of the total RCI equity. But we now owned a little less of a much, much bigger company with far greater potential.

At the end of 2004, the revenue of RCI broke down this way across the three lines of business: cable at 44 percent, wireless at 34 percent, and media at 22 percent. In terms of operating profit, or EBITDA, it was cable at 52 percent, wireless at 39 percent,, and media at 11 percent.

In only three years, by year-end 2007, these numbers had changed dramatically. Revenue: wireless 54 percent, cable 35 per cent, and media 11 percent. Operating profit: wireless 70 percent, cable 27 percent, and media 3 percent.

Wireless is a juggernaut. If we had not won Fido, our company would now be worth half of what it is worth today. In the first part of 2008, RCI chairman Alan Horn, who is a master with numbers, mentioned to me that RCI's market capitalization—what it's worth on the stock market—was $26 billion that day and he placed the value of media at $1 billion, cable at $6 billion and wireless at $19 billion, which are amazing numbers.

For years, the business press has slotted me as a cable guy or media owner, but the lion's share of the company is wireless now. Wireless is three times the size of cable and 19 times media, where we started almost 50 years ago with that once tiny CHFI-FM. Imagine that. Is it any wonder why I say the Fido deal is the greatest surprise of my business life? It has helped propel RCI into the vaunted investment-grade category with the ability to churn out profits and pay out dividends of a dollar per share. Perhaps most importantly, the company has moved into a position where it will ensure the Rogers name stays at the forefront of Canadian communications for generations to come.

There is still much work to be done, not least of which is planning for the inevitable day when I will no longer be chief executive officer and controlling shareholder of Rogers Communications Inc.

Chapter 20

MOVING FORWARD

have alluded to the fact that I have had health challenges much of my life. I will lay out some of the bigger problems, as a reminder to everyone that we should never take our health for granted. It is so precious.

I am asked often about my health and sometimes about stress and how I handle it, with billions of dollars of debt and thousands of families depending on Rogers Communications to put a roof over their heads and provide them with a good life. Do I walk around feeling the weight of the world on my shoulders? No, I do not. I have learned little things to help me deal with stress. I am still learning.

I was a sickly child and I lost most of the sight in my right eye in my first year. I was also a skinny little fellow and was forced to eat sugar pills and other things to fatten me up until I was about six years old. So, right from the get-go I never took my health for granted.

My biggest health challenge has been heart failure. Heart failure is something quite different from a heart attack, which occurs when an artery is blocked and culminates in a coronary event. A massive heart attack will likely kill you, a lesser one not necessarily: you may not even know you've had a heart attack. I actually had one of those "silent" heart attacks in 1985 just before the launch of our wireless phone business. Not long after that heart attack we discovered that I had heart failure.

It began at a board meeting of fine-china maker Josiah Wedgewood & Sons (Canada) Ltd. when I was overcome with nausea. I went to the washroom and sat in the stall in great discomfort and remembered that something similar had happened to my friend and neighbour Don Hunter of Maclean Hunter. Don passed out in the washroom and wasn't found for an hour or so. He survived that episode, thankfully, but died some years later from cancer, as I have described elsewhere in this book.

Remembering Don's heart attack story startled me enough to get up immediately and head home to bed, which is exactly the wrong thing to do if you have had a heart attack, even a mild one. You should go immediately to the hospital. I didn't know this at the time, but 25 percent of people who go to sleep never wake up.

The next day, I was presenting the Rogers Award at Bishop Strachan School, where my three daughters attended. John Black Aird, who was Ontario's lieutenant-governor at the time, was there. I said hello and chatted with him for a few moments. Later he told John Graham that I looked terrible, to which I replied that he didn't look so hot either.

I had no idea I had had a heart attack until two weeks later when I was in San Diego at a Sigma Chi gathering with John Graham, who insisted I go to the Scripps Clinic for a checkup. After a battery of tests, I was starting to get dressed when a doctor and a nurse came running down the hall, shouting: "Don't leave! Don't put your clothes on! You've had a heart attack!"

And that was the beginning of numerous procedures and operations over the next 20-plus years, including a quadruple bypass in 1992 at the Mayo Clinic. It seems like I am undergoing some sort of medical procedure every six months or so related to heart failure, or to aneurysms, melanoma, glaucoma and other things.

Heart failure is still the biggest concern. What happens with heart failure is that the little arteries, or wires, in the heart gradually die off one by one. As the process continues, you have less and less energy, and the weakened heart cannot do things like pump the water from your feet and ankles. I have a defibrillator in my chest the size of a cigarette package and we have the external paddle defibrillators at home, at the office and cottage, and aboard the jet and yacht. (My internal defibrillator saved my life when I collapsed on August 14, 2003, the night of the great blackout in Ontario and the northeastern U.S. With the city in darkness, I was taken to our private jet and flown down to the Mayo Clinic, where Dr. Bernie Gosevitz had alerted them of my condition.)

My doctor and I are constantly changing and upgrading various types of pills, and looking at advanced procedures at acclaimed medical facilities in North America and Europe. But we have to measure the benefits versus the risk. For example, in the summer of 2006 I enrolled in a new heart technique procedure at the Mayo Clinic. Right at the last minute, Bernie and I decided it wasn't worth the risk in my particular case. The guy who took my place died not long after leaving the Mayo.

The fact remains, we're all going to die sometime. I'm doing my best to optimize what time I have left. I am now 75 years old and have lived twice as long as my father and longer than my mother, who had a history of short lifespans in her family.

How do I deal with stress? Exercise, diet and sleep. Nothing unique there. I try to exercise up to four times a week. I try to eat properly and avoid eating too much. I do my best to base my diet on vegetables, grains and fruits, though I do enjoy a good steak periodically. I sleep eight hours a night and lately I have even taken to napping in the afternoon. Adjoining my office is a little room with a daybed. I got this idea from J.S.D. Tory, the great Toronto lawyer and father of John A. Tory.

Another trick I learned over the years is to train myself not to go to bed worrying about things because when I can't sleep properly that just adds to the stress. I'm not a paragon of virtue here. I am learning all the time not to worry about things at night. I simply keep reminding myself I will be better able to deal with the problem in the morning after a good night's sleep. I am leaving colleagues fewer voice mail messages in the middle of the night, too.

When a founder, controlling shareholder and CEO reaches 75 years of age, the question of succession frequently arises. This question is always difficult for me because I love what I am doing and am awed by the growth that our team has accomplished.

From an early age, I knew I was an entrepreneur. I've always had the drive to get things done. It is who I am. I'm not trying to be modest, but I'm amazed at how we got here. I've never had some great plan, some entrepreneurial map. Each step along the way was just that: a step. At every step I simply took advantage of the moment and the opportunities at hand.

When I refer to succession at Rogers, I am really talking about two separate successions. The first is the succession of a new CEO. It has long been agreed that this will be handled by a RCI board committee that will interview some members of our excellent and deep management team, as well as any external candidates who might be identified. It is my belief that an internal candidate will become CEO because there is a wealth of talent within our senior management team. But that decision will be up to the search committee and, ultimately, the full board of directors of RCI. During this search period, an acting CEO will be appointed, someone who will not be a candidate for the job of permanent chief executive officer. At the time of this book's publication, the interim CEO named is RCI chairman Alan Horn, but again that could change, depending on when these events unfold. As of 2008, my recommendation to the board is that it consider a five-year contract with the new CEO, renewable on an annual basis.

To transition into the next phase of the company's management, I have set up something called the "Office of the President," which consists of RCI chairman Alan Horn, CFO Bill Linton and COO of the Communications Group, Nadir Mohamed, and me. We meet every Tuesday for three hours and more often, if needed, to discuss company matters. The point I am making is that a plan and procedures are in place should I get hit by a bus tomorrow and be unable to fulfill the duties and responsibilities of chief executive officer.

The second succession is the most important to me and other family members, as it involves succession as controlling shareholder. I have two fundamental beliefs as far as ownership of the controlling shares of Rogers Communications Inc. is concerned. The first conviction is that I would like to see the Rogers family keep control of this company that I worked so damned hard to build over 50 years for as long as feasible under today's tax law regime. I have done everything I can to cause this to happen within the law. It is not my wish that the controlling Class A shares be divvied up between our children or grandchildren. Such distributions would fast track the Rogers family to lose control of the company. The only way to avoid this is to have the Class A shares held by family trusts.

We have worked very, very hard on this plan and I am proud of it. I started planning for this inevitability way back in 1968, when I was only 35 years old and Loretta and I had our first child. I never knew how long I would have the good fortune to be on this earth. Along the way, I have received excellent advice from John A. Tory, Alan Horn and other brilliant legal and financial minds, who, in addition to those skills, are decent and fair people. We've involved the children as best we can at appropriate ages, and here I owe a debt of gratitude to John H. Tory, who bridges the generations between me and the children, because as a lawyer he sat down with each child at age 21 and explained the Rogers family trusts and my wishes, in case something happened to me. Now that the kids are older, ranging from their mid-thirties to early forties, we have regular meetings to discuss various issues on this matter. It has been good to hash things out now while I am still around.

The plan has inevitably changed over the years and may continue to evolve in the future. Does today's plan meet with universal applause and contentment in the family? No! But as we work through things, I ask all of the family to give me their thoughts and comments. I don't promise to do all the things they ask me to do, but I do promise to respectfully spend sufficient time with my advisors on thinking through all suggestions before coming back with an answer. People want a sense of fairness and I think this process provides that.

We've employed the most common form of estate planning, which is called an estate freeze. There are Rogers family ownership trusts that hold all the equity shares. I own the preferred shares, which control the holding company and will be held by a separate non-equity control trust, under the terms of my will. It sounds complicated but the plan supports my two fundamental wishes: keep RCI under Rogers family control and ensure someone is in charge.

There are 15 advisors to this trust, each with a vote, including my wife Loretta and all four of our children. Each year, the person who heads the control trust—the controlling shareholder—comes up for renewal, so to speak. He or she must be doing the job functions as laid out in my will, acting in the best interests of the family. If not, he or she can be replaced by a two-thirds vote, so long as there is also a two-thirds vote on the replacement. These are the checks and balances. It is somewhat like the checks and balances between the U.S. president and the Senate and the House of Representatives. The president has the most power and can veto any bill, but the Congress should always be consulted, because it can override the veto with enough votes.

One of the great advantages of a family-controlled company is that its horizon for strategy and planning is normally much longer term than that of widely held public companies, whose managements, by necessity, have to concentrate on the current month's and quarter's profit and loss—sometimes at the cost of long-term growth. Ideally, there is a balance with the controlling shareholder being focused on long-term planning, with an excellent management team to drive growth, reduce costs and improve profitability.

The second fundamental conviction is that there should be someone in charge of the controlling shareholder position. There has to be an individual controlling shareholder to whom the board of directors and the chief executive officer can turn when needed. Under my current will, my son, Edward, will hold this controlling shareholder position for the first two years after my death. My will has changed many times over the years and may again, but that is the plan as it stands now.

———————

Loretta and I both believe strongly in the need to give back to the community. We have been so fortunate in life and think it is our obligation to help others. We also believe we should target our philanthropy in areas that can instill pride, passion and hope within people. For that reason, we have made education our number one priority. My first significant charitable donation of my life was in the 1950s when I gave $200 in my dad's name to the University of Toronto.

Things have changed a lot since then, but not my priority on education. Our largest donations to date have been to the University of Toronto and Ryerson University. (Loretta served two terms on the board of governors of Ryerson.) Between these two fine institutions, we have bequeathed about $60 million. We've also donated about $1 million to the University of Western Ontario where all four of our children did their undergraduate studies. In 2006, Loretta and I gave $100,000 to the University of New Brunswick after Wallace McCain asked us to help in his fundraising. Loretta has also been inspirational in her time and fundraising efforts at

Bishop Strachan School, the oldest independent girl's school in Canada, where Lisa, Melinda and Martha all attended. We've also given to Upper Canada College and there is a clock tower at UCC named in honour of the extended Rogers family.

Though some of the money donated has gone to capital projects at the U of T's Edward S. Rogers Sr. Department of Electrical and Computer Engineering, the John W. Graham Library at Trinity College U of T, and the Ted Rogers School of Management at Ryerson University, most of the money goes to scholarships so that bright, passionate young people can get a chance even if their families are short on money. I can think of few things worse than good minds not developing to their full potential because of economic reasons. Education can remake a city, a province or a country and can produce a growing middle class in only one generation

Outside of our commitment to education, Loretta was a founding director of Sheena's Place, an agency supporting those affected by eating disorders. My sister, Ann, was also the president of Sheena's Place. The Jays Care Foundation, which Melinda brilliantly chairs, has invested more than $1 million in helping underprivileged children get access to activity programs in their neighbourhood parks. Martha is involved in various environmental sustainability causes and non-profit organizations. Edward and his wife, Suzanne, are co-founders of the Canadian OneXOne Foundation, a non-profit organization working to make life safer for children in Canada and around the world. They were recently honoured by the British royal family for their leadership, and naturally I am very proud. We have started the Rogers Foundation, which gives money to worthwhile non-profit organizations primarily in education, health and environmental sustainability. It has an endowment of $25 million and will grow well beyond $50 million from contributions in my will. I was delighted recently when Lisa, who worked for Rogers 15 years ago, realized stock options worth about $500,000 and insisted the money go to the foundation.

With the support of Phil Lind, all the companies inside Rogers Communications promote a culture of community involvement and public generosity. Over the years, Rogers employees have been tremendous in giving back, from making Internet safety for children a priority to using our networks to help find missing children. I'd like to point out two endeavours I find special.

For 25 years, the Rogers Pumpkin Patrol has served its cable communities by distributing "safety loot bags" in schools, which contain things like reflective armbands, and on Halloween night, Rogers employees give up their time to patrol neighbourhoods in the red Rogers trucks watching out for kids' safety. The other is the Jolly Trolley program, which provides children with mobile entertainment units, complete with TVs, video games, DVDs and new-release movies in 34 children's hospitals across Canada.

In 2002, the Toronto Chapter of the Association of Fundraising Professionals honoured Loretta and me with the Outstanding Philanthropists of the Year award. They were gracious in their remarks by stating that "our gifts launch people, places and ideas and their vision draws others into the dream and the reality of creating a changed and dynamic community." This has always been our intent, and I hope I will be judged to have lived my life that way and that our children pass the value of community-giving along to future generations of Rogers. Just to nudge them along, Loretta and I have decided that the Rogers Foundation will match any charitable gift of up to $50,000 a year made by Rogers children and by future generations and hopefully they will be active in these particular charities. We did this because we want them to give away some of their dough, too, and not just the foundation's money.

Throughout my life, my business drive has been emotional—to get my father's name back as a leader in communications. Most of my financial efforts have been to survive. Risky levels of debt were a consequence, not a choice. I am truly amazed how well it has turned out!

If my dad had lived a normal lifespan, I am sure I would not have had that emotional drive. And just driving to make money is not nearly as strong as an emotional drive. This is proven time and again. If your drive is simply to make money, it peters out after a while. It is not sustainable. In Canada, we've seen people come from abroad and want to prove themselves to their parents who are still back in the old country. They do whatever it takes. They start by digging trenches and end up owning thousands of acres and are huge developers. Or, they work in a factory and end up owning it. We all know these stories. What drives them is that emotional need to prove to their parents, whether they are still alive or not, that they have achieved something in their name. The same applies to me.

All my life, almost from birth, I have been battling poor health of one sort or another. Only after age seven was I expected to survive. But I've learned never to give up and to keep my hand on the tiller of the company as long as possible because I love it so much. I am a hands-on detail-oriented manager fighting the odds, whether in business or health, always believing and hoping that the best is yet to come. One day, my daughter Lisa said, "The best way to describe you is in racetrack terms. You're not the horse people would bet on, yet you find ways to win, over and over again." She must have gotten her artistic eloquence from her mother.

If my life has a lesson for others, I think it is that everyone has a shot. Don't follow a dream; live it. No matter what it is you want, take your best shot. Be passionate and work hard, maybe harder than you ever dreamt, but the opportunity is there. You've got to be lucky at times and having a supportive spouse and solid family sure helps.

Someone recently asked me what messages I would most like to give future generations of Rogers, either those too young to read now or those not even born. I thought about it and came up with these: Get a job and work very hard. Give back to the community. Keep the

Rogers' company together and the family traditions alive for years to come. And live a balanced life between family and business.

I recognize the irony of Ted Rogers giving advice on leading a balanced life, but as I look back at age 75 I am finally beginning to become a little more balanced, spending much more time thinking about the future rather than the day-to-day.

As of late 2008, we have built a company that is strong and capable of moving forward with annual revenue of more than $11 billion and cash flow (EBITDA) of more than $4 billion per year. After years of tumultuous growth, we've finally been producing profits and paying dividends of $1 a share. The company is a far cry from that which started with a loan of $85,000 to buy CHFI-FM in 1960. All of my business life, Rogers has been the underdog, and we'll always think of ourselves that way.

We're the country's biggest wireless company with 7.5 million customers; and the biggest cable company with 2.3 million basic subscribers, 1.5 million high-speed Internet subscribers and 1 million Home Phone telephone customers, the bulk of whom use our cable telephony. In addition, our media holdings are stellar, including the five urban Citytv stations we bought in 2007, five multicultural OMNI stations and four Sportsnet regional stations plus an HD feed, the Shopping Channel, Biography, G4 Tech TV, Outdoor Life Network, 52 radio stations coast-to-coast, 70 magazines and trade journals, and the Toronto Blue Jays and Rogers Centre.

And we're poised for still more growth. We're adding more than 50,000 Home Phone customers each quarter. Close to 60 percent of cable customers have digital set-top boxes but it will be 100 percent, especially as the benefits of high-definition television and personal video recorders spread via word of mouth. Wireless data (currently 15 percent of our wireless network revenue) is just taking off in Canada toward levels in other markets in Europe and Asia that are around 25 percent. And this data will grow well beyond even these current numbers in other markets. At Rogers, we hold some of the largest contiguous blocks of wireless spectrum in North America, which was beneficial when we rolled out the latest high-speed 3G wireless in late 2007 and early 2008 to 25 Canadian markets. Globally, 85 percent of wireless is now GSM and Canada is the seventh-most-travelled-to destination in the world, according to federal government numbers I've seen, which means that more than eight out of 10 visitors with a wireless device will be connecting into our network when they come to Canada.

Innovation has been the hallmark of Rogers for almost 50 years. Innovation continues unabated. We're the first wireless carrier in North America to offer full-motion video calling where callers can see and hear each other. We're the first in Canada to convert voice mails into text and email the message to customers' handheld devices. We innovate by doing simple things like turning a Home Phone and wireless voice mailbox into one so customers pick up messages in only one place. Or we offer no long-distance charges between Home Phone subscribers.

It all comes back to one of my entrepreneurial philosophies, the one about customers and finding needs and filling them. We are not smarter than the folks at Bell or Telus, but we work hard at finding and delivering products and services customers want.

It would be easy to toss out more and more numbers proving this point about innovation and the future. But the fact is that Rogers Communications Inc. is now so much bigger than its founder. I know I will not be around forever. No one is. But I am comfortable in the thought that the next Rogers CEO, and the one after that, and the one after that will take the company beyond where it is today.

And each one will have to continue to ring alarm bells and plan for rain even when the sun is shining, as it has been the last few years. In the meantime, I am still here doing just that because I truly believe in this company and that . . .

the best is yet to come!

AFTERWORD

Four weeks after the initial publication of this book, Ted Rogers developed a major rhythm disturbance of his heart, which put him into Stage 4 heart failure, a level that is extremely difficult, if not impossible, to cure. Ted was admitted to hospital at the Cleveland Clinic on October 29 and was transferred by air ambulance to the Toronto General Hospital on November 3. The man who lived by the credo "never give up" finally succumbed in his fight with congestive heart failure on December 2, 2008, but not before battling in hospital to regain enough strength to get back to his Toronto home to die. He was 75.

Though his death was not a surprise, it was most definitely still a loss for many, many people, from family and friends to employees, customers and even competitors. More than 2,000 people attended his funeral, including Prime Minister Stephen Harper, former prime minister Brian Mulroney, and a host of other dignitaries and high-profile guests from the Canadian business community. Perhaps the most moving part of the service was when three of Ted's four children—Edward, Melinda and Martha—undertook the difficult task of speaking about their father. Each spoke eloquently from the heart and turned a Canadian icon into simply a dad for all those in attendance. Ted's eldest daughter, Lisa, gave a reading and added some personal reflections about her father. After the funeral, 600 more people posted personal stories about

Ted on the website honouring his legacy, www.tedrogerstribute. com. At the time of this writing, more than four months after Ted Rogers' death, people continue to post stories. *Relentless* co-author Robert Brehl offers the following account of Ted's final days and his perspective of working on the book with a truly great Canadian.

———————

It was Friday, November 14, 2008, and I was driving home after the year's final game of golf. It was chilly; winter was on its way. It was more than two weeks since Ted Rogers had been hospitalized after crashing into the most severe stage of heart failure. The outside world did not know the exact details, but anyone familiar with Ted and his company knew his condition was serious because he had stepped down as chief executive officer of Rogers Communications Inc.

As I drove along the highway, I began to think about Ted— particularly about how he didn't care for golf. I smiled, remembering how he had often teased me about my passion for the game, saying I was wasting my time on the golf course when I could be working. He'd always end the jab with some line about it being good to be passionate about something, or the importance of having balance in your life, just so that I knew his teasing wasn't serious.

It's funny what comes into your head when people you care about are sick. It made sense to be thinking of Ted. He was in the hospital. But why think of golf? Ted and golf didn't mix. It made no sense that I was thinking of the two at the same time. I had sent Ted a get-well card but had not spoken with him since the book launch on October 6, and a lot had happened in his life in those five weeks. Just then my cell phone rang.

It was Ted's assistant, the marvellously efficient Jeannie Hastie. "I have Mr. Rogers on the other line from his hospital room. May I connect you?" she asked.

"Of course," I said, and before I knew it, that big, energetic voice boomed through the car's speaker phone.

"Bob, it's Ted Rogers here," he said.

"This is a wonderful surprise," I replied, not quite sure what else to say.

"It's great to hear your voice," Ted said, and then he paused. "And considering where I am, it's great to hear my voice, too." I laughed. "Good one, eh?" he added with a chuckle. "I've used that line quite a bit lately."

His optimism and good humour were contagious. When in Ted Rogers' presence—or even when speaking with him on the phone—you always felt anything was possible. This time, just hearing his voice made me think, *Maybe things aren't that dire. Maybe he will pull through, like he has so many times before.* That's how powerful his optimism was. I have never met anyone as optimistic in my life, and I don't know if I ever will. (If he were reading this, he'd probably say, "Why would you resign yourself to the fact that you won't meet someone else as optimistic? That is not a positive way of looking at things.")

During our 15-minute telephone conversation that November afternoon, his voice waxed and waned, but what struck me most was that it was far more robust than I would have imagined, considering what he had gone through the past couple of weeks. He touched on many topics—his heart failure, the wonderful care he had received at the Toronto General Hospital, his decision to step down as CEO of the multi-billion-dollar company he had built, the financial decision-making at one of the charities he had supported with millions of dollars.

At one point, I said, "We should write a new chapter, an epilogue, for the paperback edition of *Relentless*." This turned out to be the reason he had called me in the first place. Ted was the grandmaster, always several moves ahead in the game of chess.

"Will you come down for a visit and a talk?" he asked.

"Certainly," I responded. "When?"

"It will have to be soon. But I can't say for sure right now. I'm having good days and not-so-good days. I'll call you back and let you know," he said.

With that, we ended the call, and I started thinking about a lot of things, especially about how fortunate I had been to work with Ted for nearly the last two years. I had known him, his family and his company for at least 15 years, first as a reporter and then as a consultant who wrote speeches and other corporate material. But this project was altogether different. While chronicling his life, we would sit and talk for hours, and I would have his undivided attention all the while. These times were special; I knew it then and I know it now even more. Sometimes it felt like I was walking "through the looking glass" into the personal life of one of the most powerful people in the country, and into a world to which I was unaccustomed. Other times I felt I was in the world of a "regular Joe," a man who had achieved so much yet was at his core a genu- inely nice person, someone who treated people as equals, regardless of their standing. Ted Rogers was no rich snob; in fact, he abhorred snobbishness. What an endearing quality in such a powerful man, a man who had his ring kissed daily on so many occasions.

Not long into this project, I came to realize that, although Ted Rogers was extraordinary in business, he was in many ways an ordi- nary guy who loved his family and friends. He was an icon and a "brand" to the public, as well as a gentleman in the truest sense of the word. And yet he was enigmatic, too. He was a gracious host but could also be an unremitting tease. I recall one dinner at his winter home, when I was one of half a dozen guests. One couple began talking about fishing, and the wife made the mis- take of commenting on how much time her husband spent angling. The hook was baited for Ted. Within minutes, through a series of apparently innocent questions, he had the couple arguing across the table about the merits and demerits of fishing. As voices and tensions rose, Ted's wife, Loretta, stopped the argument by direct- ing everyone to look at the end of the table, where Ted sat back, arms crossed, wearing a Cheshire-cat grin. The true nature of his coy questioning, which had precipitated the argument, had been revealed—and he loved it! I will never forget the look on his face. It was so mischievous and playful.

I also quickly realized that the Ted Rogers I was spending time with was not the Ted Rogers of 20 or 30 years earlier. That younger man had inspired many stories of door-slamming and shouting matches with workers and bankers. His drive to get things done and his temper were legendary. Yes, the Ted I knew was still relentless and driven. But by the time we worked together he was well into his 70s and much mellower, a man who knew his body was giving out but whose mind was sharp, with the added clarity and perspective of what is really important in life.

He was an incredibly emotional man, too. Tears often flowed freely. The first time I saw this side of him, we were sitting in his Toronto home talking about his mother, Velma, who had fought the bottle and won, and battled cancer and ultimately lost. Before I knew it, tears were rolling down Ted's cheeks and he was too choked up to continue. Remembering my own mother's death from cancer, I also became too upset to speak. We just sat there in silence, sniffling, for about five minutes, until we were able to go on. A few days later, I received the transcript from the recorded interview. It made me chuckle. Halfway through, it contained the following note from the transcriber: "Mechanical trouble. No audio for long portion."

We had a lot of laughs working on *Relentless*. Ted could tell great stories. He loved to laugh and he wasn't afraid to laugh at himself, either. There was the anecdote about the time Rogers Media President Tony Viner picked a Toronto restaurant where the two were to hold a dinner meeting. When Ted arrived, he pulled out a coupon for a free entrée and presented it to the waiter. Ted didn't like wasting money!

Another funny incident started out as an embarrassment for me. One Sunday, I offered Ted a ride home from his office. After he accepted, I realized I was driving the old family van that day. It had McDonald's french fries ground into the carpet and kids' toys all over the place. A little sheepishly, I stopped the van in front of Ted's office building. I had the air conditioning on full blast because it was stinking hot outside and I hoped the air might cover up some of the stale smell in the van. Ted got in and immediately put his window down all the way. I thought he did it because of the smell, but unbeknownst to me, his window had so much dog slobber on it he could hardly see out of it. Once I realized that, we had a good laugh. I was impressed that a man of Ted's stature could so easily roll with the situation. I told him I had just learned that dog slobber, and a person's reaction to it, could tell you a lot about that person. He laughed and launched into a story about one of his golden retrievers. He was a real dog lover.

So many thoughts popped into my head after that phone call with Ted from his hospital bed. After the weekend, on Monday, November 17, his daughter Lisa called and said he was feeling good that day and wondered if I could come down to see him at the hospital.

When I arrived, Ted was being moved from the intensive care unit's "step-down" area to his own room. His daughters, Lisa and Martha, were there, as well as his great friend and personal physician, Dr. Bernie Gosevitz. I went into Ted's room and he was sitting up in bed. He greeted me with a surprisingly firm handshake. All things considered, he looked good.

Always business, Ted started our conversation by saying he had just called the chairman of the CRTC, Konrad von Finckenstein, with a suggestion to improve Canada's broadcasting system. "He thought I was crazy. We'll see. It isn't that bad an idea," Ted said.

"He was probably surprised that you were calling, given everything you've been through lately," I said.

"Well, I'm not dead yet," he said, his voice filled with that patented determination.

He came by that determination honestly. He had developed it long ago. When he was a young man of 21, he and his mother got into a fight at the family cottage on Tobin Island in Muskoka. To teach him a lesson, his mother told him to find another way home and left for Toronto without him. Ted canoed to the mainland, hitch-hiked home and got back in time to open the front door for her.

In Ted's hospital room, we chatted awhile. Then, when all the other people left the room, he dropped this bombshell on me: "The doctors say there is nothing more they can do. I could make it to Christmas, but not much longer than that," he said.

His frankness caught me off guard, even though we had talked about his death many times before.

"They've guaranteed you until Christmas?" I asked.

"No," he said. "There are no guarantees. They think I can make it to Christmas. But I want to make it to May 27 and see one more birthday."

Ted loved celebrating birthdays, especially his own. Because his father had died so young and Ted had fought his own health challenges throughout his life, seeing each new birthday was very important to him. Knowing how much birthdays meant to him, his family, friends and workmates would throw several parties for him each year. The week of May 27 was known as "Holy Week" around Rogers Communications because there would be a daily birthday celebration for the boss from Monday to Friday.

"If anyone can defy the odds the doctors have laid down, you can," I said.

"Don't bet on it, but I'll try," he said.

What followed was an incredible 45-minute conversation. He said he just wanted to talk first, and we'd determine the next steps towards an epilogue for the book later. Afterwards, from our conversation, I did complete a draft of the epilogue in the first person and sent it to him. But since his health deteriorated shortly after,

I doubt he read it. He died exactly two weeks after that meeting. What follows is the essence of my last conversation with Ted Rogers.

At first, he wanted to step back and tell me about October 29, when his downward spiral began while he was in Ohio for scheduled medical procedures at the Cleveland Clinic. The crisis happened while he was in bed at the hotel near the hospital. Ted didn't even know about it at the time. All he could recall was being awakened at 8 a.m., feeling weaker than usual. Dr. Bernie Gosevitz, who was staying at the hotel in a room down the hall, took him in a wheelchair down to a waiting car and drove the short distance to the Cleveland Clinic.

Once there, Ted was hooked up to a bunch of beeping and blinking medical paraphernalia. A nurse told him, "Your defibulator has gone off. It went off on October 29. That's today! You've had a massive rhythm disturbance today. Actually, you've had three of them."

While Ted slept that morning, the little defibulator, which was the size of a cigarette package and was implanted inside his chest, had saved his life yet again. But things were about to get worse, much worse. His condition quickly deteriorated; had he not been right there with all that medical equipment and expertise around him, he would have died in Cleveland.

Within 48 hours, the company put out a press release stating that Ted was in hospital and was stepping down as chief executive officer of Rogers Communications Inc., a role he had held for 50 years. Chairman Alan Horn was named interim CEO. This was a salient move and an emotional one. For Ted to step down, it had to be serious. (In March 2009, Nadir Mohamed was named permanent CEO.)

The news that Ted had stepped down sent the Canadian business media into a lather. In fact, the next day, during the evening of November 1, a reporter from none other than the *Toronto Star*, which had long been at odds with Ted, phoned Ted's hospital room at the Cleveland Clinic. Bernie answered the phone, telling the reporter politely, but sternly, that Ted was in no condition to be interviewed and that she should get updates through the company spokespeople. "Say what I will about my old nemesis, the *Star*," Ted said later, "they certainly train their journalists to be dogged. I have to admire that, but, my goodness, considering all the battles the Rogers family has had with that newspaper over the years, it made me chuckle when I heard they called looking for an interview when I was in such dire straits. Was it ironic or apropos that it was the *Star* calling? I don't know. But it was funny in a strange sort of way."

A few days later, Ted was flown back to Toronto by medical helicopter. The ride was bumpy due to windy weather, but the helicopter landed safely on the roof of Toronto General Hospital, right downtown. Coming across the lake and above all the skyscrapers made for a remarkable view of the city, "but seeing it the way I did is not something I would recommend," Ted said. The chopper was so small that no one from the family, or even his doctor, Bernie Gosevitz, was with him.

At Ted's insistence, on November 6, Rogers Communications issued a second news release, stating that he had returned to Canada and that his condition had stabilized. "I am grateful for the quality of care I am receiving at the Toronto General Hospital, a world-class facility," he said. The main point of the release was to publicly state how terrific the care was at this Canadian hospital. Though he had received treatments over the years in U.S. facilities such as the Mayo and Cleveland Clinics, Ted was truly impressed by the staff at the Toronto General Hospital. Moreover, he said, "It was just so good to be home in Canada."

Though his condition stabilized, it certainly didn't mean he was out of the woods. It wasn't long until he had another massive rhythm disturbance, which pushed him deeper into Stage 4 heart failure. This disturbance he remembered. "It was so painful; it felt like heavy weights were pushing down on my chest and knife-like stabs were coming from *inside* my body," Ted said afterwards.

At the time, doctors discussed the options with the family—his wife, Loretta, and his children, Lisa, Edward, Melinda and Martha, who were all by his side during the crisis—including unhooking the medical equipment that was keeping him alive. As Ted faded in and out of consciousness, he asked for one more day before making any decision. "I did not want my loved ones to face—and ultimately make—such a difficult decision at that point," he said later. Ted had been such a fighter his entire life. Within the next 24 hours, his condition improved and the family was not forced to make the decision that day.

After this crisis passed, Ted said his next goal was to regain enough strength to go home. He knew he was down to days, maybe weeks. As I sat at his bedside, his fortitude amazed me. He talked about for being so thankful for having the time to prepare for the inevitable and being around to take part in so many wonderful personal, business and family occurrences throughout 2008. His last year really was his opportunity to tie up loose ends.

First and foremost was family. At Thanksgiving that past October he and Loretta had taken 31 members of both families, the Rogers and the Robinsons (Loretta's side of the family), to Barbados. It was a celebration of several milestones: Ted and Loretta's forty-fifth wedding anniversary, Lisa's birthday and Ted's sister Ann's birthday, which all fell around that time. It was a splendid holiday, reminiscent of a trip his in-laws had taken 30 years earlier, but it was emotional at times, especially as the families gathered for dinner. Reflecting on their time together, Ted said, "I am not a perfect man, and no family is perfect. But let me say that I love my family and I am very secure in the knowledge that each member will do his or her best to ensure the Rogers name remains at the forefront for years to come. That was my life's dream and life's work, and they all know that."

Ted also talked about the spectacular birthday parties his family and friends had thrown him in May 2008. At the private party on May 24, organized by his daughter Melinda, Ted and about 300 friends were treated to surprise performances by Harry Connick Jr., Paul Anka and Harry Belafonte. Ted sat in the chair reserved for him, the guest of honour, in great spirits, at one point clapping to the music as Anka took Loretta for a spin on the dance floor. At the big staff party, several thousand Rogers employees gathered at the Rogers Centre on May 27, his actual birthday, to offer their best wishes. Ted never thought he would see his 75th birthday, so he revelled in the celebrations. Later, from his hospital bed, he enjoyed looking back at those times.

Ted made a great effort in 2008 to complete this book, not for some sort of ego gratification but because he wanted to chronicle the story for future generations of Rogers and current and future Canadian entrepreneurs. If reading his story helped even one or two entrepreneurs build their businesses, adding to Canada's prosperity, the project was well worth it, he said.

On August 22, 2008, Loretta and Ted gave a $1-million-dollar cheque to the Woodstock Hospital Foundation in honour of his mother, Velma. The donation would pay for an automated medication system for a hospital that was being built in her hometown. It was with great pride that Ted made the donation in her name. The three-storey, 39,000-square-foot wing of the new hospital will be named in honour of Velma. It will include the pharmacy department, a chemotherapy suite, beds for acute patients and a palliative care department. Ted witnessed his mother's valiant struggle with cancer; he believed she'd be pleased with this new quality-care institution for cancer patients in her beloved Woodstock, in southwestern Ontario.

Also in 2008, Ted and Loretta gave their support to additional Canadian hospitals. On September 16, the Loretta Anne Rogers Critical Care Centre at the Toronto Western Hospital opened its doors after undergoing a complete renovation, one that saw the facility outfitted with greatly improved infection-control capabilities. The Rogers' $5-million-dollar donation helped turn the centre into a modern unit with additional bed space and a central nursing station to optimize clinical care for the most critically ill patients.

The day before, on September 15, the Rogers' contribution of $7.5 million to the Sunnybrook Health Sciences Centre was announced. This money would help tackle the most common causes of blindness in Canada by supporting research into three major conditions that result from the uncontrolled growth of blood vessels in the eye: age-related macular degeneration, vision complications stemming from diabetes and vision complications arising from premature birth. These conditions affect more than one million Canadians. Ted had vision problems his entire life, so this initiative meant a lot to him personally. Even more meaningful is the fact that the research centre is named in honour of his great friends John and Liz Tory, who are working so hard to raise money for Sunnybrook, one of their many community efforts.

After finishing with healthcare, Ted turned to another topic he was very passionate about: education. "For years, I have believed that education can change the fabric of society and it can change it quickly. There is nothing more important than presenting educational opportunities to all young people with the desire to learn. Economic situations should never, and I mean never, be a barrier to bright young people getting the opportunity to learn and work hard to expand their horizons," he said.

As 2008 came to a close, the world was falling deeper and deeper into recessionary times. Ted could foresee tougher times ahead, too. But he warned that education for Canada's young people must not be a casualty of these tough times in any way, shape or form. For example, he said, Ryerson University in Toronto, with its populist view of opportunity afforded to young minds, regardless of their families' economic standing, is a great model for learning in the years ahead in Canada. His daughter Martha may have said it best at a recent Ryerson event: "Our family loves Ryerson. We believe education is a right for all Canadians and we're lucky to have an institution like Ryerson." Though he was too sick to attend the event, Ted was so pleased that both Martha and Lisa represented the family at Ryerson in November 2008, giving out the Rogers Awards to 50 talented students that year to help them pay for their schooling.

After tossing accolades Ryerson's way, Ted also had a few sharp words for the institution. In May 2007, he and Loretta had given $15 million to the university with the majority used to establish 52 new undergraduate and graduate student awards and scholarships. He wanted the Rogers donation to work for the students, with the principal amount of money generating annual income to be handed out in the way of awards. Now, with the stock market turmoil, the value of the Rogers gift had declined and the administrators wanted to protect their principal and temporarily cut back on the money given to qualifying Ryerson students until the markets improved. "I know these bureaucrats mean well, but to heck with that," Ted said to me in the hospital. "When they outlined this new plan I told them this: Loretta and I gave the money to work for the students. Make it work. Don't stop the scholarships and awards because the stock market is down. If you need more money, we'll deal with that when the time comes."

Ted said that he told this story for two reasons: First, because it was parents' responsibility to do whatever they could to ensure their children got the best possible education. They should fight for this education, not only by saving money for it, but also by ensuring the accountability of administrators to guarantee the best possible education. Second, governments in Canada at every level should never look to cut education when times got tough. That was incredibly short-term thinking. "In business, I would classify that as quarterly thinking, not strategic long-term thinking," he said. "Sure, there are places within the education system where things may be done more wisely, where money can be better spent. But education is an investment, and to order across-the-board edicts to cut back is sowing the seeds for a less prosperous Canada tomorrow."

At this point in our conversation, I turned to Ted and said: "You must be so proud of where your company stands today." In turbulent times, the so-called financial experts and media have called Rogers Communications "a safe haven" and a "safe port" for investors. Many of these same people labelled Rogers "debt-soaked" not that long ago.

He smiled and said, "You know I don't like braggarts. But, yes, I am proud of what we have achieved."

Then he changed the subject to his family and warm and pleasant memories. Some memories involved coming home from a long workday and getting down on his hands and knees to play with his children when they were young. He used to enjoy wrestling or playing horsey with them. His daughter Melinda recently told me how much she loved that too, and it was a side of his personality she cherished. Other memories included trips to Europe and Asia with the family.

He chuckled when we talked about the surprised looks on the faces of chauvinistic businessmen in South Korea after Loretta sat down beside him for a lunch when they were meeting to discuss new products in the late 1980s. (Of course it was a holiday, but he couldn't help working for part of it.) Loretta had every right to be there as his business partner and a member of the Rogers board of directors. Edward, who was still a teenager at the time, mentioned during this book project that he was so proud of his mother for sticking to her guns.

We ended our last meeting by talking about Canada. I admit that until I worked so closely with him on this book, I always thought he was a little over-the-top with all his talk about Canada and wrapping his company in the maple leaf. But the more I spoke with him, the more I came to realize this was not an act. He truly loved Canada and thought it the best place on earth to live and call home.

By now, Ted was getting tired and I knew it was time to leave. I told him I would write up a last chapter and come back to go over it with him soon. We shook hands and I left, firmly believing I would see him again. As I said, he had this ability to make anyone in his presence feel anything was possible. He died fifteen days later.

Ted Rogers was a great and unique Canadian. He was a man with the common touch who could relate to anyone—from prime ministers and captains of industry to university students receiving Rogers awards and call centre representatives on coffee break in the company cafeteria. He lived life large, fought hard in every endeavour, achieved lifelong goals and died at home with all his loved ones around him.

After his funeral, I thanked Lisa for calling me and getting me down to the hospital to see him one last time.

"Bob, it wasn't me," she said.

"What do you mean? You called me that Monday morning," I said.

"Yes, it was me who phoned you, but what I mean is that it was dad. He told me to call you to come down. You were on his list of people he wanted to see one last time," she said.

That was Ted: Despite what he had achieved and built, and all the wealth and power he had accumulated, it didn't matter what anyone's status was in life. He could be friends with anyone; even some schmoe who drove around in a dog-slobbered beater of a van and was addicted to a game he thought was a waste of time.

I truly wish I could sound more optimistic and say Canada will produce more like him, but there likely won't be another person quite like Ted Rogers.

—Bob Brehl
April 2009

TIMELINE

1927   Edward Rogers Sr. founds Toronto radio station CFRB—the call
letters stand for "Canada's First Rogers Batteryless"—three years
after he creates the world's first plug-in radio.

1933   Edward Samuel Rogers Jr.—"Ted"—is born on May 27.

1939   Edward Rogers Sr. dies suddenly three weeks before Ted's sixth
birthday.

1940   At age seven, Ted is sent to boarding school in Quebec and then to
Upper Canada College in Toronto, blocks from the family home.
He remains there until age 17.

1941   Velma Rogers, Ted's mother, marries John Webb Graham, who
becomes Ted's second father and life long business mentor.
The family radio businesses are sold.

1950   Ted hooks up an antenna on the roof of his dormitory at Upper
Canada College and brings in American television from Buffalo,
charging classmates to watch programs in his room.

1954   Ted, along with his friend William C. Boultbee, is detained in
Miami during the McCarthy red scare era under suspicion of being
a Communist after Ted tells U.S. authorities that he is a "Progressive"
Conservative.

1956   Ted works tirelessly on his hero John Diefenbaker's third (and
successful) bid to lead the federal Progressive Conservatives.

1957   Ted meets Loretta Anne Robinson, the daughter of a highly
respected British member of Parliament, in Nassau, Bahamas, and
they begin to date.

1960   While articling at the Bay Street law firm Torys, Ted buys CHFI,
the country's first FM radio station, for $85,000. Together with John
Bassett, the Eaton family and Joel Aldred, Ted wins the licence for
the first private TV station in Toronto, CFTO.

TIMELINE

1961 CFTO goes on air for the first time on January 1.

1963 Ted creates space on the AM dial for CHFI-AM at 680 and wins the licence. He and Loretta marry on September 25. He has to cut short his honeymoon in Kenya to return to Ottawa for the radio license hearing in October.

1967 Rogers is granted cable TV licences for three Ontario markets—parts of Toronto, Brampton and Leamington; he partners with the Bassetts and the Eatons.
Oldest daughter, Lisa Anne, is born October 9.

1969 Because of their other media holdings, the Bassetts and the Eatons are forced by the CRTC to get out of Rogers cable, which leads to Ted's closest brush with bankruptcy in 1971.
Edward Samuel Rogers III is born June 22.

1971 Daughter, Melinda Mary, is born January 27.
Velma Rogers Graham, who taught her son, Ted, to never give up and inspired him to get back what the family had lost, dies in November.

1972 Youngest child, Martha Loretta, is born April 6.

1979 Rogers becomes a public company when it acquires control of Canadian Cablesystems through a reverse takeover that makes it the biggest cable company in Canada, a perch Rogers has never relinquished.

1981 Rogers cable makes its first foray into the U.S. cable market and for a brief period becomes the largest cable company in the world.

1985 Cantel, the predecessor to Rogers Wireless, introduces Canada's first cellular service on July 1. Rogers is one of three partners. Just days earlier, Ted has a "silent" heart attack that marks the beginning of his heart ailments.

1986 Rogers Broadcasting acquires CFMT-Toronto, the first multicultural, multilingual television service in Canada. (CFMT is renamed OMNI Television in 2002 and expands to five channels by 2008.)

1989 Rogers Communications sells its U.S. cable assets and records a $1 billion profit on the decade-long venture. Rogers buys 40 percent of CNCP Telecommunications (later Unitel) to compete in long-distance against Bell Canada and invests other U.S. cable profits into the Canadian wireless industry.

1992 Ted undergoes quadruple-bypass heart surgery at the Mayo Clinic in Rochester, Minnesota.

1993 CFTR-AM changes its format and becomes 680 News, an all-news station.

1994 Rogers launches a hostile bid for Maclean Hunter, which encompasses cable, radio, TV, magazines and the *Sun* newspapers, ultimately paying $3.1 billion. Just before Christmas, Rogers is given final approval for the merger.

1995 Unitel restructures. Rogers walks away after losing $500 million. Rogers introduces the first high-speed Internet service in North America in Newmarket, Ontario, just north of Toronto.

1998 Rogers shares fall to $4.80 amid staggering losses at Rogers Cantel and fears that the company can't service its $5-billion debt.

1999 Rogers receives a huge boost—financially and in the public's perception—when Microsoft, AT&T and British Telecom each invests in parts of the company for a total of $2 billion.

2000 Rogers' $5-billion stock deal to take over Quebec cable company Groupe Vidéotron is defeated by Quebecor Inc. and a giant Quebec pension fund. Rogers bags a $241-million breakup fee and acquires the Toronto Blue Jays baseball team and Cable Atlantic in Newfoundland. Rogers and Shaw swap $4 billion of cable assets in Ontario, New Brunswick and British Columbia to each solidify clusters in western and central Canada.

2004 Rogers spends $1.8 billion to buy AT&T's 33 percent stake in Rogers Wireless and, one week later, announces a $1.6-billion deal for Microcell, the "greatest success" of Ted's business life.

2005 Rogers Home Phone is officially launched with the acquisition of Call-Net Enterprises.

2007 Wireless becomes the juggernaut of Rogers Communications with 70 percent of operating profit to cable's 27 percent and media's 3 percent. Ted's "media mogul" and "cable czar" monikers are supplanted by "wireless wizard"—the name given to his father in the early days of radio.
Rogers Media acquires five Citytv over-the-air television stations operating in Toronto, Winnipeg, Calgary, Edmonton and Vancouver.

2008 Ted Rogers celebrates his seventy-fifth birthday and, later in the year, his forty-fifth wedding anniversary.
The company records annual revenue of more than $11 billion and introduces the popular iPhone into Canada.
Ted Rogers dies on December 2.

ACKNOWLEDGEMENTS

There are so many people to whom I am grateful and indebted for helping make Rogers Communications Inc. the company it is today, a far cry from what it was when we started in 1960 with $85,000 of borrowed money to buy radio station CHFI. There are simply too many people to name here, but all know who they are, and many will see references to themselves throughout these pages. As for this book project specifically, I would like to thank my children— Lisa, Edward, Melinda and Martha—for coming up with this idea to mark my seventy-fifth birthday in 2008. It was a delightful and thoughtful gift. Loretta and I are both so pleased.

—ESR

First and foremost, I would like to thank Lisa, Edward, Melinda and Martha for not only coming up with the book idea but for entrusting me with helping their father tell his story. It was a pleasure to work with Melinda, the family member who took the file and guided the project from beginning to end.

Naturally, I am indebted to my beautiful wife, Cobi, and children, Aidan and Charlotte, for putting up with me during this project, giving me time to be away or alone when needed. Many friends and family were also there when I needed advice or help over the months the book was written, including my six siblings;

Jim Brehl, Mary Katherine Whelan, Michael Brehl, Bill Brehl, Joan Steele and Paul Brehl; as well as Mary Ladner, Todd Ladner, Bill Fanjoy, Rob Bracey, Geoff Rowan, Eric Rothschild, Art Chamberlain, Gordon Pitts, Iain Grant, Nick van Rijn, Lorraine Campbell, Rob Thompson, Stephen Elgee and Mark Coombs.

I am also appreciative of my other clients, including Paul Barter, George Horhota, Jay Rosenzweig, Jennifer Reinhard and Jessica Hougentogler, for their patience as demanding deadlines for the book approached at various times. And I thank both Natalia Smalyuk and James Lewis for being there to help when needed. Thanks also to the *Relentless* editor, Jim Gifford, and copy editor Anne Holloway.

I would like to express my sincere appreciation to so many people at Rogers who in one way or another helped with this project, especially Jan Innes, vice-president of communications. If there is anyone better at such a demanding job, I have yet to meet him or her. Ian Anthony, the Rogers historian, has been an incredible resource and I am truly thankful for his help. Both Jeannie Hastie and Maria Selina were wonderful at so often fitting me onto Ted's incredibly busy calendar, and they were a delight to deal with, even when I posed questions about where Ted was on certain days 10, 20, even 30 years ago. Mary Treacey, Jan's assistant, has been invaluable in tracking down important bits of information and background, as have Elizabeth Hunter and Melinda's assistant, Melanie Kenrick.

I am beholden to so many friends and associates of Ted who gave me insight into the man, both in formal interview sessions and simply informal chatting. These include Phil Lind, the Torys (both John A. and John H.), Dr. Bernie Gosevitz, Bob Buchan, Dwight Aranha, Dick Thomson, Robin Korthals, Colin Watson, Alan Horn, Nadir Mohamed, Bill Linton, Tony Viner, Missy Goerner, Ann Graham, Toby Hull, Ron Besse and, of course, Loretta Rogers and her children. Lastly, thanks to Ted Rogers, perhaps Canada's greatest entrepreneur over the last century or so. At the start of this project, he gave me two rules: "Don't get bogged down with endless details

ACKNOWLEDGEMENTS

that nobody gives a damn about; and ask me anything you like and feel free to put any of my answers in the book and we'll see what stays and what goes in the end." In all honesty, his memory is uncanny and his candour is refreshing. As we worked through drafts of the manuscript together, Ted changed things here and there (always to the better, I might add) and in the end, he cut nothing out.

—RGB

INDEX

INDEX

INDEX